Dreamweaver® CS6
FOR
DUMMIES®

Dreamweaver® CS6

FOR

DUMMIES®

by Janine Warner

WILEY

John Wiley & Sons, Inc.

Dreamweaver® CS6 For Dummies®

Published by
John Wiley & Sons, Inc.
111 River Street
Hoboken, NJ 07030-5774
www.wiley.com

Copyright © 2012 by John Wiley & Sons, Inc., Hoboken, New Jersey

Published by John Wiley & Sons, Inc., Hoboken, New Jersey

Published simultaneously in Canada

For general information on our other products and services, please contact our Customer Care Department within the U.S. at 877-762-2974, outside the U.S. at 317-572-3993, or fax 317-572-4002.

For technical support, please visit www.wiley.com/techsupport.

Wiley publishes in a variety of print and electronic formats and by print-on-demand. Some material included with standard print versions of this book may not be included in e-books or in print-on-demand. If this book refers to media such as a CD or DVD that is not included in the version you purchased, you may download this material at http://booksupport.wiley.com. For more information about Wiley products, visit www.wiley.com.

Library of Congress Control Number is available from the publisher.

ISBN 978-1-118-21233-2 (pbk); ISBN 978-1-118-22873-9 (ebk); ISBN 978-1-118-23135-7 (ebk); ISBN 978-1-118-26601-4 (ebk)

Manufactured in the United States of America

10 9 8 7 6 5 4 3 2 1

WILEY

About the Author

Janine Warner is an author, a speaker, and a web designer.

Since 1995, she's written and coauthored more than a dozen books, including every edition of *Dreamweaver For Dummies, Web Sites Do-it-Yourself For Dummies,* and *Teach Yourself Visually Dreamweaver.* She is the host of a growing collection of training videos for web design, Adobe Dreamweaver, and Cascading Style Sheets. She has also created videos for Kelby Training and Total Training. You can learn more about her books and videos, and find many free tutorials on web design, social media, and SEO on her website at www.DigitalFamily.com.

Janine is a popular speaker at conferences and events throughout the United States and abroad, and she's been a guest lecturer at more than 20 universities. An award-winning journalist, her articles and columns have appeared in a variety of publications, including *The Miami Herald, Shape Magazine,* and *Layers* magazine.

Janine has extensive Internet experience working on large and small websites. From 1994 to 1998, she ran Visiontec Communications, a web design business in Northern California, where she worked for a diverse group of clients including Levi Strauss & Co., AirTouch International, and many other small- and medium-sized businesses.

In 1998, she joined *The Miami Herald* as their Online Managing Editor. A year later, she was promoted to Director of New Media. She left that position to serve as Director of Latin American Operations for CNET Networks, an international technology media company.

Since 2001, Janine has run her own business as a writer, speaker, and consultant. She lives and works with her husband in Los Angeles. To learn more, visit www.JanineWarner.com or www.DigitalFamily.com.

Dedication

To all those who aspire to share their stories and passions on the web: May all your dreams come true.

Author's Acknowledgments

More than anything, I want to thank all the people who have read my books or watched my videos over the years. My readers and students are my greatest inspiration, and I sincerely enjoy it when you send me links to your websites. You'll find my e-mail address on my site at www.DigitalFamily.com.

Special thanks to David LaFontaine, my partner in all things digital and analog, whose patience and support keep me fed, loved, and (mostly) sane, even when I'm up against impossible deadlines.

For their contributions to this book, a heartfelt thanks to designer Beth Renniessen (http://www.ChameleonEngine.com); to photographer Jasper Johal (www.jasperphoto.com); to artist Amy Baur (www.inplainsightart.com); to underwater photographer Ken Riddick (www.cousinswest.com), and my father, Robin Warner (www.DexterTreeFarm.com).

Thanks to the entire editorial team on this book: Susan Pink for her helpful and proactive editing style; Jeff Noble for his attention to the technical details; and Bob Woerner for shepherding this book through the development and publishing process (again and again and again).

Over the years, I've thanked many people in my books — family, friends, teachers, and mentors — but I have been graced by so many wonderful people now that no publisher will give me enough pages to thank them all. So let me conclude by thanking everyone who has ever helped me with a website, a book, or any other aspect of the writing and research that go into these pages. Okay, now I think I can go to sleep tonight without fearing I've forgotten anyone. Thank you, thank you, thank you.

Publisher's Acknowledgments

We're proud of this book; please send us your comments at http://dummies.custhelp.com. For other comments, please contact our Customer Care Department within the U.S. at 877-762-2974, outside the U.S. at 317-572-3993, or fax 317-572-4002.

Some of the people who helped bring this book to market include the following:

Acquisitions and Editorial

Project Editor: Susan Pink

(Previous Edition: Rebecca Huehls)

Acquisitions Editor: Bob Woerner

Copy Editor: Susan Pink

Technical Editor: Jeff Noble

Editorial Manager: Jodi Jensen

Editorial Assistant: Amanda Graham

Sr. Editorial Assistant: Cherie Case

Cover Photo: © iStockphoto.com / Cary Westfall

Cartoons: Rich Tennant (www.the5thwave.com)

Composition Services

Project Coordinator: Katie Crocker

Layout and Graphics: Melanee Habig, Jennifer Henry

Proofreaders: Melissa Cossell, Jessica Kramer, Shannon Ramsey

Indexer: BIM Indexing & Proofreading Services

Publishing and Editorial for Technology Dummies

Richard Swadley, Vice President and Executive Group Publisher

Andy Cummings, Vice President and Publisher

Mary Bednarek, Executive Acquisitions Director

Mary C. Corder, Editorial Director

Publishing for Consumer Dummies

Kathleen Nebenhaus, Vice President and Executive Publisher

Composition Services

Debbie Stailey, Director of Composition Services

Contents at a Glance

Table of Contents

Introduction

*I*n the last few years, the Internet has experienced extraordinary growth and has gone through incredible changes. As more and more users access the web with smartphones, tablets, Google TV, and Apple TV, web designers have been forced to design sites that work on tiny mobile screens as well as giant television sets.

Simultaneously, the technologies that work best on the web are changing. The once popular design tool Adobe Flash is losing its audience because videos and animations created in Flash don't work on the iPad or iPhone. Fortunately, emerging new technologies, including HTML5 and CSS3 (the latest flavors of the Hypertext Markup Language and Cascading Style Sheets, respectively), make it possible to add new design features and greater interactivity without the need for Flash.

I can't cover every detail of all these technologies in this book, but I do give you a solid introduction to modern web design. You discover how the newest features in Dreamweaver CS6 make it easier to create web pages that meet modern standards and adapt to all the screens used to view websites today.

In this fully updated version of *Dreamweaver For Dummies,* I added a new chapter to introduce CSS3 and help you transform the boxy look of old-fashioned web pages into the smoother styles made possible by CSS3 additions, including rounded corners, drop shadows, and almost any font you want.

Over the years, web design has evolved into an increasingly complex field, and Dreamweaver has evolved with it, adding features that go way beyond the basics of combining a few words and images. Adobe's dedication to keeping up with changing standards and adding new features with each new version is why Dreamweaver is such a popular program among professional web designers, as well as among a growing number of people who want to build sites for their hobbies, clubs, families, and small businesses.

In the 15-plus years that I've been writing about web design, I've seen many changes — from the early days (before Dreamweaver even existed) when you could create only simple pages with HTML 1.0, to the elaborate designs you can create with Dreamweaver today using HTML, CSS, jQuery, multimedia, and more.

If you're not sure what those acronyms mean yet, don't worry. I remember what it was like to figure out all this stuff, too, so I designed this book to introduce you to the basic concepts before you get into the more advanced features. To prepare you for the ever-changing world of web design, I show you how to use Dreamweaver to create websites that take advantage of the latest advances in web technology — including CSS3, covered in the new Chapter 7.

One of the challenges of web design today is that web pages are not only displayed on different kinds of computers but also downloaded to computers with monitors as big as widescreen televisions — or as small as the little screens on cell phones. As a result, creating websites that look good to *all* visitors is a lot more complex than it used to be — and standards have become a lot more important. This book shows you not only how to use all the great features in Dreamweaver but also how to determine which of those features best serve your goals and your audience.

About This Book

I designed *Dreamweaver CS6 For Dummies* to help you find the answers you need when you need them. You don't have to read through this book cover to cover, and you certainly don't have to memorize it. Consider this a quick study guide and a reference you can return to. Each section stands alone, giving you easy answers to specific questions and step-by-step instructions for common tasks.

Want to find out how to change the background color in page properties, design CSS style rules to align images, or add an interactive photo gallery with the Swap Image behavior? Jump right to the pages that cover those features. (Hint: the Table of Contents and index can help you find the sections that interest you most.) Don't worry about getting sand on this book at the beach or coffee spilled on the pages at breakfast. I promise it won't complain!

You find templates, artwork, and other goodies to use with this book at www. DigitalFamily.com/bonus.

Using Dreamweaver on a Mac or PC

Dreamweaver works almost identically on Macintosh or Windows computers. To keep screenshots consistent throughout this book, I've used a computer running Windows 7. However, I've tested the program on both platforms, and whenever I find a difference in how a feature works, I indicate that difference in the instructions.

Conventions Used in This Book

Keeping things consistent makes them easier to understand. In this book, those consistent elements are *conventions*. Notice how the word *conventions* is in italics? I frequently put new terms in italics and then define them so you know what they mean. It just makes reading so much nicer.

When I type actual *URLs* (web addresses) within regular paragraph text, they look like this: www.digitalfamily.com.

I also assume that your web browser doesn't require the introductory http:// for web addresses. If you use an older browser, remember to type that quaint prefix before the address (also make sure you include that part of the address when you're creating links in Dreamweaver).

Even though Dreamweaver makes understanding HTML pages easier, you may want to wade into HTML waters occasionally. I include HTML code in this book when I think it can help you better understand how things work in Design view. Sometimes it's easier to remove or edit a tag in Code view than Design view. When I do provide examples — including filenames, file extensions, attributes, and tags, such as the following code that links a URL to a web page — I set off the HTML in monospaced type:

```
<a href="http://www.digitalfamily.com">Learn more about
          Dreamweaver at Janine's DigitalFamily website</a>
```

When I introduce you to a new set of features, such as options in a dialog box, I set those items apart with bullet lists so you can see that they're all related. When I want you to follow instructions, I use numbered step lists to walk you through the process.

What You're Not to Read

If you're like most of the web designers I know, you don't have time to wade through a thick book before you start working on your website. That's why I wrote *Dreamweaver CS6 For Dummies* in a way that makes it easy for you to find the answers you need quickly. You don't have to read this book cover to cover. If you're in a hurry, go right to the information you need most and then get back to work. If you're new to web design or you want to know the intricacies of Dreamweaver, skim through the chapters to get an overview — and then go back and read what's most relevant to your project in greater detail. Whether you're building a simple site for the first time or working to redesign a complex site for the umpteenth time, you find everything you need in these pages.

Foolish Assumptions

Although Dreamweaver is designed for *professional* developers, I don't assume you're a pro — at least not yet. In keeping with the philosophy behind the *For Dummies* series, this book is an easy-to-use guide designed for readers with a wide range of experience. If you're interested in web design and want to create a website, that's all I expect from you.

If you're an experienced web designer, *Dreamweaver CS6 For Dummies* is an ideal reference for you because it gets you working quickly with this program — starting with basic web-page design features and progressing to more advanced options. If you're new to web design, this book walks you through all you need to know to create a website, from creating a new page to publishing your finished project on the web.

How This Book Is Organized

To ease you through the learning curve associated with any new program, I organized *Dreamweaver CS6 For Dummies* as a reference. This section provides a breakdown of the four parts of the book and what you can find in each one. Each chapter walks you through the features of Dreamweaver step by step, providing tips and helping you understand the vocabulary of web design as you go along.

Part I: Creating Great Websites

Part I introduces you to the basic concepts of web design as well as the main features of Dreamweaver. In Chapter 1, I give you an overview of the many approaches to web design, so you can best determine how you want to build your website before you get into the details of which features in Dreamweaver are best suited to any particular design approach. In Chapter 2, I start you on the road to your first website — including creating a new site, importing an existing site, creating new web pages, applying basic formatting, and setting links. To make this chapter more interesting and help you see how all these features come together, I walk you through creating a real web page as I show you how the features work.

In Chapter 3, I move on to graphics, with an introduction to creating graphics for the web, an overview of the differences in formats (GIFs, JPEGs, and PNG files), and detailed instructions for adding and positioning graphics in your pages. In Chapter 4, you discover Dreamweaver's testing and publishing features, so you can make sure that all your links work and that your website will look good in the most important web browsers. You also find everything you need to start uploading pages to the Internet.

Part II: Creating Page Designs with Style

Chapter 5 provides an overview of how Cascading Style Sheets work and how they can save you time. CSS has become *the* way to create page designs and manage formatting on web pages, and these features have been nicely improved in Dreamweaver CS6. In this chapter, you find descriptions of the style definition options available in Dreamweaver as well as instructions for creating and applying styles. In Chapter 6, I take you further into CSS, introducing you to the power of `<div>` tags, how to create CSS layouts, how to create centered CSS designs and fluid layouts, and how to use Dreamweaver's newest CSS testing features. In Chapter 7, I introduce the newest features in Dreamweaver and show you how to add some of the hot new design options, such as drop shadows and gradients, which were made possible by CSS3.

In Chapter 8, I introduce you to some of my favorite Dreamweaver features, including sophisticated template capabilities that enable you to create more consistent designs and make global updates across many pages at once. I also cover Dreamweaver's Library items, which come in handy for commonly used elements, such as the copyright on all of your web pages. In Chapter 9, you discover how to use HTML table features (and when they're still recommended on the web).

Part III: Making Your Site Cool with Advanced Features

In Part III, you discover how cool your site can look when you add interactive images, audio, video, and drop-down menus. In Chapter 10, you find instructions for creating an interactive photo gallery with the Swap Image behavior, as well as how to use other features in Dreamweaver's Behaviors panel — including the Open New Browser behavior. In Chapter 11, you discover how great the Spry features are for adding AJAX interactivity to your site. You find instructions for creating and customizing drop-down lists, collapsible panels, and more. In Chapter 12, you find out what it takes to add multimedia to your web pages, including how to insert and create links to a variety of file types — from Flash to video and audio files. In Chapter 13, I cover Dreamweaver's HTML form options, which you can use to add feedback forms, surveys, and much more.

Part IV: The Part of Tens

Part IV features two quick references to help you develop the best websites possible. Chapter 14 provides a collection of online resources where you can register domain names and find hosting services, as well as a few services that can help you take care of more advanced challenges (such as setting up an e-commerce system). In Chapter 15, you find ten ways to promote your website, from search engine optimization to social media and beyond.

Icons Used in This Book

This icon points you toward valuable resources on the web.

This icon reminds you of an important concept or procedure that you'll want to store away in your own memory banks for future use.

This icon signals technical stuff that you may find informative and interesting, though it isn't essential for using Dreamweaver. Feel free to skip over this information.

This icon indicates a tip or technique that can save you time and money — and a headache — later.

This icon warns you of any potential pitfalls — and gives you the all-important information on how to avoid them.

Where to Go from Here

To familiarize yourself with the latest in web design strategies and options, don't skip Chapter 1, which guides you through the many ways to create websites that you have to choose from today. If you're ready to dive in and build a basic website right away, jump ahead to Chapter 2. If you want to find out about a specific trick or technique, consult the Table of Contents or the index; you won't miss a beat as you work to make those impossible web design deadlines. Most of all, I wish you great success in all your web projects!

For technical updates to this book, visit `www.dummies.com/go/dreamweavercs6fdupdates`.

Part I
Creating Great Websites

The 5th Wave — By Rich Tennant

"Just how accurately should my website reflect my place of business?"

*C*hapter 1 compares different layout techniques you can use in Dreamweaver and provides an introduction to the toolbars, menus, and panels that make up Dreamweaver's interface. In Chapter 2, you dive into setting up a website, creating web pages, and adding text, links, and meta data for search engines.

In Chapter 3, you find an introduction to web graphics with instructions for using Photoshop (or Photoshop Elements) to optimize images in GIF, PNG, and JPEG formats. Chapter 4 covers managing, testing and publishing your site, so you can make sure that everything works beautifully before you publish your site to a web server.

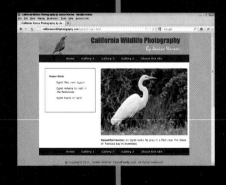

The Many Ways to Design a Web Page

In the mid-1990s, learning to create websites — and teaching others how to do it — was easy. More than a dozen years and a dozen books later, the process is a lot more complex. I've come to realize that one of the first things to understand about web design is that there isn't just one way to create a website anymore.

In this chapter, I being with an introduction to the many ways you can create a website and the tools Dreamweaver offers to make those designs possible. I also introduce you to the basics of HTML and how websites and browsers work. At the end of this chapter, you find a quick tour of the Dreamweaver CS6 interface to help you get comfortable with the workspace.

Understanding How Web Design Works

In a nutshell, building a website involves creating individual pages and linking them to other pages. You need to have a *home page,* the first page visitors see when they arrive at your web address, (also known as your URL), and that page needs to bring them into the rest of the pages of the site, usually with links to each of the main sections of the site. Those pages, in turn, link to subsections that can then lead to deeper subsections.

After you create a website, you can test all the links on your own hard drive and then upload the pages to a web server when everything is ready and working well. You can read more about setting up a site and using Dreamweaver to create pages on your local computer in Chapter 2. In Chapter 4, you discover how to upload your pages to a web server when you're ready to publish your site on the Internet.

The most important thing to remember is that you need to create a folder on your local computer that will mirror your website on your web server when you publish your site. That's why the site setup process in Chapter 2 is so important — because it sets up Dreamweaver to help you create these two versions of your site: the version you create and edit on your computer and the copy you need to maintain on the web server.

Although you have to save all the files in your site in one main folder, you can create subfolders to organize the site. Thus a key part of planning a website is determining how to organize the pages of your site into sections and how those sections should link to one another. Dreamweaver makes creating pages and setting links easy, but how you arrange the pages and links is up to you.

If you're just planning to create a small website, you may think you don't need to worry about how your site will grow and develop. Think again. All good websites grow, and the bigger they get, the harder they are to manage. Planning the path of growth for your website before you begin can make a tremendous difference later. Neglecting to think about growth is probably one of the most common mistakes among new designers. This oversight becomes even more serious when more than one person is working on the same site. Taking a little time to organize the structure of your site, and developing a few consistent conventions for tasks such as naming files, can make everything else go more smoothly.

Managing your site's structure

Managing the structure of a website has two sides: the side that users see, which depends on how you set up links, and the side that's behind the scenes, which depends on how you organize files and folders.

What the user sees

The side that the user sees is all about design and navigation. When users arrive at your home page, where do you direct them? How do they move from one page to another in your site? A good website is designed so that users navigate easily and intuitively and can make a beeline to the information most relevant to them. As you plan, make sure that users can

- ✔ Access key information easily from more than one place in the site
- ✔ Move easily between pages and sections
- ✔ Return to main pages and subsections in one step

Setting links is easy in Dreamweaver; the challenge is to make sure that those links are easy for visitors to follow. One of the best ways to ensure that visitors can easily move around your site is to create on every page of your site a navigation or menu bar that includes links to the main pages of your site. You find instructions in Chapter 6 for creating a menu bar with CSS. In Chapter 11, you find out how to use Dreamweaver's Spry features to create a menu with a drop-down list using AJAX. And in Chapter 8, you find instructions for using Dreamweaver's template and library features, which make menus easier to include on your pages — as well as faster to update if you add or change a menu link later.

What's behind the scenes

The second side to managing your website structure happens behind the scenes (where your users can't see the information, but you want some kind of organizational system to remember what's what). Before you begin designing and linking the pages in your site, think about how to keep track of all the text, images, animations, and other files that make up your site. At minimum, consider the following:

- ✔ **A file-naming system:** For example, naming image files consistently can make them easier to find if you need to edit them later. For example, if you use small, thumbnail images as well as bigger versions, give both files similar names to make it easier to match them later. An easy way to do that is to add *th* to the thumbnail versions, like this: `bird.jpg` and `bird-th.jpg`. Similarly, giving the main section pages in your site names that match the text of the links on your pages can make setting the links easier. For example, if the navigation bar on your home page includes an About Us page and a Contact page, you can easily figure out what page a link should point to if your pages are named `aboutus.html` and `contact.html`.

- ✔ **A folder structure:** When your website grows past a handful of pages, organizing them in separate folders or directories can help you keep track. Fortunately, Dreamweaver makes this easy by providing a Files panel where you can see all the files of your site — and even move and rename files and folders (see Chapter 2 for more on how to use Dreamweaver's Files panel).

Exploring HTML, XHTML, and HTML5

Contrary to popular belief, HTML isn't a programming language. Rather, it's a *markup* language: That is, HTML is designed to mark up a page, or to provide instructions for how a web page should look. HTML is written by using *tags*, which are markup instructions that tell a web browser how to display the page. For example, to apply italic formatting to text, you (or Dreamweaver) insert the HTML tag <em>, which stands for emphasis, where you want the italics to begin and end. Most tags in HTML include both an open tag and a close tag, indicated by the forward slash /. Thus, to make the name of this book appear in italics, I would write the code like this:

```
<em>Dreamweaver CS6 For Dummies</em>
```

Another challenge of HTML is that the tags have changed over time, and so has the acronym. When I'm referring to the code in a general way, I use the acronym HTML, but the two most popular versions of HTML today are really called XHTML and HTML5.

XHTML, a stricter version of HTML, is the recommended language to use for most websites today. HTML5, which has garnered lots of hype, is the newest version. However, HTML5 hasn't yet been approved as a standard and many of its tags are not yet supported by web browsers, so Dreamweaver (and I) still recommend you do most of your design work today in XHTML.

Although I don't recommend that everyone start using HTML5 yet, because the advantages don't outweigh the challenges today, I'm bullish about the new design features of CSS3. As you discover in Chapter 7, you have little reason to hold back on adding the wonderful design enhancements made possible by the new rules in CSS3, no matter what version of HTML you use.

You have two ways to see what the code behind a web page looks like:

- ✔ In most browsers, choose View➪Source.
- ✔ If you're using Dreamweaver (as shown in Figure 1-1), you can click the Split button (upper-left corner of the workspace) to see the code and the design areas of the program at the same time in *Split view*.

If you want to see only the code, click the Code button. However, while I'm working on the site design, I find Split view is a useful way to keep an eye on what's going on behind the scenes — and, as a bonus, you can learn a lot of HTML as you go along.

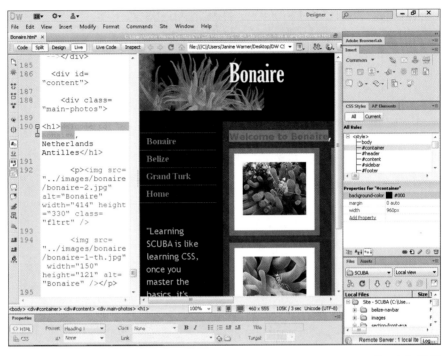

Photos by Ken Riddick

Figure 1-1: Use Split view in Dreamweaver to display the page design and the code behind the page.

Dreamweaver offers four view options:

- ✔ **Code view:** In code view, you see only the HTML and other code.

- ✔ **Split view:** In Split view, the page is divided so you can see the code in one part of the workspace and a view of how the page should be displayed in a web browser in the other part.

- ✔ **Design view:** In Design view, you see only the page as it should be displayed in older web browsers.

- ✔ **Live view:** In Live view, you get a more accurate preview of how your pages will look in the latest web browsers, and you get an interactive view, where you can test rollovers and other interactive features without having to leave Dreamweaver and launch another program.

In Dreamweaver's Split view, the Code and Design views are completely integrated. If you select something in Design view — say, the headline shown in Figure 1-1 — you see the same text highlighted in Code view, enabling you to find your place easily in the code.

How web browsers work

Web browsers such as Internet Explorer, Firefox, Chrome, and Safari are designed to decipher HTML, CSS, JavaScript, and other code — and display the corresponding text, images, and multimedia on a computer screen. Essentially, browsers read the code in a web page and interpret how to display the page to visitors. Unfortunately, because web browsers are created by different companies and the code they display has evolved dramatically over the years, not all web browsers display web pages the same way. Differences in browser display can lead to unpredictable (and often frustrating) results because a page that looks good in one browser may be unreadable in another. For more information on browser differences and testing your pages to make sure they look good to all your visitors, see Chapter 4.

Here are a few points to help you better understand the similarities and differences among older versions of HTML, XHTML, and the latest, HTML5:

- **All versions of HTML include tags that are designed to be hierarchical.** Examples are the `<h1>` (heading 1) through `<h6>` (heading 6) tags, which are ideally suited to formatting text according to its importance on a web page. Reserve the `<h1>` tag for the most important text on the page, such as the top headline. The `<h2>` tag is ideal for subheads or secondary headings, `<h3>` for the third level of headings, and so on. A headline formatted with the `<h1>` tag looks like this:

  ```
  <h1>This is a headline</h1>
  ```

- **HTML5 adds new tags.** HTML5 adds a collection of tags designed to make webpages more *semantic*, or more meaningful. New tags, including `<header>` and `<footer>`, can be used to identify the type of content in a webpage.

- **XHTML tags must be written in lowercase.** HTML5 and older versions of HTML are not case sensitive.

- **In XHTML, all tags must include the closing slash.** A few tags can stand alone, such as the `<br />` tag, which adds a line break. As a rule, XHTML tags must have a close tag, even if there's only one tag, and the close tag must always contain a forward slash (/). Thus the line break tag is `<br>` in HTML and `<br />` in XHTML.

- **Some tags are more complex, and the open and close tags don't always match.** More complicated tags, such as the tags used to create links or insert images into pages, are more challenging to use because they include link information, and the close tag doesn't always match the open tag. For example, the code to create a link to another website looks like this:

```
<a href="http://www.digitalfamily.com">This is a link to
          DigitalFamily.com</a>
```

At their heart, all versions of HTML are just text — and believe it or not, you can write HTML in a plain-text editor as simple as Notepad, SimpleText, or TextEdit. However, you have to be careful to type all the code perfectly because there is no room for error or typos in HTML. After writing code yourself, even to create a simple page, you're sure to appreciate how wonderful it is to let Dreamweaver write the code for you.

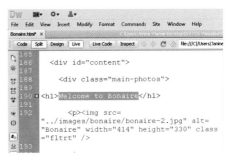

Figure 1-2: A heading 1 tag highlighted in Code view.

If (at first glance) you think that HTML code looks like hieroglyphics, don't give up too quickly. With just a little practice, you can start to recognize at least the most common tags, such as `<h1>` (heading 1) tag used to format the headline shown in Figure 1-2.

Comparing Static and Dynamic Sites

Websites fall into two very broad categories: static sites, which are generally built with a program such as Adobe Dreamweaver, and dynamic sites, which combine advanced programming with a database to generate web pages dynamically.

A *static site* is like a unique book, where each page has been created by hand. The process can be compared to illuminated manuscripts, where monks toiled for years and each page was an individual work of art. Static websites are made up of a collection of individual pages with the .html or .htm extension. You might think that all websites are made up of individual pages (and in a way they are), but with static site, each page is saved as a separate file.

In contrast, a *dynamic site* works more like a warehouse full of words, images, videos, and colors with a super-fast clerk who can run at light speed through the aisles, grabbing items and assembling them into pages as you read them. With a dynamic site, the pages you view in a web browser are created as they are delivered to the browser, so they're not saved as individual pages but as pieces of pages that can be mixed and matched. That gives dynamic sites many advantages, but it also makes them a lot more complicated to create. On a large website such as Amazon.com, for example, this dynamic process makes it possible for Amazon to create a page with recommended books for you that looks different from the page it recommends to me, even though we're both entering the same URL into a web browser.

If you're just creating a simple profile or small business site, go with a static site. Dynamic websites are often not worth the extra effort, unless you're creating a site that you expect to grow to 100 pages or more.

Although you can create custom dynamic websites in Dreamweaver using popular technologies such as PHP or ASP.NET, most programmers who are creating sites with this level of complexity use more advanced programming tools, such as Eclipse or Microsoft Visual Studio.

I used to teach the basics of dynamic site creation in Dreamweaver, but today better options exist. Instead of reinventing the wheel by creating their own dynamic site system with Dreamweaver, many web designers are using Content Management Systems (CMS), such as WordPress and Joomla.

Following are some of the most popular content management systems:

- **WordPress (**www.wordpress.org**):** WordPress.com offers WordPress on a free hosting service; at www.wordpress.org, you can download the WordPress program for free and install it on your own server. One of the most popular and powerful blogging tools, WordPress is increasingly used as a CMS for more complex sites. You'll find many great extensions for WordPress. After a site is built, teaching people to use the administrative tools to update the site (even if they don't know HTML) is relatively easy, making this an especially popular tool among web designers who are creating sites that they want their clients to be able to update themselves.

- **Joomla (**www.Joomla.org**):** Joomla offers many of the features of WordPress. Joomla is a good choice for magazine-style sites and directories because it enables you to create categories and subcategories far more easily than in WordPress.

- **Drupal (**drupal.org/**):** Designed by programmers for programmers, Drupal offers more advanced functionality for creating highly complex, interactive websites. If you're a designer, not a programmer, the learning curve for Drupal is steeper than for WordPress or Joomla.

You can use Dreamweaver to create and edit templates for any of the content management systems listed here. Before you do, however, you have to set up a web server on your local computer. You learn more about how to work with these programs in the section, "Working with Templates in Dreamweaver," later in this chapter.

If you're interested in learning more about WordPress, check out *WordPress For Dummies,* 4th Edition, by Lisa Sabin-Wilson (Wiley).

Most of this book is dedicated to helping you create static websites — but that doesn't mean you can't get many of the same benefits of dynamic sites, including the capability to update pages quickly. As you find in this book, you can combine CSS (covered in Chapters 5–7) with Dreamweaver's `.dwt` template features (covered in detail in Chapter 8) and get many features of a big-budget website without all the complicated programming skills. (You find a general description of Dreamweaver's template features, as well as a look at the differences among templates, in the next section.)

Static pages work well for small and medium-sized websites, such as a professional profile or online gallery. Because static web pages are written in plain text, you can create them in a program as simple as Notepad or SimpleText, although tools such as Dreamweaver make designing pages a lot easier because you don't have to remember all the cryptic HTML tags.

A static website offers a few advantages, especially if you're just starting out. A static website

- ✔ **Is easy to learn to develop:** Anyone who can resize a photo has a head start on the skills needed to create and arrange graphic elements on a static page.

- ✔ **Gives you complete control over the design of each page:** You can tweak the size, colors, fonts, and arrangement of the elements on each page individually, and you can edit templates for these kinds of sites more easily than the templates for dynamic sites.

- ✔ **Is easy to build, test, and publish to a web server:** You can create and test static web pages on any personal computer and then host them on any commercial web server — and you need only FTP access (built in to programs such as Dreamweaver) to publish pages to the Internet.

Working with Templates in Dreamweaver

The term template is used in different ways for different kinds of design work (on and off the web), but essentially a *template* is a shortcut in the design process. By working with Dreamweaver templates, you can set or adjust almost any aspect of a site's design or functionality, including a header, logo, navigation bar, or sidebar. Whatever you include in a Dreamweaver template, you can then apply to any new page based on the template, which automatically applies the settings you want to appear throughout your site. Moreover, if you want to adjust the overall settings in your site, you can make those updates once in the template, update your pages, and — voila — all pages based on the template are updated automatically.

But not all templates are created equally. Although they all share those basic characteristics, many kinds of templates are in use on the web today. For example, templates for static websites (which you find instructions for creating in Chapter 8) are quite different from the kinds of templates you would use if you were creating a blog with WordPress.

You can download many kinds of templates from the web, but they don't all work in all programs. For example, if you download templates designed for Adobe Flash, you won't be able to use them in Dreamweaver (although you can insert Flash files in Dreamweaver, as you discover in Chapter 12).

You can edit many kinds of templates in Dreamweaver. Before you start using Dreamweaver to create or edit templates, however, it's helpful to better understand how they are different. The following sections cover two of the most common types of templates in use on the web today (and what you should know about how they differ). See the nearby sidebar, "So many Dreamweaver template options," for a complete list of template options.

Creating and editing Dreamweaver templates

Dreamweaver templates (extension .dwt) offer many advantages without requiring advanced programming skills. When you create Dreamweaver templates with the .dwt extension, you can use HTML and CSS to create static websites that include many of the high-end features found on dynamic sites — such as the capability to create new pages quickly and to update every page in your site with the click of a button.

Although you can use Dreamweaver to create templates that use advanced programming (such as PHP or Java), the .dwt Dreamweaver template is a much simpler option that's ideal for small- to medium-size websites — which is why I've dedicated much of Chapter 8 to making the most of Dreamweaver templates.

Editing WordPress, Joomla, and Drupal templates

Templates like the ones you get with a blogging program such as WordPress use the extension .php because they're written in the PHP (Hypertext Preprocessor) programming language. Although you can create PHP pages and templates in Dreamweaver and use them for more than just WordPress, these types of files are far more complex to create than .dwt Dreamweaver templates.

So many Dreamweaver template options

Dreamweaver supports many kinds of technologies, as well as the templates that go with each. When you create new pages in Dreamweaver by choosing File⇨New, you have the option to create a blank page or a blank template. When you create a simple HTML template, Dreamweaver uses the `.dwt` extension. Dreamweaver also supports Microsoft ASP and ASP.NET, and you can create templates using either ASP JavaScript or ASP VBScript (both of which use the `.asp` extension) — or you can use ASP.NET C# or VB (which use the `.aspx` extension). The templates for a site created using Java end in `.jsp`. And if you use Adobe's ColdFusion technology, your templates end in `.cfm`.

The big lesson is this: Make sure you have the right kind of template for the kind of site you're creating — and rest assured that Dreamweaver supports just about any kind of technology you can use to create a website today.

Because so many people use WordPress (such as the blog shown in Figure 1-3) and so many sites offer WordPress template downloads, many people are confused about why WordPress templates don't work in Dreamweaver in the same way that `.dwt` Dreamweaver templates work.

Figure 1-3: The Sips from the Firehose blog was created with WordPress.

WordPress templates offer many of the same benefits as Dreamweaver templates — except that templates for blogs such as WordPress draw their content from a database. As a result, they include HTML and CSS (as do the Dreamweaver templates), plus much more complicated code in the PHP programming language, which describes how content from the database should be displayed in a web page.

As a result, to make WordPress, Joomla, or Drupal templates work in Dreamweaver, you must first set up your computer as a web server and install MySQL and WordPress. Because so many people are using these programs, you can get all the software you need in one nifty package from MAMP.com (for Mac) and XAMP.com (for Windows). You will find links to these tools, as well as instructions for using them to set up your computer as a web server, at `www.digitalfamily.com/cms-blogs/setting-up-a-web-server.html`.

Comparing Tables, Frames, and Layers

If you've already done a little web design, you may be wondering what happened to some of the old ways of creating web page layouts. For years, web designers used the HTML feature called tables to create page layouts. Then frames came along, and many people were excited by the capability to display multiple pages in one browser window (which frames and iFrames make possible). Then came layers, which were especially popular among designers because they seemed to offer precise design control.

Today, most professional designers agree that the best way to create a web page design is to use HTML with Cascading Style Sheets, which are covered in detail in Chapters 5–7.

Over the years, all these other options have become less desirable except in a few special cases. In this section, you find a quick review of when tables, frames, and layers may still be useful.

Creating page designs with HTML tables

In the early days of web design, most page layouts on the web were created with tables. By merging and splitting table cells and even adding background images, designers created complex web designs. CSS expands upon this concept by adding many new design options — including the capability to add precise margins and padding around elements, which offers better control of how and where background images appear.

Figure 1-4 provides an example of an old-school site created with the HTML `table` tag. Most designers turn off table borders by setting the table border to 0 to create cleaner layouts, but in Figure 1-4, I've set the borders to 2 pixels so you can see the outline of the table. Table cells surround each of the photos and captions in this two-column layout; I've merged the columns at the top of the design to make room for the banner image, which spans the full width of the page. I also merged two rows to create a space for the large photo on the right side of the page.

Although tables are no longer recommended for creating page layouts, they're still considered the best way to format tabular data like that you'd find in a spreadsheet program. You can use tables to format a consistent collection of information — such as the list of birds with their photos, names, and habitats, as shown in Figure 1-5.

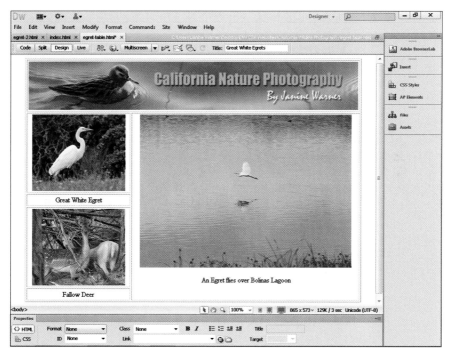

Photos by Janine Warner

Figure 1-4: In the old days, complex web page designs used HTML tables to control text and image placement.

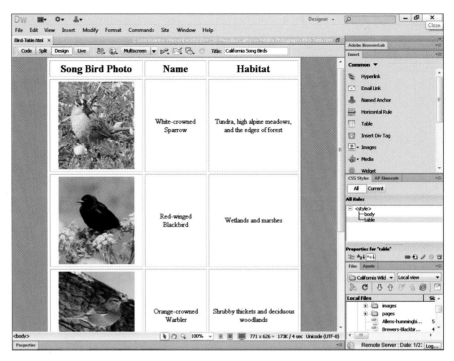

Figure 1-5: Tables are still the best way to display tabular data in columns and rows.

Although I recommend that you redesign sites like the one shown in Figure 1-4 with CSS and `<div>` tags, I do understand that some designers still find it easier to create layouts with tables, and not everyone has time to redesign their websites right away. I have to admit, I've been guilty of leaving online a few sites designed with tables long after I knew better. I recommend using only CSS today for all your web page layouts — except when you're creating a layout for tabular data. Even then, I still urge you to use CSS to add any styling (such as background colors or padding) that you might want in your tables. In Chapter 9, you discover how to create tables like the one shown in Figure 1-5.

Considering design options with HTML frames

You won't find any instructions in this book for creating websites that use frames, such as the Cold War Museum site shown in Figure 1-6. Frames enable you to display multiple web pages in one browser window. Among web designers, frames are a little like the Cold War itself — a part of history. Although frames are still used on a few sites on the web, most designers don't like them because they can make navigation confusing to site visitors.

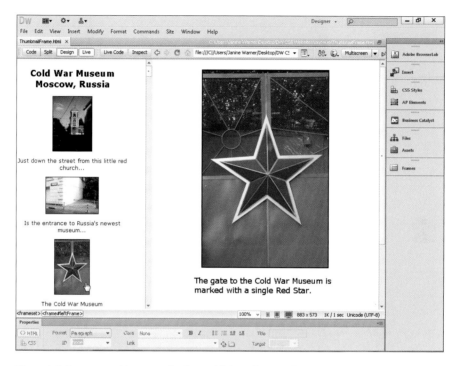

Figure 1-6: Frames enable you to display multiple web pages in one browser window.

Frames are also problematic because when you use frames, the URL at the top of a web browser does not change, even when you click links and change the pages displayed within the frames. As a result, you can only *bookmark* (create a link to) the first page of a site that uses frames. Worse yet, search engines have a hard time properly indexing a site designed with frames — which can diminish your site's search engine ranking.

Appreciating the Benefits of Cascading Style Sheets

The concept of creating styles has been around since well before the web. Desktop publishing programs (such as Adobe InDesign) and even word processing programs (such as Microsoft Word) have long used styles to manage the formatting and editing of text on printed pages. In a word processor, you can create and save styles for common features, such as headlines and captions. In print design, styles are great timesavers because they enable you to combine a collection of formatting options (such as Arial and bold and italic) into one style — and then apply all those options at once to any selected text in your document, using only a single style. The advantage is that if you change a style, you can automatically apply the change everywhere you've used that style in a document.

On the web, you can do all that and more with CSS — because you can use style sheets for more than just text formatting. For example, you can use CSS to create styles that align images to the left or right side of a page, add padding around text or images, and change background and link colors. You can even create more than one style sheet for the same page — say, one that makes your design look good on computers, another for cell phones, and a third for a printed page.

For all these reasons (and more), CSS has quickly become the preferred method of designing web pages among professional web designers. One of the most powerful aspects of CSS is that it enables you to make global style changes across an entire website. Suppose, for example, that you create a style for your headlines by redefining the <h1> tag to create large, blue, bold headlines. Then, one fine day, you decide that all your headlines should be red instead of blue. If you aren't using CSS, changing all your headlines could be a huge undertaking — a matter of opening every web page in your site to make changes to the font tags around every headline. But if you're using CSS in an external style sheet, you can simply change the style that contains formatting information for the <h1> tag in the style sheet and all your headlines turn red automatically. If you ever have to redesign your site (and believe me, every good site goes through periodic redesigns), you can save hours (or even days) of work if you created your design with CSS in the first place.

A website designed with CSS separates content from design. Keeping the content of site (such as the text and headings) separate from the instructions that tell a browser how the content should look benefits both you as a designer and your site visitors. Here are some of the advantages:

- ✓ **CSS simplifies design changes.** CSS styles can be saved in the header section at the very top of an HTML page, or they can be saved in a separate file that can be attached to multiple HTML pages. Either way, if you use a style to format many headlines, you can make formatting changes by simply editing the style.

- ✓ **Separating content from design enables you to create different style sheets for different audiences and devices.** Today's websites are as likely to be viewed on giant, wall-size screens as they are to be seen on screens small enough to hide in the palm of your hand during a lunch date. CSS enables you to create web page designs that are more adaptable so they look good on big *and* small screens, as well as everything in between.

  As you get more advanced with CSS, you can even create multiple style sheets for the same web page. For example, you can create one that's ideally suited to a big computer monitor, another that's designed to get the best results when the page is printed, and yet another designed with a larger font size for anyone who may have trouble reading the small print that's so common on web pages.

✔ **Using CSS makes your site comply with the current standards.** Today, the W3C, which sets standards for the Internet, recommends using CSS for nearly every aspect of web design because the best CSS designs are accessible, flexible, and adaptable.

✔ **Websites designed in CSS are accessible to more visitors.** Today, a movement is growing among some of the best designers in the world to get everyone to follow the same standards, create websites with CSS, and make sure sites are accessible to everyone.

When web designers talk about *accessibility,* they mean creating a site that anyone who might ever visit your pages can access — including people with limited vision who use special browsers (often called *screen readers*) that read web pages aloud, as well as many others who use specialized browsers for a variety of other reasons.

If you work for a university, a nonprofit, a government agency, or a similar organization, you may be required to create accessible designs. Even if you're not required to design for accessibility, know that pages that meet accessibility standards also tend to score better in search engine rankings because accessible designs also enable search engines to access and interpret site content more easily.

In Chapters 5 and 6, you find an introduction to creating styles and page designs with CSS. In Chapter 7, you find an introduction to some of the new features introduced in CSS3.

Understanding Browser Differences

HTML was created to share information in a way that could be displayed on every computer on the planet — one of the greatest advantages of the web. However, for web designers, this advantage is also a challenge because not all those computers use the same browsers, the same fonts, or the same monitor size. On top of that, a lot of older web browsers that can't display the latest web features are still in use and even newer browsers don't all display pages that use those features in the same way. So before you start creating web pages, know that no matter how carefully you create your designs, your pages will never look exactly the same to every possible visitor to your site.

If you want to create page designs using the latest technology and reach the broadest possible audience, pay special attention to Dreamweaver's Live view, browser preview, and compatibility features — and be prepared to move on to training that's more advanced than this book. Entire books and websites are dedicated to creating highly complex CSS layouts that are displayed well on various computers and browsers — and to combining CSS and other special code to make complex pages look good in older and newer web browsers.

In Chapter 4, you find more information about browser differences, as well as Dreamweaver's testing and compatibility features, which can help ensure that your pages work well for a broad audience.

Introducing the Dreamweaver CS6 Workspace

Dreamweaver can seem a bit overwhelming at first. You can easily get lost with so many features spread among so many panels, toolbars, and dialog boxes. If you prefer to build an understanding by poking around, have at it (and feel free to skip to Chapter 2, where you start building your first web page). If you want a tour before you get started, read this last section, which introduces you to the interface and gives you a quick overview of the features in this powerful program.

When you launch Dreamweaver, the Welcome screen, shown in Figure 1-7, appears in the main area of the program (and reappears anytime you don't have a file open, unless you close the Welcome screen by selecting the Don't Show Again option). After you select an option on the Welcome screen (these options are explained in Chapter 2), Dreamweaver creates a new blank HTML page in the main workspace, the main area of the program where you design your page. The *workspace* consists mainly of a Document window, which displays the page you're working on and is where you add text, images, and other elements that will appear on your web pages. The *Document window* is surrounded by a collection of panels, toolbars, and menus that provide easy access to Dreamweaver's many features. Details of these controls follow.

Changing workspace layouts

In Dreamweaver CS6, you can choose from 11 preset workspace layouts, reflecting the increased complexity of the job of a web designer. Recent additions include the App Developer Plus, Fluid Layout, and Mobile Applications views.

These layouts arrange the many toolbars, panels, and other features in popular configurations. You can change layouts by choosing Window➪Workspace Layout and then selecting one of the listed layouts. Or choose a layout from the drop-down list at the top of the Dreamweaver window, such as Designer (which is selected in Figure 1-7) or Coder Plus (shown in Figure 1-8).

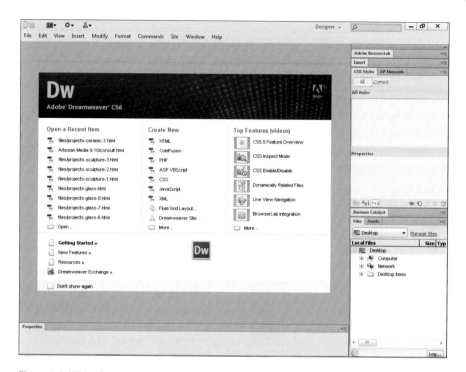

Figure 1-7: When Dreamweaver opens, the welcome screen provides easy access to commonly used items, such as recently opened files.

In addition to the preset workspace layouts, you can create your own by following these steps:

1. **Open, close, or move any of the panels, inspectors, or other features, as described in the following sections.**

2. **Choose Window⇨Workspace Layout⇨New Workspace.**

3. **Give your new workspace a name and click OK.**

   Your custom workspace is added to the Layout menu so you can easily reset the program to match your favorite settings.

The name that the Layout menu displays will match the last layout you chose and used. If your last choice was Designer, it says Designer; if your last choice was Coder, it says Coder.

If you move a panel or inspector and then want to return it to its original location, use the Layout menu: Choose Reset and then choose the name of the workspace layout you want to restore.

At the end of the drop-down list are the two options that control the display of the list of options in the Insert panels:

- ✔ **Color Icons:** Restores the color to the icons

- ✔ **Hide Labels/Show Labels:** Enables you to display the names of the Insert panel features next to each icon, or to remove the names

The Property inspector

The Property inspector is docked at the bottom of the workspace in Dreamweaver. If you prefer, you can click the gray bar at the top of the inspector and drag it to detach it so it floats in the workspace. You can move the inspector anywhere on the screen or you can drag and dock it in the panel group. When you dock the Property inspector with the other panels, you can expand and collapse it just as you would any other panels. To restore the inspector to its original location, choose Window⇨Workspace Layout⇨Reset. (I rather like that the Property inspector is handy but out of the way, at the bottom of the screen.)

The Property inspector displays the *properties,* or options, for any selected element on a page, and it changes based on what's selected. For example, if you click an image, the Property inspector displays image properties. If you click a Flash file, the Property inspector displays Flash properties.

For many elements, the Property inspector is split into two sections, one for HTML features and the other for CSS. Use the CSS and HTML buttons on the left side of the Property inspector (as shown in Figure 1-10) to switch from one to the other. (You find detailed instructions for how to use these two modes of the Property inspector in Chapters 5–7.)

Figure 1-10: The status bar and the Property inspector in CSS mode.

At the bottom-right corner of the Property inspector, you see a small arrow. Click this arrow to reduce or expand the inspector to hide or reveal additional attributes, such as the image map options when a graphic is selected. Click the gray bar at the top of the inspector to close and open the inspector.

The status bar

The status bar is located at the bottom of the Document window and just above the Property inspector, as shown in Figure 1-10. The status bar includes access to a number of features that control the display of a page in Dreamweaver's workspace:

- **Tag selector:** On the far left of the status bar, as shown in the top of Figure 1-10, you find the tag selector, which displays the HTML tags and CSS rules that apply to any selected element on the page. In Figure 1-10, the cursor is inside a text block that's formatted with the <h1> tag, which is inside a <div> tag with a #container ID, which is inside the <body> tag.

  - *Clicking* any tag in the tag selector selects the tag and all its contents in the workspace.

  - *Right-clicking (Control-clicking on a Mac)* a tag opens a pop-up menu with options to add or remove tags and CSS rules.

- **Select tool, Hand tool, Zoom tool, and Magnification pop-up menu:** You can use these tools, which are toward the middle of the status bar, to move (Select tool) or resize (Hand tool, Zoom tool, and Magnification menu) the display of a page in the workspace.

- **Mobile, Tablet, and Desktop Size preview buttons:** These buttons provide a quick view of what your web design might look like when viewed using one of these three platforms. The results are not exact: So many possible screen resolutions exist that your computer screen couldn't hold buttons for them all.

- **Download Size/Download Time tool:** Found on the far-right side of the status bar, this tool displays the total size of the web page, including all images and other elements on the page — and the estimated time downloading the page will take, based on the connection speed specified in Dreamweaver's preferences. By default, the connection speed is set to estimate the download time of a page over a 384K modem (which is now the low end of broadband access and about what you can get from a stable 3G connection on a mobile phone). You can set a faster or slower speed by changing the preferences, as shown in the following section.

Changing preference settings

The more you use Dreamweaver, the more you're likely to appreciate how readily you can customize its features. Remember that you can always change the workspace to better suit the way you like to work, and you can easily alter Dreamweaver's preference settings using the Preferences dialog box.

To open the Preferences dialog box, choose Edit⇨Preferences on a Windows computer, or Dreamweaver⇨Preferences on a Mac. Dreamweaver includes 19 categories in the Preferences dialog box and makes it possible to change the appearance, default settings, and many other options throughout the program.

twitter
None
Paragraph
Heading 1

2

twitter
None
Paragraph
Heading 1

Opening and Creating Sites

In This Chapter

▷ Starting with the site setup process

▷ Creating new web pages

▷ Inserting and formatting text

▷ Creating links

▷ Adding search engine keywords to meta tags

*W*hether you're building a new site or need to make changes to an existing site, this chapter is the place to start. Here you discover an important preliminary step: the *site setup process* that enables Dreamweaver to keep track of the images and links in your site. After you complete the site setup process, you're ready to create web pages, insert text and images, set links, and more. (You find instructions for doing all those things in this chapter, too.) But whatever you do, don't skip the first step of defining a site — the process takes only a minute or two.

nnect with Janine

Although you can use Dreamweaver without doing this initial site setup, you run the risk of breaking links when you publish your site using the built-in FTP features. Other features, such as templates, automated link checking, and the Library, won't work at all.

facebook
Profile

The best approach to web design with Dreamweaver is to first create a website on your computer's hard drive, where you use Dreamweaver's preview options to test the site in any browser on your computer before you publish it on the Internet. That's why this chapter starts with setting up a folder on the hard drive where you'll keep your site files. When you're ready to publish the completed site, you transfer it to a web server. A *web server* is a computer with a permanent connection to

twitter
None
Paragraph

The goal is to simply select the folder so that Dreamweaver can identify where all the files and folders for your site will be stored. When you've completed this step, the name of the folder and the path to that folder's location on your hard drive appear in the Local Site Folder field.

5. Click Save to close the Site Setup dialog box and save your settings.

If the folder you selected as your local site folder already contains files or folders, all the files and folders in your site are displayed in the Files panel. As you see in Figure 2-2, I already had many files in my personal profile site, which I'm using as the example in this chapter, so they are listed in the Files panel. If I were creating a new site with a new empty folder, the Files panel would contain only the main site folder.

If you haven't selected the Enable Cache option, a message box appears asking whether you want to create a cache for the site. Choose Yes to speed up Dreamweaver's site management features.

Figure 2-2: When site setup is complete, the files and folders are displayed.

Switching among Sites

You can set up as many sites as you like in Dreamweaver and change from one site to another by selecting the site name in the Files panel. To load a different site into the Files panel, use the drop-down arrow next to the site name and choose the name of the site you want to display.

In Figure 2-3, I'm selecting Janine Warner Website from a list of defined sites. When you select a site, the files in that site replace the ones of any currently open site in the Files panel. Selecting a site in the Files panel before you start working on it is always best.

Figure 2-3: Define multiple sites and change the active site.

Managing Sites in Dreamweaver

After you complete the site setup process covered in the preceding exercise, you can make changes and additions to a site setup by choosing Site⇨Manage Sites to open the Manage Sites dialog box, as shown in Figure 2-4. The Manage Sites dialog box was changed in version 6, but the features are similar.

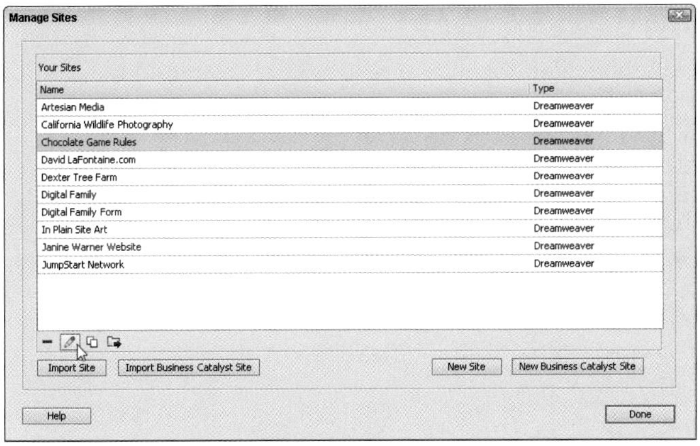

Figure 2-4: You can edit any site setup.

To edit a site that you've already set up, select the name of the site in the Manage Sites dialog box, and then click an icon at the bottom left of the dialog box to manage your site. The icons, from left to right, are as follows:

- ✔ **The minus sign icon** deletes a site from the Manage Sites dialog box. When you delete a site from the list, you don't delete the site's files or folders from your hard drive; you simply remove the site setup in Dreamweaver.

- ✔ **The Edit icon** looks like a pencil and opens the site in the Site Setup dialog box, where you can change the name by replacing the text in the Site Name field and change the local site folder by clicking the Browse icon (which looks like a file folder) and selecting a different folder. In Figure 2-4, I selected the Chocolate Game Rules site and my cursor is on the Edit (pencil) icon.

- ✔ **The Duplicated icon** (the third icon from the left) makes a copy of the site setup but does not make a new copy of the site on your hard drive.

- ✔ **The Export icon** (the fourth icon from the left) exports the site definition. Similar to the duplicate option, the option does not create a copy of the files in the site. Instead, the Export icon exports the .ste file, which can be used to share site setup information from one computer to another.

At the bottom of the Manage Sites dialog box, you find four buttons:

✔ **Import Site:** The Import Site button lets you import a .ste file to add site setup information to Dreamweaver.

✔ **New Site:** Click this button to define a new site. (The process is the same as choosing Site⇨New Site, as explained in "Setting Up a New or Existing Site," earlier in this chapter.

✔ **Business Catalyst buttons:** You also find two buttons specifically for importing and creating new sites using Adobe's Business Catalyst service. Business Catalyst is a hosted web service that extends the features of Dreamweaver to include advanced features, such as a shopping cart ecommerce service. You can learn more at www. BusinessCatalyst.com.

Creating New Pages

Every website begins with a single page. Visitors are first greeted by the front page — or *home page* — of your site, and that page is usually a good place to start building.

Dreamweaver makes creating new pages easy: You can work from the Welcome screen or use the New Document window, which provides more options. The following sections explain both methods, and you find details about the best names to use for new pages so that they'll work well when you publish your site to the web.

Starting from the Welcome screen

When you open Dreamweaver, a Welcome screen greets you with shortcuts to many handy features for creating new pages in a variety of formats:

✔ **The left column provides a handy shortcut to recently opened files.** Click the name of any file in the list to open the file in Dreamweaver.

✔ **If you want to create a simple, blank web page,** choose HTML from the Create New list in the middle column (see Figure 2-5). Remember that choosing HTML doesn't mean that you have to write the HTML code yourself. Rather, you're just telling Dreamweaver that you want to create a page written only with HTML, not with one of the more complex technologies, such as PHP or ASP.NET. You still have the option to work in the code editor or the visual editor and let Dreamweaver write the underlying HTML for you.

✔ **If you're creating a dynamic site,** choose ColdFusion, PHP, or one of the other dynamic site options from the list in the middle of the Welcome screen.

✔ **The Top Features list on the right side of the dialog box** includes links to a collection of video tutorials where you can learn more about Dreamweaver's most popular features.

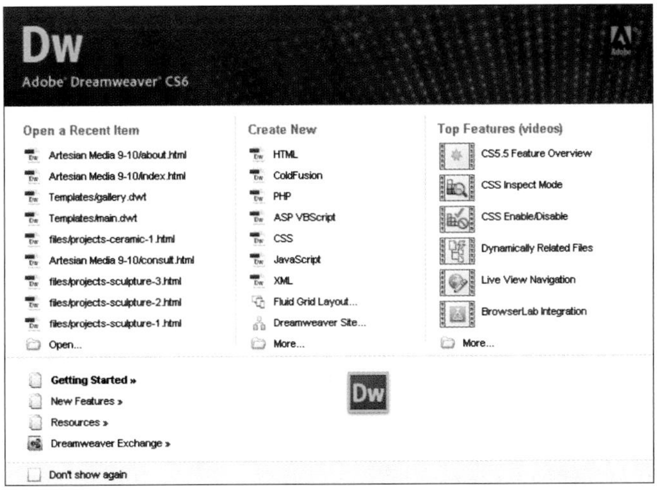

Figure 2-5: View a list of shortcuts for creating files or opening pages.

If you prefer not to use the Welcome screen, you can turn it off by selecting the Don't Show Again check box in the bottom-left corner.

Creating an HTML page with the New Document window

You can also create a new HTML page by using the New Document window, which offers more options than the Welcome screen, including access to any templates you've created with Dreamweaver (covered in Chapter 8), as well as a collection of predesigned layouts, which can give you a head start on your designs.

You can create many kinds of files using the New Document window, and you can mix and match some, but not all, options. This versatility can be confusing at first. Essentially, if you choose an option under Page Types that creates a web page, including HTML, HTML Template, or any of the ASP, ColdFusion, JSP, or PHP options, you can also choose one of the page layouts from the Layout list. If you choose any of the other options, such as Library, CSS, JavaScript, or XML, the layout options are not available because you would not include a layout in any of these types of files. Also note that the layouts are all created with CSS, which Dreamweaver generates as it creates the new web page. You find instructions for altering the CSS to edit these layouts in Chapter 6.

To create a new, blank HTML file, follow these steps:

1. **Choose File⇨New.**

   The New Document window opens, as shown in Figure 2-6.

2. **From the left side of the screen, select Blank Page.**

3. **From the Page Type list, select HTML.**

4. **From the Layout section, choose <none>.**

5. **Use the drop-down list next to DocType if you want to change the document type.**

   By default, Dreamweaver creates pages using the XHTML 1.0 Transitional doctype, which is the best option for most web pages today. If you are working on a site that requires strict HTML pages or are using HTML5, however, make sure to change this setting.

6. **Click Create in the bottom right of the window.**

   The New Document window closes, and a new blank page is created and opened in the workspace.

   In this example, I'm creating a blank page by choosing <none>, but I often start new pages by using one of Dreamweaver's many great layouts. You find instructions for creating and editing pages with these layouts in Chapter 6.

   Note: If you are using a Macintosh, the Create and Cancel buttons are swapped.

7. **Choose File⇨Save to save your page and give it a filename.**

   Dreamweaver automatically names all new files Untitled, followed by a 1, 2, etc. in the order created. I highly recommend you get in the habit of giving your files names that have more meaning to you. Also note that in general, you should not include spaces or special characters in filenames in your website (although the hyphen and underscore are okay). For more on how best to name files and folders in your website, see the upcoming sections "Naming new page files" and "Naming the first page index.html."

Get in the habit of saving new web pages in your local site folder as soon as you create them, even though the pages are still blank. As you create links or add images to your pages, Dreamweaver needs to be able to identify the location of your page within your site folder. Although Dreamweaver sets temporary links until your page is saved, saving a page first is best because many other Dreamweaver features won't work until a page is saved.

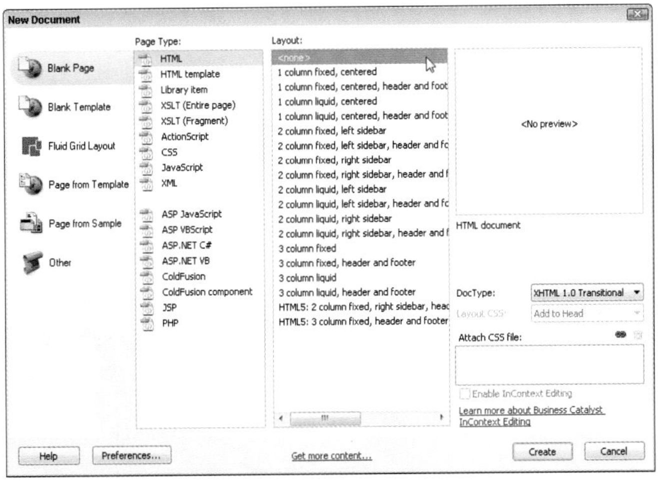

Figure 2-6: The New Document window offers more options when creating a page.

Naming new page files

Over the years, I've received many e-mail messages from panicked web designers because of broken links caused by filename conflicts. These problems usually don't occur until after a website is published on a server, so they can be especially confusing and difficult to understand. If you're publishing your website to a web server that runs on a Mac or under Windows, the following may not apply to you. But if you're using a web server that runs Unix or Linux (used by many commercial web-hosting companies), the following instructions are especially important. If you're not sure, be safe and follow these rules when you save web pages, images, and other files on your site:

✔ **Include an extension at the end to identify the file type.** Examples include .html for HTML files and .gif for GIF images. Dreamweaver automatically adds the .html file extension to the end of HTML files, which works for most web servers. However, in the rare case that you need to change the extension to .htm for your web server, you can do so in Dreamweaver's Preferences dialog box by choosing Edit⇨Preferences (Windows) or Dreamweaver⇨Preferences (Mac). See the "Displaying file extensions in Windows" sidebar for tips on how to view file extensions, which are hidden in Windows.

✔ **Don't use spaces or special characters in filenames.** For example, don't name a web page with an apostrophe, such as cat's meow page. html. If you want to separate words, you can use the underscore (_) or the hyphen (-). For example, meow-page.html is a fine filename. Numbers are okay in most cases, and although capital letters don't generally matter, most designers stick with lowercase. Doing so keeps filenames consistent and makes setting and checking links easier because the name of the file and its reference in any links must match.

Displaying file extensions in Windows

Unless you change the settings on a Windows computer, you won't see the file extension of your GIFs, JPEGs, or HTML pages (although these extensions will be displayed in the Files panel in Dreamweaver). To change these settings, open the Folder Options dialog box, as shown in the following figure, choose the View tab, and then look through the long list of options and deselect Hide Extensions for Known File Types. How you open the Folder Options dialog box depends on which version of Windows you're using. You should be able to find the dialog box easily if you search for Folder Options in the Help section.

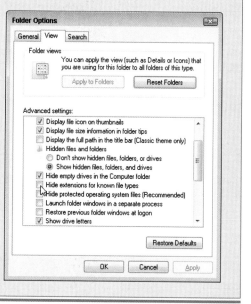

The reason for all this fuss? Filenames are especially important in websites because they're included in the HTML code when you set links. Links with spaces and special characters work just fine when you test pages on a Mac or a PC computer, but many web servers on the Internet use software that doesn't understand spaces or special characters in links. Thus, links that don't follow these rules may get broken when you publish the site to a web server. By following these rules, you ensure that the filename and the code in the link match.

Naming the first page index.html

Another confusing rule — and one of the most important — is that the main page (or the front page) of your website must be called index.html (on some Windows-based servers, the first page should be named default. html). Most servers are set up to serve the index.html or default.html page first.

Essentially, when a web browser comes to a domain name, such as DigitalFamily.com, the first page that opens is index.html. Similarly, when a web browser is directed to a subfolder within a site, it also displays the index page first. As a result, if you create a subfolder with the name books, for example, and inside that subfolder you create a page named index. html as the main page, you can tell visitors to your site to simply enter **www.DigitalFamily.com/books** to arrive at the books page within your site. If you name the first page anything else, such as books.html, visitors have to type **www.DigitalFamily.com/books/books.html** to open the page. The rest of the pages in your site can be named anything you like, as long as the names don't include spaces or special characters (except the hyphen or underscore).

It doesn't matter if you use uppercase or lowercase letters when typing a domain name, but everything that comes after the .com (or .net, or whatever the ending of your domain name) must match the case of the file and folder names. Thus, www.DigitalFamily.com and www.digitalfamily. com are the same, but if you create a folder named books, the address typed into a browser must use a lowercase *b,* as in www.DigitalFamily.com/ books. If someone enters www.DigitalFamily.com/Books in a browser, he or she will get a 404 error, indicating that the link is not valid.

Bestowing a page title

When you create new pages, adding a page title right away is also good practice. A *page title* is the text that appears in the title bar when a visitor opens your site in a browser window.

In Dreamweaver, you can add a page title by changing the text in the Title box at the top of the workspace. This detail is easy to forget, but page titles play an important role in your site's appearance as well as behind the scenes:

- The title won't appear in the main part of your web page, but it does appear at the top of a browser window, usually just to the right or left of the name of the browser. Pages on the web look unfinished when the words *untitled document* appear at the top of the browser window.

- The page title is also the text that appears in a user's Favorites or Bookmarks list.

- Many search engines give special priority to the words that appear in the title of a web page, so including the name of your site and a few keywords can help you score better in search results.

Changing Page-Wide Styles with the Page Properties Dialog Box

You can change many individual elements on a page in the Property inspector. If you want to make changes that affect the entire page — such as changing the background color of the entire page or changing the way links and text are formatted — use the Page Properties dialog box.

As shown in Figure 2-7, the Page Properties dialog box includes a list of categories on the left. Each of these reveals different options for specifying page settings. Some of these options are covered in other parts of the book, such as the Background Image feature, covered in Chapter 3.

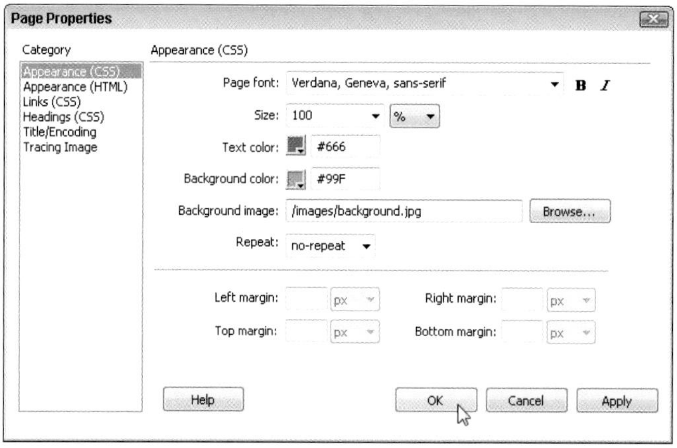

Figure 2-7: Specify text color, font face, font size, background, and margins.

Changing background and text colors

This section focuses on changing the background and the text colors available from the Appearance categories, as shown in Figure 2-7. Note that the CSS options are recommended over HTML options. When you use the Appearance (CSS) options, Dreamweaver creates corresponding styles for the body tag automatically.

Although you can apply global settings, such as text size and color, in the Page Properties dialog box, you can override those settings with other formatting options in specific instances. For example, you could set all your text to Helvetica in Page Properties and then change the font for an individual headline to Arial with the Font field in the Property inspector.

To change the font settings, background color, text color, and page margins for an entire page, follow these steps:

1. **Choose Modify⇨Page Properties.**

   The Appearance (CSS) category of the Page Properties dialog box appears (refer to Figure 2-7).

2. **In the Page Font drop-down list, specify the fonts you want for the text on your page.**

   In this example, I set the font face to the collection that begins with the Georgia font. If you don't specify a font, your text appears in the font specified in your user's browser, which is usually Times. (You find instructions for using custom fonts in Chapter 7.)

3. **If you want all the text on your page to appear bold or italic, click the B or I (respectively) to the right of the Page Font drop-down list.**

   If you select one of these options, all your text appears bold or italic in the page.

4. **In the Size drop-down list, specify the font size you want for the text on your page.**

   Again, you can override these settings for any text on the page.

   I recommend that you specify the size of the text on your pages using the percent or ems measurement because these size options create more adaptive text, a useful strategy on the web where font sizes vary from computer to computer. You find more information about the many size options in Chapter 5.

5. **Click the Text Color swatch box to reveal the color palette. Choose any color you like.**

   The color you select fills the color swatch box but won't change the text color on your page until you click the Apply or OK button.

6. **Click the Background Color swatch box to reveal the color palette. Choose any color you like.**

   The color you selected fills the color swatch box, but the color doesn't fill the background until you click the Apply or OK button.

7. **If you want to insert a graphic or photograph into the background of your page, click the Browse button next to the Background Image box and select the image in the Select Image Source dialog box.**

   When you insert a background image, it automatically repeats, or tiles, across and down the page unless you choose the No-Repeat option from the Repeat drop-down list or use CSS to further define the display.

8. **Use the margin options at the bottom of the dialog box to change the left, right, top, or bottom margins of your page.**

   Entering **0** in all four of these fields removes the default margin settings that automatically add margin space at the top and left of a web page, enabling you to create designs that begin flush with the edge of a browser.

9. **Click the Apply button to see how the colors look on your page.**

10. **Click OK to finish and close the Page Properties dialog box.**

Changing Link Styles with Page Properties

If you're like many designers, you probably don't like the underline that automatically appears under all the linked text in a web page. In this section, you discover how easy it is to remove that underline and change the color, font face, and size for the links with Dreamweaver's Page Properties dialog box. You can also change other page-wide settings, such as the background color and page margins, from the Page Properties dialog box.

The easiest way to alter all your link styles at once is to change them in the Page Properties dialog box. When you use this option, Dreamweaver creates the corresponding tag selector styles automatically and lists them in the CSS Styles panel. Other page-wide settings in this dialog box work similarly.

To change hyperlink and other styles with the Page Properties dialog box, open an existing page or create a new one and follow these steps:

1. **Choose Modify⇨Page Properties.**

   Alternatively, you can click the Page Properties button in the Property inspector. The Page Properties dialog box appears.

2. **Select the Links (CSS) category on the left of the Page Properties dialog box, as shown in Figure 2-8.**

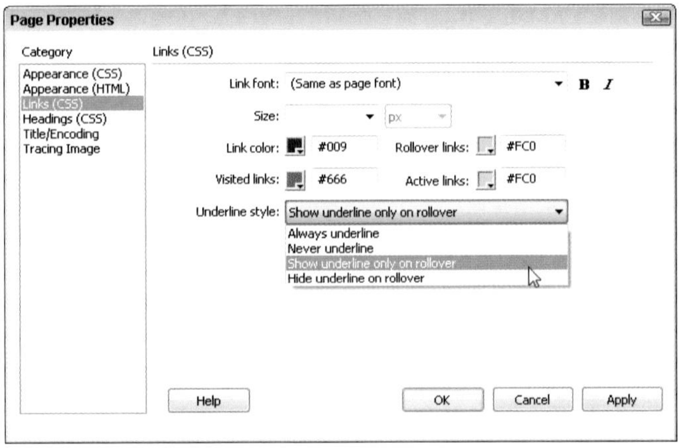

Page Properties

Category   Links (CSS)

Appearance (CSS)
Appearance (HTML)   Link font: (Same as page font)   ▾ **B** *I*
Links (CSS)
Headings (CSS)   Size: ▾ px ▾
Title/Encoding
Tracing Image   Link color: ■ #009   Rollover links: □ #FC0

Visited links: ■ #666   Active links: □ #FC0

Underline style: Show underline only on rollover   ▾

Always underline
Never underline
Show underline only on rollover
Hide underline on rollover

Help   OK   Cancel   Apply

Figure 2-8: Change the style definitions for all four hyperlink states.

3. Specify a font face and size for your links.

If you want to use the same font size and face for your links as you use in the rest of the text on your page, it's best to leave these options blank. Then, if you change the text settings for the page, you won't have to remember to change them for your links as well.

4. Specify colors for each hyperlink state by clicking in the corresponding color well and selecting a color from the Color dialog box.

You can change any or all link color settings. If you don't specify a link color, the browser uses the default link color. Here's an explanation of each of the four link states:

- **Link Color:** The color in which your links appear when the page is first loaded and the linked page hasn't yet been visited by the browser. The corresponding HTML tag is <a:link>.

- **Visited Links:** The color your links change to after a browser has already viewed the linked page. The corresponding HTML tag is <a:visited>.

- **Rollover Links:** The color a link changes to as a user rolls a cursor over a link. The corresponding HTML tag is <a:hover>.

- **Active Links:** The color a link changes to as a user is actively clicking a link. The corresponding HTML tag is <a:active>.

5. Select a style from the Underline Style drop-down list.

By default, links displayed in a web browser are underlined. Many designers prefer to remove the underline that automatically appears

If I wanted to link to that same anchor named `dreamweaver` on another page in my site, and my list of books appeared on an HTML page with the filename `books.html`, to create the link, I would type *books. html#dreamweaver* in the Link text box.

Linking to another website

To link to a page on another website — sometimes called an *external link* — all you need is the URL of the page to which you want to link, and you're most of the way there.

To create an external link, follow these steps:

1. **In Dreamweaver, open the page where you want to create the link.**

2. **Select the text or image that you want to act as the link.**

3. **In the Link text box in the Property inspector, type the URL of the page you want your text or image to link to.**

   The link is set automatically. In the example in Figure 2-12, I created a link using the text *Erin Manning* to link to `www.erinmanning.com`, the website of the person who took this photo, my friend Erin Manning.

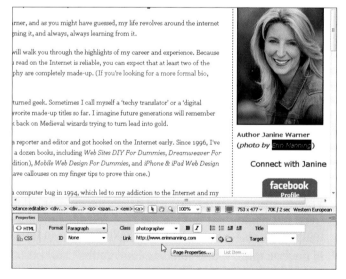

Photo by Erin Manning

Figure 2-12: In the Link text box, enter the URL of any website to which you want to link.

Although you don't have to type the `http://` or even the `www.` at the beginning of a website address to get to a site in most web browsers, you must always use the full URL, including the `http://`, when you create a link to another website in HTML. Otherwise, the browser can't find the correct external site address, and the visitor will probably end up on an error page.

Setting a link to an e-mail address

Another common link option goes to an e-mail address. Visitors can send you messages easily with e-mail links. I always recommend that you invite visitors to contact you because including contact information helps establish credibility on the web and because visitors to your site can point out mistakes and give you valuable feedback about how you can improve your site. Setting a link to an e-mail address is just as easy as setting a link to another web page. All you need to know is the e-mail address you want to link to and what text or image you want to use when you set the link.

To create an e-mail link, select the text you want to link and then click the E-mail Link icon in the Common Insert panel. In the E-mail Link dialog box, enter the e-mail address in the Link field and then click OK. If you want to use an image as an e-mail link, select an image in Dreamweaver's main work area, click the Hyperlink icon in the Common insert panel, and then type the e-mail link into the Link field.

You can also set e-mail links using the Link field in the Property inspector, but you must enter the code `mailto:` (no `//`) before the e-mail address, as shown in Figure 2-13. For example, if you typed a link to my e-mail address into the Property inspector, you'd need to type **mailto:janine@digitalfamily. com**. Here's what the full line of code behind that e-mail link would look like:

```
<a href="mailto:janine@digitalfamily.com">Send a message to
          Janine</a>
```

When visitors to your website click an e-mail link, their computer systems automatically launch their e-mail program and create a blank e-mail message to the specified e-mail address. Although this trick is cool, your users may find an e-mail's sudden appearance disconcerting if they don't expect it to happen, and the e-mail link won't work if your users don't have e-mail programs on their computers. That's why I always try to let users know when I use an e-mail link. For example, instead of just linking the

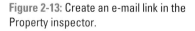

Figure 2-13: Create an e-mail link in the Property inspector.

words *Contact Janine,* I link the words *E-mail Janine.* Even better, I often link the actual e-mail address.

When you create an e-mail link on a web page that will be displayed on the public Internet, you open yourself to spammers, some of whom use automated programs to "lift" e-mail addresses off web pages. Spam is the reason many sites don't include e-mail links, but instead use one of the following methods to provide visitors with contact info:

- ✏ **Text worded for people (not bots):** An example is *Send e-mail to Janine at digitalfamily.com.* Using text to describe the e-mail address instead of including the actual address can help thwart spammers, but it does make it a little harder for your visitors to send you e-mail.

- ✏ **Code that hides your e-mail address from bots:** The online service AddressMunger makes it easy for you to add special code using JavaScript to hide your e-mail address from spammers. Visit `www.AddressMunger.com` to read more about this free service.

- ✏ **Forms:** By setting up a form with a script that delivers the form's contents to an e-mail address, you can shield your e-mail address from *scrapers* (people who use automated programs to copy e-mail addresses posted on websites) because the address is included in a script, not in the HTML code, which is easy to copy from a website. Using a form is also a way to ask visitors to your site to include more information, such as their mailing address or the product they are interested in. Using a form requires that you set up a script on a web server, which is more complicated than simply adding an email link to a web page. You read more about form mail scripts and how to create the HTML code needed for forms in Chapter 13.

Understanding the HTML behind links

You don't have to learn HTML code to use Dreamweaver, but the ability to recognize important snippets of code behind your pages is often helpful. Because links are so important to web pages and the Internet as a whole, I include this section to help you understand the code behind your links.

Here's an example of what the code looks like for a relative link from the home page on my website at `www.DigitalFamily.com` to the Dreamweaver page in the books section, which is contained in a folder named `books`. Note that you are essentially telling the browser to enter the subfolder named `books` and find the page named `dreamweaver.html`:

```
<a href="books/dreamweaver.html">Dreamweaver Books</a>
```

and

```
<a href="/books/dreamweaver.html">Dreamweaver Books</a>
```

If you link to a page on a different website, the link includes the full Internet address of the other site. Here's an example of what the code would look like if you created a link from your site to the Dreamweaver page in my books section:

```
<a href="http://www.digitalfamily.com/books/
        dreamweaver.html">Janine's Books on
        Dreamweaver</a>
```

If all that `href` code stuff looks like Greek to you, don't worry. Remember Dreamweaver sets links like this for you so you don't even have to look at this code if you don't want to. (I include these final tips because I think it's helpful to have a little understanding of what's happening behind the scenes, not because you have to memorize any of this stuff.)

Adding Meta Tags for Search Engines

If you've heard of meta tags, you probably associate them with search engines, and you'd be right. Meta tags are used for a variety of things, but one of the most common uses is to provide special text in the code at the top of the page. This code doesn't appear in a web browser when your page is viewed but can be read by crawlers, bots, and other programs that scour the web cataloging and ranking web pages for Bing, Google, and a long list of other search-related sites.

In Dreamweaver you find features that help you add meta tags for keywords and descriptions. Here's a brief explanation of each tag; the steps for filling each tag with text are coming up:

- ✔ **Meta keyword tag:** A meta keyword tag enables you to include a list of keywords you would like search engines to match if someone searches for those words. Unfortunately, meta keywords have been so abused by web designers attempting to mislead visitors about the true content of their web pages that most search engines ignore the meta keyword tag and its contents. That said, using this meta tag won't hurt your ranking with any search engines and many search engine experts still include them.

- ✔ **Meta description tag:** This tag is important and should be included in every page in your website. The meta description tag is designed to let you include a written description of each page — a worthwhile endeavor because most search engines, including Google, use the meta description as the brief description that appears in search results pages. Make the description a call to action, almost like a short advertisement, for the page that will get potential visitors to click your link when they are reading through a list of matches to a search. If you don't include your own text in a meta description tag, many search engines use the first several words that appear on your page as the description. Depending on your design, the first few words may not be the best description of your site.

The advent of social media has made the meta description tag even more important. When someone posts your web page by entering the URL into a social media site, the text you include in the meta description tag is included automatically with their post. Similarly, the meta description is included when someone shares a page on your site using a social media icon. (See Chapter 15 for tips on adding social media icons to your website.)

You can include the same meta description on every page of your site, but the best strategy is to include a description specific to the contents of each page on your site.

Follow these steps to add a meta description tag to your page:

1. **Open the page where you want to add a meta description.**

2. **Choose Insert⟿HTML⟿Head Tags⟿Description.**

   The Description dialog box appears.

3. **In the Description text box, enter the text you want for your page description.**

   Don't add any HTML to the text in this box. Most search engine experts recommend that you limit this text to no more than 160 characters because that is all that will be included in the search results page on sites such as Google.

4. **Click OK.**

   The description text you entered is inserted between the <head> tags area at the top of the page in the HTML code. Meta content doesn't appear in the body of the page, but you can find it just below the <title> tag if you look at the code behind the page.

If you want to add keywords, repeat Steps 1–4, choosing Insert⟿HTML⟿Head Tags⟿Keywords in Step 2. Type a list of keywords, separated by commas, in place of a description in Step 3.

Dreamweaver's meta tag tools are somewhat limited. You can use them to add these tags but not to edit them. To edit the text in meta description or keyword tags after you've inserted them, you have to view the code in Dreamweaver and edit the text in Code view. You'll find this text near the top of the HTML code, just below the `<title>` tag in the area surrounded by the `<head>` tags.

3

Creating Web Graphics

In This Chapter

▶ Creating and optimizing images for the web

▶ Inserting and aligning images

▶ Editing images in Dreamweaver

▶ Including a background image

*N*o matter how great the writing on your website may be, the graphics always get people's attention first. The key to making a good first impression is to use images that look great and download quickly.

If you're familiar with using a graphics-editing program, such as Adobe Photoshop or Fireworks, to create graphics for the web, you're a step ahead. If not, you'll appreciate this chapter's pointers on how to convert images for the web, what image formats to use, and how to optimize images for faster download times. The examples in this chapter were created using Adobe Photoshop CS5, but the features I used are nearly identical in both Photoshop CS5 and Photoshop Elements, so you can use the same instructions in either program. (See the sidebar "Comparing Adobe web graphics programs" to find out more about the differences.)

If your images are already in GIF, JPEG, or PNG format and ready for the web, you can jump ahead to the "Inserting Images in Dreamweaver" section, where you find out how to place and align images and use an image as a background. You also discover some of Dreamweaver's built-in image-editing features, which enable you to crop images and even adjust contrast and brightness without ever launching an external image-editing program.

Comparing Adobe web graphics programs

Most professional designers strongly prefer Adobe Photoshop, although I have to say I've been impressed with Photoshop Elements, which is a "light" version but offers many of the same features for a fraction of the cost. The following is a list of some of the most popular image-editing programs on the market today. All these image programs are available for both Mac and Windows:

✔ **Adobe Photoshop** (www.adobe.com/photoshop): By far the most popular image-editing program on the market, Photoshop is a widely used standard among graphics professionals. With Photoshop, you can create original artwork, edit and enhance photographs, and so much more. Photoshop has a wealth of powerful painting and selection tools, special effects, and filters that enable you to create images far beyond what you can capture on film or create with many other illustration programs. In previous versions, Photoshop came bundled with a program called *Image Ready,* a companion program designed for web graphics. In CS3, those web features were included in Photoshop; and in CS4, they've been enhanced. Switching between Photoshop and Dreamweaver is easier than ever.

✔ **Adobe Photoshop Elements** (www.adobe.com/elements): If you don't need all the bells and whistles offered in the full-blown version of Photoshop, Photoshop Elements is a remarkably powerful program — for about a sixth of the price. If you're a professional designer, you're best served by Photoshop. But if you're a hobbyist or small business owner and want to create good-looking images without the high cost and learning curve of a professional graphics program, Elements is a great deal and well-suited to creating web graphics.

✔ **Adobe Fireworks** (www.adobe.com/fireworks): Fireworks was one of the first image-editing programs designed to create and edit web graphics. Created by Macromedia, the program is now part of Adobe Web Suite and is fully integrated with Dreamweaver. Fireworks gives you everything you need to create, edit, and output web graphics, all in one well-designed product. Although Fireworks lacks many of the advanced image-editing capabilities of Photoshop, Fireworks shines when creating web graphics and is especially popular among web designers who rave about the ability to create a design in Fireworks that can easily be sliced and converted into a web page in Dreamweaver.

If you have an Internet connection and want to do basic image editing for free, visit www.gimp.org or www.photoshop.com/express. Both sites make it possible to edit and optimize images online without purchasing a software program.

Creating and Optimizing Web Graphics

The most important thing to keep in mind when creating images for the web is that you want to *optimize* your images to make your file sizes as small as possible so that they download as quickly as possible.

How you optimize an image depends on how the image was created and whether you want to save it as a JPEG, PNG, or GIF. You find instructions for optimizing images with Photoshop in the sections that follow, but the bottom line is this: No matter what program, format, or optimization technique you choose, your biggest challenge is finding the best balance between small file size and good image quality. Essentially, the more you optimize, the faster the image will download, but the compression and color reduction techniques used to optimize images can make them look terrible if you go too far.

As a general rule, do any editing, such as adjusting contrast, retouching, or combining images, before you reduce their size or optimize them because you want to work with the highest resolution possible when you're editing. Also, resize an image before you optimize it. You find instructions for resizing an image in the next exercise and instructions for optimizing in the sections that follow.

Resizing graphics and photos

Resizing is important for two reasons: The images must be small enough to display well on a computer monitor, and you want them to download quickly to a user's computer. The smaller the image is, the faster it will download.

Although you can change the display size of an image in a web page by altering the height and width settings in Dreamweaver, you get much better results if you change the physical size of the image in an editor program such as Photoshop.

When you alter an image's height and width in the HTML code (by using the height and width settings in Dreamweaver), you simply instruct a web browser to display the image in a different size. Unfortunately, browsers don't do a good job of resizing images because browsers don't change the image itself but just force it to fit in the assigned space when the browser loads the page. If you set the image to display larger than its actual size, the image is likely to look fuzzy or distorted because it doesn't contain enough pixels for all the details to look good in a larger size. If you set the code to display the image smaller than it is, the image is likely to look squished, and you're requiring that your users download an image that's larger than necessary.

Reducing an image's size for use on the web requires two steps. First, you reduce the resolution of an image, which changes the number of pixels in the image. When you're working with images for the web, you want to reduce the resolution to 72 pixels per inch, or ppi. (If you're wondering why 72, see the sidebar that's appropriately named "Why only 72 ppi?") Second, you reduce the image's physical size by reducing its dimensions. You want to size your images to fit well in a browser window and to work within the design of your site.

Why only 72 ppi?

When you save images for the web, you save them at a resolution of 72 pixels per inch (better known as *ppi*). Most computer monitors display no more than 72 ppi, so any resolution higher than that is wasted on the web because you'd be making your visitors download more pixels than they can see. However, if you want to print an image, you want all the pixels you can get, usually at least 200 ppi or higher, which is why most images you see on the web look terrible if you try to print them in a large size.

Follow these steps to lower the resolution and reduce the size of an image in Photoshop. (In Photoshop Elements or Fireworks, you follow a similar process although the specific steps may vary.)

1. **With an image open in Photoshop, choose Image➪Resize.**

   The Image Size dialog box opens, as shown in Figure 3-1.

   TIP: If you don't want your original image to lose quality (or you just want to play it safe), make a copy of your image and resize the *copy* for your website.

2. **To change the resolution of your image, first deselect the Resample Image check box at the bottom of the Image Size dialog box.**

   For best results, you always want the Resample Image check box deselected when you change the resolution.

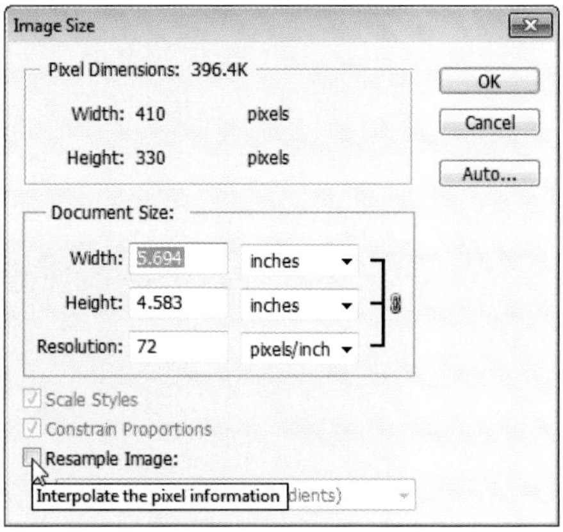

Figure 3-1: Change the image resolution to 72 ppi for a faster download.

3. **Click and drag to highlight the number in the Resolution field and replace it by typing the number** 72.

4. **Click to select the Resample Image check box.**

   With the Resample Image check box deselected, you can't change the Pixel dimensions, so it must be checked when you change the image size.

5. **Enter a height and width for the image in the Height and Width fields.**

As shown in Figure 3-2, I'm reducing the size of this image to 450 pixels wide. If the Constrain Proportions check box at the bottom of the dialog box is checked (as it is in this example), any changes you make to the height automatically affect the width (and vice versa) to ensure that the image proportions remain constant. I prefer to work this way, but if you do want to change the image and not maintain the proportions, deselect this box.

6. **Click OK to resize the image.**

   If you want to return the image to its previous size, choose Edit⇨Undo. Beware that when you save the image, the changes become permanent.

Choosing the best image format

One of the most common questions about images for the web concerns when to use GIF or PNG and when to use JPEG. Table 3-1 provides the simple answer.

Photo by Ken Riddick

Figure 3-2: Specify a new image size in pixels or as a percentage of the original size.

Table 3-1	Image Formats for the Web
Format	*Best Use*
GIF (`.gif`)	For line art (such as one- or two-color logos), simple drawings, animations, and basically any image that has no gradients or blends. GIF is also the best format when you want to display an image with a transparent background.
PNG (`.png`)	PNG generally produces better-looking images with smaller file sizes than GIF for the same kinds of limited-color images. Really old browsers, such as IE 3, don't support the PNG format, but most web designers today choose the PNG format over GIF because so few people use such old browsers.
JPEG (`.jpg` or `.jpeg`)	JPEG is the best format for colorful, complex images (such as photographs); images containing gradients or color blends; and any other images with millions of colors.

Saving images for the web: The basics

If you're new to saving images for the web, the following basics can help you get the best results from your files, your image-editing program, and ultimately your web pages. You can

- **Convert an image from any format into the GIF, PNG, or JPEG format.** For example, turn all your TIF, BMP, and PSD image files into a web-friendly file format.

- **Optimize images that are already in GIF, PNG, or JPEG format.** Even if your files are already in a web-friendly format, following the instructions in this chapter to optimize images with Adobe's Save for Web and Devices dialog box further reduces their file sizes for faster download over the Internet.

- **Use many programs to create web graphics.** However, Photoshop is one of the most popular ones to use. Under the File menu in Photoshop (and Photoshop Elements), you'll find the Save for Web and Devices option. (In versions of Photoshop before CS4, the option is Save for Web.) Fireworks provides a similar feature, and although each program's dialog boxes are slightly different, the basic options for compressing and reducing colors (which are covered in this chapter) are the same.

  See the upcoming sections "Optimizing JPEG images for the web" and "Optimizing images in GIF and PNG formats" for details about using the Save for Web and Devices feature.

- **Make image edits before you optimize.** When you're editing, using the highest quality image possible is always best. Make sure to do all your editing, sharpening, and resizing before you use the Save for Web and Devices option. Similarly, if you want to make further changes to an image after you've optimized it, you'll achieve the best results if you go back to a higher resolution version of the image rather than editing the version that's been optimized for the web. (When you use the Save for Web and Devices feature, Photoshop creates a new copy of your image and leaves the original unchanged.)

Optimizing JPEG images for the web

The JPEG format is the best choice for optimizing continuous-tone images, such as photographs and images with many colors or gradients. When you optimize a JPEG, you can make the file size smaller by applying compression. The more compression, the smaller the image, but if you compress the image too much, the image can look terrible. The trick is finding the right balance, as you discover in this section.

If you have a digital photograph or another image that you want to prepare for the web, follow these steps to optimize and save it in Photoshop (in Photoshop Elements or Fireworks, the process is similar although the specific steps may vary):

1. **With the image open in Photoshop, choose File⇨Save for Web and Devices (or File⇨Save for Web).**

   The Save for Web and Devices dialog box appears.

2. **In the top-left corner of the dialog box, choose either the 2-Up or 4-Up tab to display multiple versions of the same image for easy side-by-side comparison.**

   In the example shown in Figure 3-3, I chose 2-Up, which makes it possible to view the original image on the left and a preview of the same image as it will appear with the specified settings on the right. The 4-Up option, as the name implies, displays four different versions for comparison.

3. **On the right side of the window, just under Preset, click the small arrow to open the Optimized File Format drop-down list and choose JPEG (this dialog window is open in Figure 3-3).**

4. **Set the compression quality.**

   Use the preset options Low, Medium, High, Very High, or Maximum from the drop-down list. Or use the slider just under the Quality field to make more precise adjustments. (The slider appears when you click the arrow.) Lowering the quality reduces the file size and makes the image download more quickly, but if you lower this number too much, the image will look blurry and blotchy.

   Photoshop uses a compression scale of 0 to 100 for JPEGs in this dialog window, with 0 the lowest possible quality (the highest amount of compression and the smallest file size) and 100 the highest possible quality (the least amount of compression and the biggest file size). Low, Medium, and High represent compression values of 10, 30, and 60, respectively.

5. **Specify other settings as desired (the compression quality and file format are the most important settings).**

6. **Click Save.**

   The Save Optimized As dialog box opens.

7. **Enter a name for the image and save it into the images folder in your website folder.**

   Photoshop saves the optimized image as a copy of the original and leaves the original open in the main Photoshop work area.

Repeat these steps for each image you want to optimize as a JPEG.

Photo by Ken Riddick

Figure 3-3: Use JPEG for photographs and other images with millions of colors.

At the bottom of the image preview in the Save for Web and Devices dialog box, Photoshop includes an estimate of the time required for the image to download at the specified connection speed. In the example shown in Figure 3-3, the estimate is 7 seconds at 13 Kbps. As you adjust the compression settings, the size of the image changes and the download estimate will automatically adjust. You can change the connection speed used to make this calculation by clicking on the small arrow just to the right of the connection speed and using the drop-down list to select another option, such as 256 Kbps for cable modem speed. Use this estimate as a guide to help you decide how much you should optimize each image.

Optimizing images in GIF and PNG formats

If you're working with a graphic that can be displayed in 256 colors or less, such as a logo, cartoon character, or drawing, your best bet is to use the PNG format and reduce the total number of colors used in the image as much as possible to reduce the file size. (If you're concerned about visitors using a very, very old web browser, use GIF instead.)

To help make up for the degradation in image quality that can happen when colors are removed, GIF and PNG use a dithering trick. *Dithering* involves alternating pixels in a checkerboard-like pattern to create subtle color variations, even with a limited color palette. The effect can smooth the image's edges and make it appear to have more colors than it actually does.

To convert an image to a GIF or a PNG in Photoshop, follow these steps (in Photoshop Elements or Fireworks, the process is similar although the specific steps may vary):

1. **With the image open in Photoshop, choose File⇨Save for Web and Devices (or File⇨Save for Web).**

   The Save for Web and Devices dialog box appears.

2. **In the top-left corner of the dialog box, choose the 2-Up or 4-Up tab to display multiple versions of the same image for easy side-by-side comparison.**

   In the example shown in Figure 3-4, I chose 4-Up, which makes it possible to view the original image (in the upper-left corner), as well as three different previews of the same image.

3. **Select a preview image to begin changing its settings.**

   Changing the preview images in the 4-Up view enables you to compare the original image with up to three different color settings.

4. **On the right side of the dialog box, just under Preset, click the small arrow to open the Optimized File Format drop-down list and choose PNG.**

5. **In the Colors box, select the number of colors.**

   The fewer colors you use, the smaller the file size and the faster the image will download. But be careful; if you reduce the colors too much (as I have in the bottom-right preview shown in Figure 3-4), you lose details. The ideal number of colors depends on your image; if you go too far, your image will look terrible.

6. **If you want to maintain a transparent area in your image, select the Transparency check box.**

   Any area of the image that was transparent when you created the image in the editor appears transparent in the preview window. If you don't have a transparent area in your image, this setting has no effect.

   Transparency is a good trick for making text or an image appear to float because a transparent background doesn't appear on the web page. You can select transparency as a background option in the New File dialog box when you create a new image in Photoshop or Photoshop Elements.

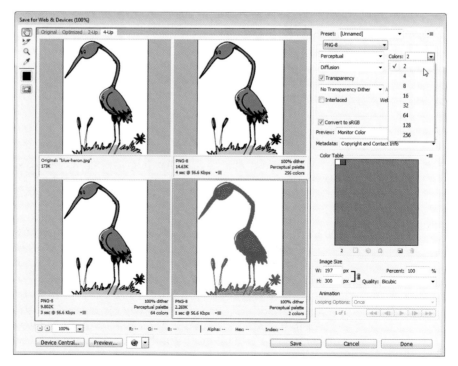

Illustration by Tom McCain

Figure 3-4: GIF and PNG are best for images with limited colors.

7. **If you choose Transparency, also specify a Matte color.**

   You want the matte color to match the background of your web page so that the dithering along the transparent edge will blend with the background. If you don't specify a matte color, the transparency is set for a white background, which can cause a halo effect when the image is displayed on a colored background.

8. **Specify other settings as desired.**

   The remainder of the settings in this dialog box can be left at their defaults in Photoshop.

9. **Click Save.**

   The Save Optimized As dialog box opens.

10. **Enter a name for the image and save it into the images folder (or any other folder) in your local site folder.**

Repeat these steps for each image you want to optimize as a GIF or PNG for your site.

Trial and error is a great technique in the Save for Web and Devices dialog box. In each of the three preview windows displaying optimized versions of the cool cartoon image in Figure 3-4, I used fewer and fewer colors, which reduced the file size with an increasingly degrading effect.

How small is small enough?

After you know how to optimize GIFs and JPEGs and appreciate the goal of making them as small as possible, you may ask, "How small is small enough?" The answer is mostly subjective, but the following points are good to remember:

- ✔ **The larger your graphics files, the longer people have to wait for them to download.** You may have the most beautiful picture of Mount Fuji on the front page of your website, but if it takes forever to download, most people aren't patient enough to wait to see it.

- ✔ **When you build pages with multiple graphics, consider the cumulative download time of all the graphics on the page.** Even if each individual image is a small file size, the cumulative image size can add up. Unlike most things in life, smaller is definitely better on the web.

- ✔ **Most web pros consider anything from about 75K to 150K a good maximum *cumulative* size for all the elements on a given page.** With the increasing popularity of DSL and cable modems, many websites are starting to become a bit more graphics heavy and go beyond that size limit. However, anything over 150K is pushing the limit, especially if you expect people with dialup modems (56K and under) or those surfing on mobile phones to stick around long enough to view your pages.

To make determining the total file size of the images on your page easy, Dreamweaver includes this information in the status bar at the bottom of the Document window, as shown in Figure 3-5. In the small text at the bottom of this web page about SCUBA diving in Bonaire, the status bar shows that the total size of all the images, text, and code on the page adds up to 86K and will download in 2 seconds at the connection speed specified in Dreamweaver's preferences. In this example, the connection speed is set to 768K. (You can change connection speed by choosing Edit⇨Preferences⇨Status Bar⇨Connection Speed. On a Mac, choose Dreamweaver⇨Preferences⇨Status Bar⇨Connection Speed.)

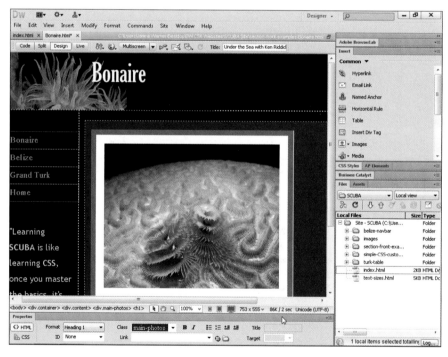

Photo by Ken Riddick

Figure 3-5: The status bar shows the total file size of all elements on a page and the estimated download time.

Inserting Images in Dreamweaver

Now for the fun part. Adding an image to your web page may seem almost magical at first because the process is so simple with Dreamweaver. The challenge with web graphics isn't adding them to your pages but creating good-looking images that load quickly in your viewer's browser. You need another program, such as Photoshop, Photoshop Elements, or Fireworks, to create, convert, edit, and optimize images. *Optimizing* images makes file sizes smaller so your images download faster. Dreamweaver provides some basic image-editing tools, but mostly you use Dreamweaver to insert and position images on your page.

Dreamweaver makes placing images on your web pages easy and provides multiple ways to do so:

✏ Click the Images icon in the Common Insert panel and then select an image using the Insert image dialog box.

✏ In the Files panel, click and drag an image name onto the page where you want the image to appear.

✏ Use the Insert menu, as I explain in the following steps.

If you don't have a web-optimized JPEG, GIF, or PNG image handy, you can download free images that are already optimized from my website by going directly to www.DigitalFamily.com/free. (You find instructions for downloading the free images when you get to this special page on my website.)

To place an image on a web page using the Insert menu, follow these instructions:

1. **Open an existing page or choose File⇨New to create a new page.**

2. **Place your cursor where you want to insert the image on the page.**

3. **Choose Insert⇨Image.**

   The Select Image Source dialog box appears.

4. **Browse to locate the image you want to insert.**

   Depending on your computer system, you can preview images as you insert them in different ways. Here are three common options:

- **On a PC with Windows XP,** choose Thumbnails from the View drop-down list to the right of the Look In field to display thumbnail versions of all the images in any open folder. You can also view a single preview of any selected image in the far right of the dialog box.

- **On a PC with Windows Vista or Windows 7** (as shown in Figure 3-6), choose one of the icon options (Small icon, Medium icon, Large icon, or Extra Large icon) from the View drop-down list to the right of the Look In field to display thumbnail versions of all the images in any open folder. You can also view a single preview of any selected image in the far right of the dialog box.

- **On a Mac,** choose the View As Columns option from the top left of the dialog, and you can view a single preview of any selected image in the far right of the dialog box.

Figure 3-6: Locate and preview images in the Image Source dialog box.

5. **To insert the image, double-click the image name or click once and then click OK.**

If you have Accessibility options turned on in Preferences (the default), the Image Tag Accessibility Attributes dialog box appears.

If you insert an image into a page and the image isn't saved in your local site folder, Dreamweaver prompts you with a warning dialog and offers to copy the image into your local site folder. (Find out how to set up a local site folder in the section "Setting Up a New or Existing Site," in Chapter 2.) Many designers create a subfolder called *images* inside the local site folder where they store all the images in their site, but you can organize images in multiple subfolders if you prefer.

6. **In the Image Tag Accessibility Attributes dialog box, enter text that describes the image in the Alternate Text field.**

   Adding alternate text in this dialog box is always a best practice. Alternate text won't appear on your web page unless the image isn't visible, but it will appear in Internet Explorer when a user holds the cursor over the image. Alternate text is also important for web surfers (such as those with limited vision) who use *screen readers,* or browsers that "read" web pages to them. For this reason, alternate text is required for accessibility compliance. A long description is considered optional under most accessibility guidelines. You can enter the address of a web page with a longer description of the image in this field. You can also add or edit alternate text in the Property inspector after clicking to select the inserted image.

7. **Click OK to close the Accessibility Attributes dialog box and insert the image.**

   The image appears in the page.

8. **Click to select the image on your web page to view image properties.**

   Image options are displayed automatically in the Property inspector at the bottom of the page when an image is selected, as shown in Figure 3-7.

Although you can change many settings, such as image alignment, by using the HTML attribute options available in the Property inspector, using CSS (covered in Chapter 5) is almost always a better option. For example, you can use the H Space attribute in the Property inspector to create a margin around an image, but H Space adds margin on both the left and right sides of an image. With CSS, you can create a style that applies margin space to any or all sides of an image, giving you more control of your design.

Table 3-2 describes the many image attributes available in the Property inspector when an image is selected. If you don't see all the attributes listed in the table on your screen, click the small triangle in the bottom-right corner of the Property inspector to reveal all the image options.

Table 3-2 *(continued)*

Abbreviation	Attribute	Function
Class	CSS Setting	Enables you to apply any class styles defined in Dreamweaver. To use this option, select any element in the workspace and then select any class style you want to apply from the drop-down list.
Original	N/A	Indentifies the original version of the image, if you are using the Smart Objects features in Photoshop or Firefox. (See your Photoshop or Firefox documentation for more on these features.)
Align	Align	Align images. (You will have more control if you use the float settings in CSS, covered in Chapter 6.)

When you insert an image file onto a page, you don't actually add a copy of the image to the page; you create a reference to the image. The underlying code looks much like the code for a link from one page to another. Both image references and links include the name of the file (the page you link to or the image you insert) and the path from the page to that file. Essentially, you're creating an instruction for a web browser to find the image when it displays the page.

Why can't I place images anywhere I want them?

You can't just place your cursor anywhere on a page and insert an image where you want it. This isn't a limitation of Dreamweaver; the way HTML is displayed on the web restricts how you can place images.

By default, all images, text, and other elements are inserted starting at the top-left corner of the browser window. To create more complex layouts and position images precisely on a page, your best option is to create a layout with CSS (which I cover in Chapters 5, 6, and 7). You can also use an HTML table to position elements on a web page (which I cover in Chapter 9).

To display an image on your web page, you need to upload both the page and the image when you publish your website. If your image files and the pages that refer to those files aren't in the same relative location on your hard drive as they are on your web server, you break the reference to your images, and an ugly Broken Image icon appears on your page. The best way to make sure that your images and files stay where they're supposed to in relation to one another is to let Dreamweaver keep track of them for you. That's why it's so important to complete the site setup process at the beginning of Chapter 2 and to make sure you never move or rename an image, except in the Files panel.

Image Editing in Dreamweaver

Dreamweaver includes basic image-editing features, including the Crop, Resample, Brightness/Contrast, and Sharpen options. You find these tools next to the Border option in the Property inspector, as shown in Figure 3-8. Image-editing features in Dreamweaver enable you to make minor changes to images without opening Fireworks, Photoshop, or any other graphics-editing program.

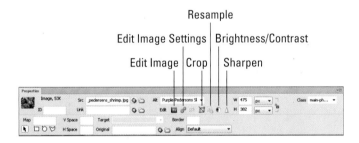

Figure 3-8: Use the image-editing tools to do basic image editing.

Before you get carried away editing your images, remember that Dreamweaver is primarily a web page-creation application and isn't really designed to edit graphics. Although these tools can be useful, they shouldn't take the place of doing serious work on your graphics in a graphics application, such as Fireworks or Photoshop.

When you use Dreamweaver's image-editing tools, beware that you're changing the actual image (not just a copy of it). Make sure you're happy with these changes before you save the page you're working on. You can use the Undo feature in Dreamweaver to revert back several steps, but after you save the page, you can't undo changes made to an image with these tools. To protect your original image, save a copy before editing it.

Cropping an image

Essentially, *cropping* an image involves trimming its edges. If you're trying to fit an image into your design and need the image to be just a touch smaller, Dreamweaver's cropping tool can come in handy. To crop a graphic or photo, follow these steps:

1. **In the Document window, select the image you want to crop by clicking it.**

   The Property inspector changes to display the image's properties.

2. **Click the Crop icon.**

   A dialog box appears, warning you that cropping changes the original image.

   Don't make the change if you're concerned about keeping the entire image available. If you're concerned, the best thing to do is to make a copy of the image before you crop it.

3. **Click OK in the warning dialog box.**

   A solid crop line with selection handles at the sides and corners appears over the image, as shown in Figure 3-9.

4. **Click and drag the selection handles to outline the area of the image you want to keep.**

   Any part of the image outside the crop line (and shaded) is deleted when the crop is completed.

5. **Double-click inside the box or press Enter (Return on a Mac).**

   The image is cropped.

You can undo cropping by choosing Edit➪Undo. However, after you save the page, changes are applied permanently to the image and can't be undone.

Figure 3-9: Drag the outline edges to define the area to crop.

Adjusting brightness and contrast

Adjusting an image's *brightness* allows you to change the overall amount of light in an image. *Contrast* controls the difference between the light and dark areas of an image.

Using Dreamweaver's editing tools permanently alters the image when the page is saved. If you're concerned, the best thing to do is to make a copy of the image and make your adjustments to the copy.

To adjust brightness and contrast, follow these steps:

1. **In the Document window, select the image you want to alter.**

   The Property inspector shows the image properties.

2. **Click the Brightness/Contrast icon (labeled in Figure 3-8).**

   A dialog box appears, indicating that the changes you make will affect the original file.

3. **Click OK in the warning dialog box.**

   The Brightness/Contrast dialog box appears.

4. **Use the sliders to adjust the brightness and contrast settings of the image.**

   Make sure to select the Preview check box if you want to see how the changes affect the image as you move the sliders around.

5. **Click OK.**

   The settings take effect permanently when you save the page.

Sharpening an image

When you apply *sharpening* to an image, you increase the distinction between areas of color. The effect can increase the definition of shapes and lines in an image.

Using Dreamweaver's editing tools permanently alters the image when the page is saved. If you're concerned, the best thing to do is to make a copy of the image and make your adjustments to the copy.

To sharpen an image, follow these steps:

1. **In the Document window, select the image you want to sharpen.**

   The Property inspector shows the image properties.

2. **Click the Sharpen icon (labeled in Figure 3-8).**

   A dialog box appears, warning that your change is made to the original file.

3. **Click OK in the warning dialog box.**

   The Sharpen dialog box appears.

4. **Use the slider to adjust the sharpness of the image.**

   Select the Preview check box to see how the changes affect the image as you move the slider.

5. **Click OK.**

   The image is sharpened, and changes to the image become permanent when you save changes to the page.

Opening an image in Photoshop or Fireworks from Dreamweaver

TIP

The Property inspector includes an icon that enables you to easily open an image in Photoshop or Fireworks from within Dreamweaver. The Edit icon changes to the icon of the program specified in Dreamweaver's preferences. To open an image in your preferred program, simply select the image in Dreamweaver, click the icon in the Property inspector, and watch your image appear as you've commanded.

Adobe has done great work integrating the Photoshop and Fireworks programs into Dreamweaver. When you save changes to the image in Fireworks or Photoshop, they're automatically reflected in the version you've already inserted into a page in Dreamweaver.

To specify the image editor you want to associate with a file type in Dreamweaver's preferences, follow these instructions:

1. **Choose Edit⇨Preferences (Windows) or Dreamweaver⇨Preferences (on a Mac).**

   The Preferences dialog box opens.

2. **On the left, select the File Types/Editors category, as shown in Figure 3-10.**

3. **In the Extensions pane, click to select .gif.**

   Dreamweaver lists a wide variety of file types here, and you can associate any or all of them with your favorite editors. To associate image editors with these graphic formats, select the GIF, PNG, and JPEG options one at a time and then continue with these steps.

4. **In the Editors pane, click to select the editor you want associated with the .gif format.**

   In the example shown in Figure 3-10, Photoshop is already highlighted, so you can simply click Photoshop to select it. If you want to associate an editor that isn't on this list, such as Fireworks, click the plus sign (+) just above the Editors pane, browse to find the program on your hard drive, and select it to make it appear on the list.

5. **With the file type and program name selected, click the Make Primary button to associate the editor with the file type.**

The editor specified as primary is launched automatically when you select an image in Dreamweaver and click the Edit button in the Property inspector.

6. **Click to select .jpeg from the Extensions pane and repeat Steps 4 and 5.**

You can continue with this process for any or all the other formats listed.

To add additional file formats to Dreamweaver, click the plus sign (+) over the Extensions pane and type the extension beginning with a dot (.).

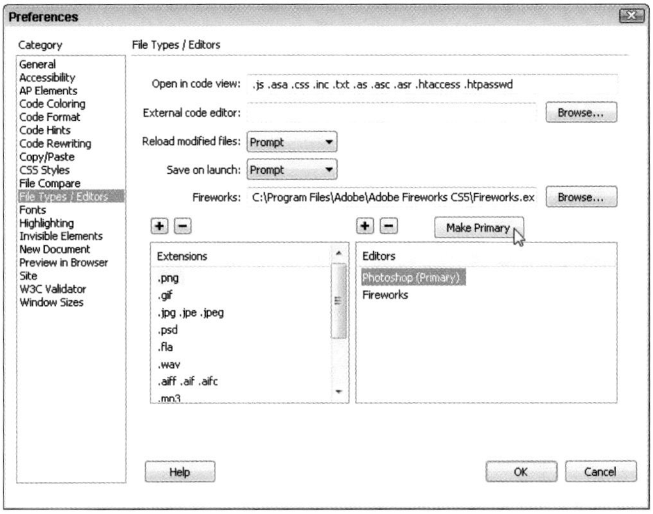

Figure 3-10: Use the preferences settings to associate your favorite image editor.

Inserting a Background Image

Background images can add depth and richness to a page design. Used cleverly, a background image that downloads quickly and efficiently helps create the illusion that the entire page is one large image. The trick is to use an image with a small file size that creates the impression of a large image. One way this works on the web is to use the default settings for a background image, which cause the image to *tile* (repeat) across and down the page (see Figure 3-11).

Text placed on certain backgrounds (such as the one shown in Figure 3-11) can be difficult to read. Choose your background images carefully and make sure your background and your text have plenty of contrast. Reading on a computer screen is hard enough.

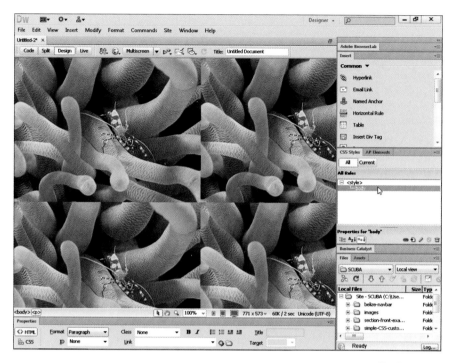

Figure 3-11: You can repeat an image across and down a page.

With CSS, you can have far greater control over the display of a background image. When you create a CSS background style, you can insert a background image that doesn't repeat or that repeats only across the Y axis or down the X axis of the page.

To insert a background image in Dreamweaver, choose Modify⇨Page Properties, click the Browse button to the right of the Background Image field (see Figure 3-12), and select the image you want to use as your background. If the image isn't already in your local site folder, Dreamweaver offers to copy it there when you click OK.

When you insert an image using Dreamweaver's Page Properties feature, you can use the Repeat drop-down list to specify how the image repeats on the page, as shown in Figure 3-12. When you specify a repeat option, Dreamweaver automatically creates a style for the page with these background settings. If you use the CSS Definition dialog box to further edit the background options in the body style (covered in Chapter 5), you can also specify where the background image is displayed on a page.

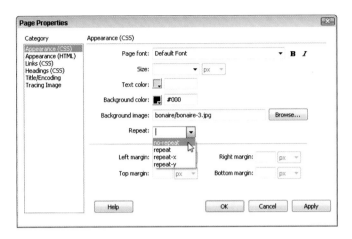

Figure 3-12: Control how a background image is repeated on a page.

Understanding browser differences

The many reasons why web pages can look different from one browser to another can be boiled down to the following:

- Over the years, web browsers have evolved to support new web technologies. Thus, many older browsers still in use have trouble displaying some newer, more advanced features that you can use on your web pages today.

- Compounding this problem, the companies that make web browsers — including Microsoft, Google, and Apple — don't all agree or follow the same rules (although most are getting better at complying with the same set of standards in their latest browser versions).

- Dozens of browsers are now in use on the web, not counting the different versions of each browser. For example, Google Chrome has become increasingly popular and is one of the best for supporting pages designed to follow modern web design standards. Unfortunately, a significant percentage of Internet users haven't yet changed or upgraded and are still using the browser that came with their computer. If that browser is IE6, your pages will face a real challenge because IE6 is notoriously bad at displaying CSS (Cascading Style Sheets) and other modern web features.

Browser limitations and differences are the root of many complications when creating and testing websites. Entire books and websites are dedicated to how best to design for the differences among browsers. I can't possibly cover all the issues or tricks to working around them in this book. However, in this chapter, I do include tips and testing sites to help you ensure that your pages look their best. In addition, throughout this book I try to stick to design strategies and techniques that most browsers in use today support.

 The best way to make sure your site looks good to your visitors is to write clean code, test it for errors (using the testing tools included in this chapter), and then preview how the site looks in a variety of web browsers. In the following sections, you find instructions for adding browsers to Dreamweaver's preview options and using online services to test in browsers that you don't have on your computer.

Targeting browsers for your design

Some web designers have decided to ignore users with older browsers or to simply include a warning message, such as: "This page looks best in the latest version of Firefox, upgrade now." Other designers carefully test their pages in dozens of browsers to make sure they look good to as many people as possible on the Internet. As you decide how to approach this issue, I suggest taking your audience into account. For example, consider the following scenarios:

- **Your visitors are advanced computer users.** If you run a website for high-end game developers or web geeks and are confident that they update their software regularly, you may not need to concern yourself with older browsers.

- **Your site attracts users from large organizations.** People at large corporations, universities, or other big organizations often are not allowed to update their own software They're stuck with older browsers until some official decides to update their systems, which can take a notoriously long time. Make sure your site is at least readable in older web browsers. That said, if you're designing a site for use by people in only one company or organization, you can often find out exactly what software they are using and design for their systems.

- **Your audience is made up of people with older computers who are unlikely to have upgraded their web browsers.** If you're designing a website for a doctor's office, real estate agency, little league team, or another group likely to attract old and young visitors, you need to design for the broadest possible audience on the Internet. Although web browsers are generally free and relatively easy to install, some people are afraid to download any software over the Internet, and many don't appreciate the benefits of using a newer browser.

The movement toward more standardized web development is growing, but getting your pages to look exactly the same on every computer on the planet is still difficult if not impossible. As a result, most designers strive to create pages that look as good as possible on as many browsers as they consider important, even if the same pages don't look *exactly* the same on all browsers.

Previewing Your Page in a Browser

Although Dreamweaver displays web pages much like a web browser, not all interactive features work in Dreamweaver. To test links, for example, you have to preview your work in a web browser.

You can test your pages using any web browser on your computer, but I recommend that you set up at least two of the latest versions of the most popular browsers: Internet Explorer, Firefox, Chrome, or Safari. (You find instructions for adding browsers to Dreamweaver in the next section.)

The simplest way to preview your work is to save the page you're working on and then click the Preview/Debug in Browser icon (it looks like a small globe), which is located at the top right of the work-space, as shown in Figure 4-3. You can also choose File⇨Preview in a Browser.

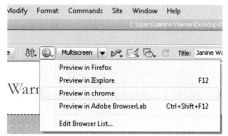

Figure 4-3: The Preview/Debug in Browser icon opens any Dreamweaver page in the selected web browser.

Adding web browsers to the preview feature

To help you test your pages, Dreamweaver makes it possible to add multiple browsers to the preview. The first step is to download and install a variety of browsers on your hard drive (see the sidebar "Downloading new browsers").

After you've installed one or more new browsers on your computer, follow these steps to add them to Dreamweaver's browser preview list:

1. **Choose File⇨Preview in Browser and then choose Edit Browser List from the fly-out menu.**

    The Preferences dialog box opens with the Preview in Browser settings displayed. ***Note:*** You must have a page open in Dreamweaver for these menu options to be available.

2. **Click the plus sign (+) at the top of the Preferences dialog box.**

    The Add Browser dialog box opens.

3. **Enter a name for the browser.**

    To help make sure you're using the latest browsers, include the version number as well as the name, as I have in Figure 4-4, where I'm adding Apple Safari 5.1.

4. **Click the Browse button.**

    The Add Browser dialog box opens.

5. **Navigate your hard drive until you find the browser you want to add.**

    Look for the browser's executable or application file (indicated with an `.exe` extension under Windows and stored in the Applications folder on a Mac). Don't use a shortcut to the actual program file.

    You can add a browser to Dreamweaver only if the browser is on your hard drive. (See the nearby sidebar, "Downloading new browsers," for more about finding and downloading new browsers for testing.)

6. **Click the name of the program file to select it, and then click Open to add the browser to the Application field in the Add Browser dialog box.**

7. **If you want this browser to be the first browser listed in the Browser drop-down list, select the Primary Browser check box. Otherwise, select the Secondary Browser check box.**

   You can also launch the designated primary browser by pressing the F12 key. To launch the secondary browser, press Ctrl+F12 in Windows or ⌘+F12 on a Mac.

8. **Repeat Steps 2–7 to add more browsers to the list.**

9. **After you add all the browsers you want, click OK to save them and close the dialog box.**

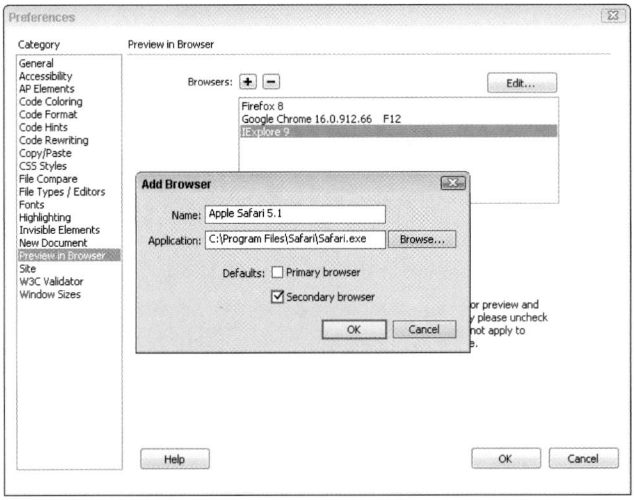

Figure 4-4: Add web browsers to the Preview in Browser list.

Previewing pages in many web browsers

When you are designing web pages for the broadest audience on the web, it's best to test your site by previewing the pages in a variety of web browsers. The following steps walk you through the process of previewing the same web page in multiple browsers:

1. **Open a web page that you want to preview in Dreamweaver.**

2. **Choose File⇨Preview in Browser, and select a web browser from the list of browser options.**

   You find out how to add more browsers to the Preview in Browser list in the preceding section, "Adding web browsers to the preview feature."

3. **Study and test the page.**

   Carefully test all links, rollovers, and other special effects to make sure that the page appears the way you want it to in this browser.

4. **Close the browser window and return to Dreamweaver to make any necessary changes to the page.**

   Often, you can make the page look better with minor changes, such as swapping the position of an image with a block of text, or adding a paragraph return using a `<p>` tag after a video.

5. **Preview the same page again in the same browser to make sure the changes you made had the desired effect.**

   Return to Dreamweaver to make further changes as necessary.

6. **Follow Steps 2–5 to preview the same page in another web browser.**

Testing sites with Adobe's BrowserLab and other online browser emulators

Unless you own a dozen computers with different operating systems and a vast collection of web browsers, you can't fully test your website — at least not on your own. Fortunately, a growing number of online services are available to help you preview your pages on many different operating systems and browsers — without your having to manage multiple computers and browsers yourself.

Downloading new browsers

So how do you put new browsers on your hard drive so that you can use them to preview your pages? The simplest way is to visit the websites of the companies that create the most popular browsers. You can download the latest version for free from each of these sites, and all four browsers are available for Mac and Windows computers:

- Microsoft Internet Explorer: `www.microsoft.com/ie`
- Mozilla Firefox: `www.firefox.com`
- Apple Safari: `www.apple.com/safari`
- Google Chrome: `www.google.com/chrome`

Like many professional web designers, I have three computers on my desk (Macs and Windows), and many different browsers installed on each. I also have an Apple iPad, a Samsung Galaxy tablet, and an iPhone because I like having several options handy to test my pages while I'm developing a design.

After a page design looks good in all the browsers and systems I have on my desk, I upload the site to a server and do a final test in even more browsers using these online services.

Following are some of the best places to test your website online:

- **Adobe BrowserLab** (browserlab.adobe.com)**:** In Dreamweaver CS5, Adobe BrowserLab is integrated into the browser preview options. You can choose BrowserLab from the list of options when you choose Edit⇨Preview in Browser. *Note:* Your computer must be connected to the Internet for this feature to work, but you can use BrowserLab to test pages that are not yet published on the Internet. You must have an Adobe ID to use BrowserLab, but at the time of this writing it was free to anyone using Dreamweaver.

  Adobe BrowserLab enables you to test any web page in the most common browsers simultaneously. At the time of this writing, that includes IE versions 6, 7, 8, and 9; Mozilla Firefox versions 5 and 7; Chrome 13 and 14; and Apple Safari 5.1. You also have a choice between the Windows and OS X operating systems.

  When you use Adobe's BrowserLab service, the result is a screenshot with a preview of the page taken in each browser. Although the screenshots enable you to spot differences quickly, you can't test interactive features, such as drop-down menus or rollover effects.

- **Browser Sandbox** (spoon.net/browsers/)**:** With Browser Sandbox, you can test a website using any of the eight most popular browsers, but you do have to go through a time-consuming installation process to use them. After you've set up each browser, you can launch it and surf the web as if the browser were installed on your computer. That means you can test interactive features, such as those that require JavaScript, AJAX, forms, and other advanced programming.

- **Cross Browser Testing** (crossbrowsertesting.com)**:** The Cross Browser Testing site takes website testing to another level. Instead of simply providing screenshots of a web page in different browsers, or letting you launch a few browsers in which to test pages, this site lets you take over other computers connected to the Internet so that you can do sophisticated testing of interactive features using a variety of browsers and operating systems. For example, suppose you use a computer that runs Windows 7 and want to see what your site will look like on a Mac. Simply choose to use a computer with the Mac OS and then view your site on that computer in any of a dozen browsers. This high-end service requires that you purchase a monthly subscription but also offers a free 30-day trial period at the time of this writing.

✔ **Browsershots** (www.browsershots.org): Browsershots is a popular online testing tool. You simply enter a page's URL and choose the options you want to use for testing. Browsershots then tests the page you submitted on each computer system selected with the specified browser and takes a screenshot. Although you can't test interactive features with this service, it's one of the easiest options and provides the largest collection of browsers to choose from. The basic service is free, but testing can take from a few minutes to a few hours. If you don't like waiting, you can upgrade to their priority processing for a fee.

Designing for mobile devices

A new audience of web page visitors has emerged. Some high-end mobile devices (think iPhone and BlackBerry Storm) are capable of loading even complex web pages and do so reasonably well. However, the screen is much smaller, and interaction with the web browser is much different. Site visitors navigate by touch or with input devices more challenging than a mouse. Lower-end mobile devices, which make up the vast majority of the market, often sport even smaller screens, have reduced color display, and allow only minimal interaction.

To best manage the dramatic differences on mobile devices, I recommend that you create a second very simplified version of your Web site designed to best serve the limited display options of mobile devices and then link your main Web site to the alternate mobile design. If you have experience writing server scripts (or can hire someone to do it for you), create an autodetect script that can determine whether visitors to your site are using a mobile phone or a computer and then direct them to the best version of your site.

Consider the following important tips when designing a version of your website for mobile devices:

✔ Keep in mind that the screen size on a mobile device is extremely limited, with less width or height than traditional computer monitors.

✔ Use a minimum of images because download times are much slower on cell phones.

✔ Avoid outdated HTML styling and layout options, such as frames and iframes, which may not be displayed at all on mobile devices.

✔ Adjust your design to require as little scrolling and user movement as possible and make your links big and separated so they can be activated by a fat fingertip. Mobile phone users point not with a mouse but with up and down arrows and at best a touchscreen.

✔ Always validate your web page code (numerous validation services are available for free online, such as the popular one at validator.w3.org). Mobile browsers are even less forgiving than traditional website browsers about errors in your code.

✔ Avoid using Flash and Flash video because many mobile devices don't support them. Use multimedia sparingly and consider using video-hosting services such as YouTube or Vimeo (covered in Chapter 12). Services such as Vimeo offer sophisticated video servers and optimize video for different devices for you.

To read more about designing for mobile devices, check out my books *iPhone & iPad Web Design For Dummies* and *Mobile Web Design For Dummies* (Wiley).

Testing your designs with Multiscreen Preview

Dreamweaver CS6 and CS5.5 include a preview feature that makes it possible to view the same web page in three screen sizes. This capability is useful when you use the latest in Cascading Style Sheet options to design HTML pages that use more than one style sheet, each designed for a different screen size.

In Chapters 5, 6, and 7, you find instructions on how to use Dreamweaver's CSS features, including how to use the CSS Media Query options to design pages that adapt to different screen sizes. Using Media Queries is an advanced topic, even for those familiar with the basics of CSS, but if you're interested in designing websites that work on mobile phones, as well as large monitors, it's worth the effort to learn how to use these features.

In Figure 4-5, you see how my web page looks when viewed in three sizes. The version in the top left is designed to be viewed on an iPhone and other small mobile devices. The top-right version is designed for the iPad, and the bottom version works well on a computer monitor. In Chapter 7, you find instructions for using Dreamweaver's Multiscreen preview, as well as tips for designing CSS style sheets that are targeted to different screen sizes.

Figure 4-5: Use the Multiscreen preview option to view a web page in different screen sizes.

Testing Your Work with the Site Reporting Features

Before you put your site online for the world to see, check your work using the Dreamweaver Site Reporting feature. You can create a variety of reports to identify problems with external links, redundant and empty tags, untitled documents, and missing alternate text, important errors that are easily missed. Before Dreamweaver added this great feature, finding these kinds of mistakes was a tedious, time-consuming task.

Follow these steps to produce a site report of your entire website:

1. **In the drop-down list at the top of the Files panel, select the site you want to work on.**

   If you already have the site you want to test open in Dreamweaver, you can skip this step. *Note:* Your site appears in the Files panel list only if you've completed the site setup process covered in Chapter 2.

2. **Make sure any documents you have open in Dreamweaver's workspace are saved by choosing File⇨Save All.**

3. **Choose Site⇨Reports.**

   The Reports dialog box appears, as shown in Figure 4-6.

4. **In the Report On drop-down list, choose Entire Current Local Site.**

   I regularly use this option to test an entire site just before publishing it to the web, but you can choose to check only a single page by opening the page in Dreamweaver and then choosing Current Document in the Report On drop-down list. You can also run a report

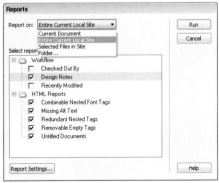

Figure 4-6: Run reports on a single page or the entire site.

on selected files or on a particular folder. If you choose Selected Files in Site, you must first click to select the pages you want to check in the Files panel.

5. **In the Select Reports section, click the check boxes to select the reports you want.**

   Table 4-1 describes the kind of report you get with each option. You can select as many reports as you want.

6. Click the Run button to create the report(s).

If you haven't already done so, you may be prompted to save your file, set up your site, or select a folder.

The Results panel appears, displaying a list of problems found on the site. To sort the list by category (filename, line number, or description), click the corresponding column heading.

7. Double-click any item in the Results panel to open the corresponding file in the Document window.

The file opens, and the error is highlighted in the workspace.

You can also right-click (Windows) or Control+click (Mac) on any line of the report and choose More Info to find additional details about the specific error or condition.

8. Use the Property inspector or another Dreamweaver feature to correct the identified problem, and then save the file.

Table 4-1	Site Report Options
Report Name	*What It Does*
Checked Out By	Lists files checked out of the site and identifies the person who checked them out. This feature is necessary only if you're working with other web designers on the same site and there's a risk of overwriting each other's work.
Design Notes	Lists Design Notes used in the site.
Recently Modified	Lists files that have been edited within a specified time period. You can set the time period for the report by selecting the Recently Modified check box and then clicking the Report Settings button at the bottom of the dialog box.
Combinable Nested Font Tags	Lists all instances where you can combine nested tags. For example, `<font color="#000000"><font size="2">Great Websites You Should Visit</font></font>` is listed because you can simplify the code by combining the two font tags into `<font color="#000000" size="2">Great Websites You Should Visit</font>`.
Missing Alt Text	Lists all the image tags that do not include Alt text. Alt text is a text description for an image tag included in the HTML code as an alternative if the image is not displayed. Alt text is important to anyone who uses a special browser that reads web pages.

Report Name	What It Does
Redundant Nested Tags	Lists all places where you have redundant nested tags. For example, `<h1>Good headlines <h1>are harder to write</h1> than you might think</h1>` is listed because you can simplify the code by removing the second `<h1>` tag to make the code look like this: `<h1>Good headlines are harder to write than you might think</h1>`.
Removable Empty Tags	Lists the empty tags on your site. Empty tags can occur when you delete an image, text section, or other element without deleting all the tags applied to the element.
Untitled Documents	Lists filenames that don't have a title. The `<title>` tag is easy to forget because it does not appear in the body of the page. Instead, the `<title>` tag specifies the text that appears at the very top of the browser window and the text that appears in the Favorites list when someone bookmarks a page. You can enter a title for any page by entering text in the Title field just above the work area or in the Title field in the Page Properties dialog box.

Finding and Fixing Broken Links

If you're trying to rein in a chaotic website or you just want to check a site for broken links, you'll be pleased to discover the Link Checker. You can use this feature to verify the links in a single file or an entire website. Link Checker can also automatically fix all the referring links at once if a link is broken. (You find instructions for creating links in Chapter 2.)

Here's an example of what Link Checker can do. Assume that someone on your team (because you would never do such a thing yourself) changed the name of a file from `new.htm` to `old.htm` without using the Files panel or any of Dreamweaver's automatic link update features. Maybe this person changed the name using another program or simply renamed it in Explorer (Windows) or Finder (Mac) the way you would change the name of most other files on your computer. Changing the filename was easy, but what this person may not have realized is that the links are now broken if he or she didn't change the links to the file when the file was renamed.

If only one page links to the file that your clueless teammate changed, fixing the broken link isn't such a big deal. As long as you remember which file the page links from, you can simply open that page and use the Property inspector to reset the link the same way you created the link in the first place.

But many times, a single page in a website is linked to many other pages. When that's the case, fixing all the link references can be time-consuming and forgetting some is all too easy, which is why the Link Checker is so helpful.

If you're working on a dynamic website that uses a database or a content management system, such as WordPress, Joomla, or Drupal, the Link Checker may not work properly. The Link Checker works best for sites with static HTML pages and sites created using .dwt Dreamweaver templates.

Checking for broken links

To check a site for broken links, follow these steps:

1. **In the drop-down list at the top of the Files panel, select the site you want to work on.**

   If you already have the site open in Dreamweaver, you can skip this step.

   You must have the entire site on your hard drive and you must have completed the site setup process (covered in Chapter 2) for the Link Checker to work properly.

2. **Choose Site⊅Check Links Sitewide.**

   The Link Checker tab, shown in Figure 4-7, opens in the Results panel at the bottom of the page, just under the Property inspector. The tab displays a list of internal and external links. The tab also lists any pages, images, or other items not linked from any other page and identifies them as unused files. Large unused files, such as images and videos, can waste space on your server, so this list is handy if you want to clean up old files you no longer use on your site.

   Remember, just because you delete a file from your hard drive doesn't mean the file is deleted from the server where you host your website. Make sure you remove files from both the Remote Site window in the Files panel as well as the Local Site panel. (For more on using FTP and synchronization to update or delete files automatically on your server, see the section "Publishing Your Website," later in this chapter.)

Fixing broken links

Broken links are one of the worst problems you can have on a website. Nothing turns off visitors faster than clicking a link and getting a *File Not Found* error page. After you identify a broken link in a site, fix it as soon as possible. Fortunately, Dreamweaver makes fixing broken links simple by providing quick access to files with broken links and automating the process of fixing multiple links to the same file.

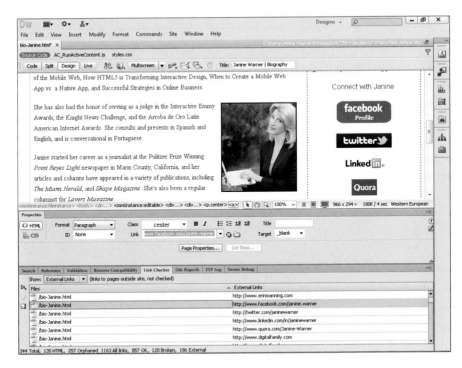

Figure 4-7: The Link Checker report displays broken links, external links, and unused files.

After using the Link Checker tab described in the preceding section to identify broken links, follow these steps to fix them by using the Results panel:

1. **With the Results panel open at the bottom of the page, double-click a filename that Dreamweaver identifies as a broken link.**

   The page and its corresponding Property inspector open. The Results panel remains visible.

2. **Select the broken link or image on the open page.**

   For example, you can fix a broken image by selecting the Broken Image icon on the page and then reinserting the image using the Property inspector to find the correct image file.

3. **In the Property inspector, click the Browse icon (which looks like a folder) to the right of the Src text box.**

   (Instead of using the Browse button to find the correct image, you can type the correct filename and path in the text box.) The Select Image Source dialog box appears.

4. Click to select the filename of the correct image and then click OK.

The link automatically changes to reflect the new filename and location. If you replace an image, the image file reappears on the page.

If the link that you correct appears in multiple pages and you fix the link using the broken link's Results panel, Dreamweaver prompts you with a dialog box asking whether you want to fix the remaining broken link references to the file. Click the Yes button to automatically correct all other references. Click the No button to leave the other files unchanged.

Finding files by their addresses

If you're not sure where you saved a file or what you called it, but you can get to it with your browser, you can determine the filename and location by looking at the URL in the browser's address bar. Each folder in a website is included in the address to a page within that folder. Folder names are separated by the forward slash, /, and each filename can be distinguished because it includes an extension. For example, the URL in the browser's address bar of the Speeches page on my site tells me that the file is named `speeches.html`. (See the URL in the top of the figure in this sidebar.)

Similarly, you can identify the name and location of any image you're viewing on a web page. If you're using Google Chrome or Firefox,

An insightful presentation that informs and inspires

Janine tailors her presentations to each audience and uses real-world stories, multimedia, and a healthy dose of humor, to create dynamic, entertaining presentations that have informed and inspired audiences all over the world.

Janine Warner delivers a keynote speech in Spanish at the Arroba de Oro Internet Awards ceremony in Panama City, Panama.

place your cursor over the image and right-click (Windows) or Control+click (Mac) and then choose Inspect element. (In Internet Explorer, choose Properties.) The Element Properties dialog box includes the specific URL of the image, which has the name and folder (path). If you're using the Safari browser on a Mac, you won't find this option, but you can Control+click any image and choose Open Image in New Window. Then, in the new window, look in the URL field and you'll find the name and path for the image.

Making Global Changes to Links

If you want to globally change a link to point at a new URL or to some other page on your site, you can use the Change Link Sitewide option to enter the new URL and change every reference automatically. You can use this option to change any kind of link, including mailto, FTP, and script links. For example, if an e-mail address that you use throughout your site changes, you can use this feature to fix it automatically — a real timesaver. You can use this feature also when you want a string of text to link to a different file. For example, you can change every instance of the words *Enter This Month's Contest* to link to `/contest/january.htm` instead of `/contest/december.htm` throughout your website.

To change a collection of links with the Change Link Sitewide feature, follow these steps:

1. **Make sure the site you want to work on is displayed in the Files panel.**

   See the preceding exercise for instructions on selecting a site.

2. **Choose Site⇨Change Link Sitewide.**

   The Change Link Sitewide dialog box appears.

3. **Enter the old address and then enter the new address, or click the Browse button to identify files where you want to change the links.**

   You can use this feature to change any link, including e-mail links, links from one page to another within a site, or links to a different website.

4. **Click OK.**

   Dreamweaver updates any documents that include the specified links.

Any changes you make to links using Dreamweaver's automated link features occur only on the local version of your site on your hard drive. Make sure you upload all affected files to your web server to ensure that all changes are included on your published site. To automatically reconcile changes on your local and remote sites, use Dreamweaver's Synchronize Files feature, which I describe later in this chapter.

Managing Files and Folders in Your Site

Dreamweaver includes a variety of tools that help you manage the files, folders, and subfolders within a site without breaking links or image references. You can use the Files panel to rename and rearrange files and folders, as well as create new folders, all with drag-and-drop ease.

You need to complete the simple site setup process for Dreamweaver's Files panel features to work. If you haven't already set up your site, turn to the instructions at the beginning of Chapter 2. (If you're getting tired of my reminding you of this point throughout this book, realize that you'd probably be even more annoyed if you didn't know the site setup process was necessary and couldn't get these features to work.)

Moving and renaming files and folders

To move or rename files and folders in a website, follow these steps:

1. **Open the site you want to work on (if it's not already open in Dreamweaver) by selecting the site name from the drop-down list at the top of the Files panel.**

   When you select a site by clicking the site name, the folders and files in that site appear in the Files panel.

2. **Click the plus sign (+) (Windows) or the small arrow (Mac) to open the local site folder or any subfolder to display the files within the folder.**

   Click the minus sign (–) to close a folder or subfolder.

3. **In the Files panel, select the file or folder you want to move or rename.**

   To *move* a selected file or folder:

   a. **Drag the selected file, group of files, or folder onto a folder.**

      Dreamweaver automatically moves the files into the folder and changes all the related links. The Files panel works much like the Explorer window on a PC or Finder on a Mac, except Dreamweaver tracks and fixes links when you move files through the Files panel.

If you move or rename files or folders in Finder or Explorer instead of in the Files panel, you will break any links set to or from those files and any image references within them.

When you move a linked file into a new folder in Dreamweaver, the Update Files dialog box appears, listing any linked pages that need to be updated, as shown in Figure 4-8.

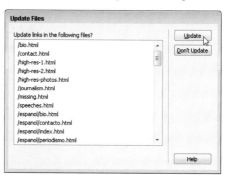

Figure 4-8: You see all files that will be changed during the update process.

> **b. To adjust the links so they don't break, choose Update.**
>
> If you choose Don't Update, any links to or from that file are left unchanged. Of course, you can always move the file back to its original location to restore the links.

To *rename* a selected file or folder:

> **a. Click twice on any filename or folder name.**
>
> Much like Finder or Explorer on your computer, you need to click twice with a slight pause between clicks to select the name (instead of double-clicking, which opens the file).
>
> **b. When a box appears around the name, edit it by typing new text, and press Enter (Return on a Mac).**
>
> Again you're prompted with the Update Files dialog box to update any links affected by the filename change.
>
> **c. Choose Update to adjust the links.**

Creating files and creating and deleting folders

In this section, you find out how to create a folder as well as how to delete folders and files:

1. **Open the site you want to work on (if it's not already open in Dreamweaver) by selecting the site name from the drop-down list at the top of the Files panel.**

   When you select a site by clicking the site name, the folders and files in that site appear in the Files panel.

2. **Click the plus sign (+) (Windows) or the small arrow (Mac) to open the local site folder or any subfolder to display the files within the folder.**

   Click the minus sign (–) to close a folder or subfolder.

3. **To *create* a new folder in the Files panel:**

   > **a. Right-click (Option-click on a Mac) the main site folder or any subfolder where you want to create a new folder.**
   >
   > A list of options appears.
   >
   > **b. Choose New Folder from the list.**
   >
   > A new, untitled folder appears inside the folder just selected in the preceding step.
   >
   > **c. Name the new folder by typing new text to replace the word `Untitled`.**
   >
   > After you've created a new folder, you can drag files or other folders in the Files panel into the new folder.

4. To *delete* a folder or file from the Files panel:

   a. **Click to select the file or folder.**

   b. **Press the Delete or Backspace key.**

This action will permanently delete the folder or file from your hard drive.

Publishing Your Website

If you're looking for the section where you find out how to upload your site (or any or all pages in your site) to your web server, you've found it.

After you create and test your website so that it's ready to publish on the web, you can put Dreamweaver's publishing tools to work. Which features you use depend on the kind of web server you use. If you're using a commercial service provider, you'll most likely need Dreamweaver's FTP features, which I cover in detail in the following section.

Note that you need the following information from your web-hosting service before you can configure Dreamweaver's FTP features. Most service providers send this information in an e-mail message when you first sign up for an account. If you don't have this information, you will need to contact your service provider for it, because it's unique to your account on your web-hosting service. Here's what you need:

- The FTP host name.
- The path to the web directory (optional but highly recommended), such as `/web/htdocs/jcwarner`.
- Your FTP login or user name.
- Your FTP password.
- Any special instructions from your server, such as if you need to use Passive FTP or any of the other advanced settings covered in Step 11 in the exercise that follows. These settings vary from server to server, so you need to ask your web-hosting service. (If you're having trouble connecting and you're not sure about these options, you can always experiment by selecting and deselecting these options to see whether a setting enables you to connect.)

Setting up Dreamweaver's FTP features

After you gather all your FTP information, you're ready to set up Dreamweaver's FTP publishing features. This process can seem daunting and often takes a few tries to get right, but the good news is that you have to do it only once.

(Dreamweaver saves these settings for you so you don't have to set them up every time you want to upload new pages to your site.)

Follow these steps to set up Dreamweaver's FTP features and publish files to a web server:

1. **Choose Site⇨Manage Sites.**

   The Manage Sites dialog box opens.

2. **In the list of defined sites, double-click the name of the site you want to publish.**

   If your site is not listed in this dialog box, you haven't set up your site. Refer to the instructions for site setup in Chapter 2 and then return to complete these steps.

3. **Select Servers from the categories listed in the left panel of the Site Setup dialog box.**

   The server list appears. If you haven't yet set up any web servers in Dreamweaver, this list is blank

4. **Click the small plus sign at the bottom left of the server list area, as shown in Figure 4-9.**

   The Basic category opens in the servers dialog box and FTP is automatically selected. (If you need to use an option other than FTP, see the list explaining all the Dreamweaver options by the Technical Stuff icon at the end of these steps.)

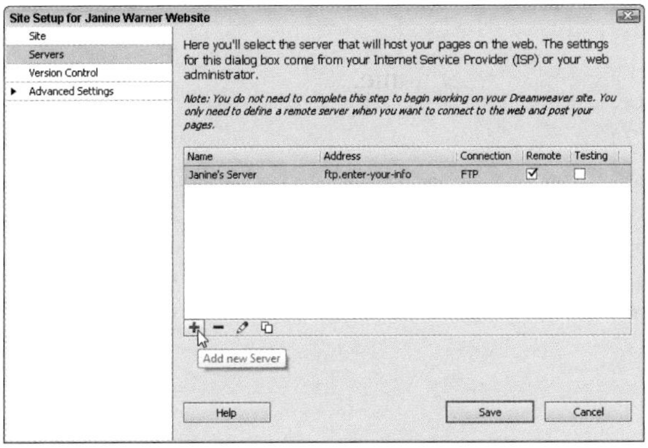

Figure 4-9: Click the small plus sign to open the Basic server configuration dialog box.

5. **Enter a name in the Server Name field.**

   You can name your server anything you like. Choose a name that will enable you to easily choose among the servers you've set up. (If you use only one web server to host your site, the choice doesn't matter as much as it does if you host your site on multiple servers — something generally done only by very large or international sites.)

6. **Enter the FTP address for your web server account.**

   Again this information depends on how your web server is set up, but most use one of the following: `ftp.servername.com`, `ftp.your domainname.com`, or simply `yourdomain.com` without anything at the beginning of the domain.

7. **In the Username and Password fields, type your username (sometimes called a login name) and password.**

   Again, this information is unique to your account on your web server.

8. **Check the Save box to the right of the Password field if you want Dreamweaver to store your access information.**

   This is handy because you can then automatically connect to the server anytime you want to upload or download pages. However, checking Save could enable anyone with access to your computer to gain access to your web server.

9. **Click the Test button to make sure you've entered everything correctly**.

   Making a mistake is easy, so the capability to test the connection and make any needed adjustments before you close this dialog box is helpful. If you connect with no problems, you see a message stating that Dreamweaver connected to your web server successfully. (**Note:** You must save the password to use the test feature, but you can deselect the Save Password box after you test if you prefer not to save the password in the program.)

   If you do have trouble connecting to your site, skip ahead to Step 11 for a few advanced options that may help.

10. **In the Root Directory field, type the directory on the remote site in which documents visible to the public are stored (also known as the local site folder).**

    The root directory usually looks something like this: `public_html/` or `www/htdocs/`. Again, how your server directory is set up may vary depending on your service provider.

If you upload your files to the wrong directory on your server, they won't be visible when you view your site through a browser. The nearby sidebar, "Why can't I see my files on the server?" helps you work around this potentially frustrating problem with tips on identifying where to upload your website after you log into your server and finding the root directory to enter in this field if you can't find it in the information you get from your web hosting company.

11. **Click the small arrow to the left of More Options, as shown in Figure 4-10.**

    You may not need to change any of these settings, but if you're having trouble connecting to your server, and you're sure you've entered your user name, password, and FTP address correctly, adjusting these settings may enable you to connect.

    I recommend selecting and deselecting each option in this area in turn, and then clicking the Test button after each change, to see if any of these adjustments makes the difference and enables you to connect to your server.

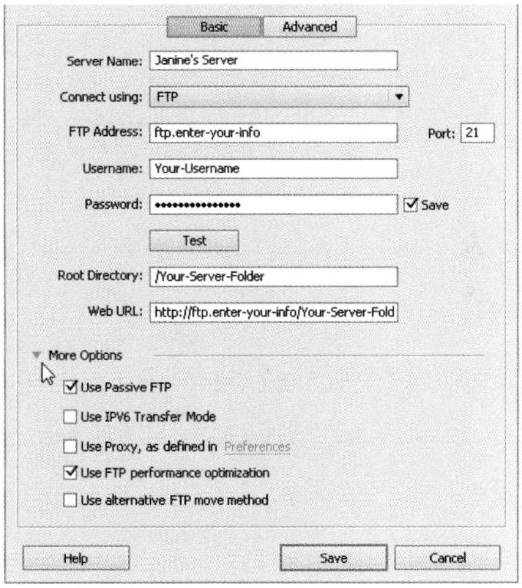

Figure 4-10: Enter all the information from your web-hosting company.

A little experimentation with settings before waiting on hold with tech support is usually worth the effort. But if you're really having trouble establishing a connection with your server, call or e-mail the tech support staff at your web server. The only people who can help you are those who run your web server, because the settings are specific to your service provider and can vary dramatically from one hosting company to another.

12. **After clicking Test successfully connects to your server, click Save to save your settings.**

Why can't I see my files on the server?

Including the root directory in Dreamweaver's FTP settings is optional, but doing so makes transferring files using Dreamweaver's Upload and Download options easier. Thus, you reduce your chances of uploading your files to the wrong directory on your server, where they won't be visible when you try to view your site through a browser.

To find the root directory and the path to that directory on your server, you may need to log into your web server and do a little experimenting before you can figure out the path to the root directory. To perform these tasks, you need to complete the steps in the "Setting Up Dreamweaver's FTP Features" and "Publishing files to a web server with FTP" sections. Trust me, the effort is worthwhile. Here's why.

When you log into most commercial web servers using the login information they provide you, you access your main folder on their server. This folder often includes several subfolders, such as a folder that stores your e-mail on the server, another folder that stores log reports of traffic to your site, and possibly several others for storing things such as CGI scripts. Among all these subfolders, finding the one in which you

need to upload your pages can be tricky. The subfolder you need is usually named something like `htdocs`, `web`, or `webfiles`. You have to upload your web pages to the right folder so that your website becomes public on the Internet and your pages are visible when you open your domain name in a web browser.

If you're not sure which folder you should use, try uploading just one file to any folder that looks like a good candidate (using the instructions in the "Publishing files to a web server with FTP" section in this chapter). Then visit your domain with a web browser to see if the page is visible. (Each time you upload another page, remember to click the Refresh button in your browser to see any changes.) After you figure out which folder corresponds to your domain name, upload all the rest of your site to that same subfolder, making sure that you mirror the local site folder on your hard drive with the main root folder on your server.

Also note that if you want to use Dreamweaver's synchronization features, also covered in this chapter, you need to include the root directory in the FTP folder.

Dreamweaver saves all your FTP settings (assuming you opted to save the password). After you enter these settings properly and know that the connection works, you never have to enter them again. You can then access your web server from the Files panel in Dreamweaver, as you discover in the exercise that follows.

Dreamweaver provides six Access options. If you work at a large company or university, you are likely to use one of these options rather than FTP. The options available from the Connect Using drop-down list in the Server Setup dialog box are as follows:

✔ **FTP:** Select this option to use Dreamweaver's built-in File Transfer Protocol features, which I cover in detail in the following section. You're most likely to need these settings if you're using a commercial web hosting service.

✔ **FTP over SSL/TLS (implicit encryption):** This option provides a more secure FTP connection, but the server can allow the client to work in an unsecure mode.

✔ **FTP over SSL/TLS (explicit encryption):** This option provides a more secure FTP connection and the server drops the connection if it is not deemed secure.

✔ **Local/Network:** Select this option if you're using a web server on a local network, such as your company or university server. For specific settings and requirements, check with your system administrator.

✔ **WebDAV (Web-based Distributed Authoring and Versioning):** Select this option if you're using a server with the WebDAV protocol, such as Microsoft IIS.

✔ **RDS (Rapid Development Services):** Select this option if you're using ColdFusion on a remote server.

Publishing files to a web server with FTP

You can upload pages to your server and download pages from your server using the built-in FTP capabilities of Dreamweaver.

To transfer files between your hard drive and a remote server (after you've successfully set up the FTP features covered in the preceding section), follow these steps:

1. **Make sure the site you want to work on is selected in the Files panel.**

2. **In the top left of the Files panel, click the Connects to Remote Host icon (labeled in Figure 4-11).**

   If you're not already connected to the Internet, the Connects to Remote Host icon starts your Internet connection. If you have trouble connecting this way, try establishing your Internet connection as you usually do to check e-mail or surf the web, and then return to Dreamweaver and click the Connects to Remote Host icon after you're connected to the Internet. When your computer is online, Dreamweaver should have no trouble automatically establishing an FTP connection with your host server.

   If you still have trouble establishing a connection to your web server, refer to the preceding section, "Setting up Dreamweaver's FTP features," and make sure that you specified the server information correctly.

3. **After you establish a connection between your computer and your web server, click the Expand/Collapse icon (labeled in Figure 4-11).**

When you click this icon, Dreamweaver displays both the local folder with your site on your hard drive and the remote folder with the site on your server. I prefer the dual view, because seeing both side-by-side makes moving files from one place to another easier. It also helps me visualize the structure of the site on the server, but it does take up more space on your computer screen.

You can also view your local site folder by choosing Local View from the drop-down list at the top right (visible in Figure 4-11). Or choose Remote View to see only the files on the server.

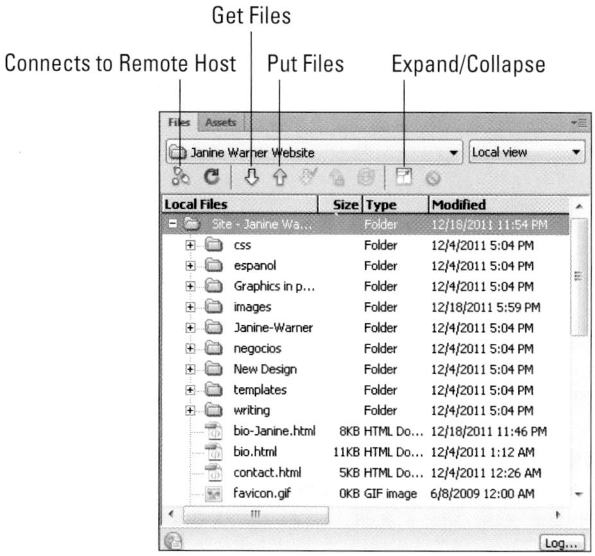

Get Files

Connects to Remote Host | Put Files | Expand/Collapse

Files	Assets

| Janine Warner Website | | Local view |

Local Files	Size	Type	Modified
Site - Janine Wa...		Folder	12/18/2011 11:54 PM
css		Folder	12/4/2011 5:04 PM
espanol		Folder	12/4/2011 5:04 PM
Graphics in p...		Folder	12/4/2011 5:04 PM
images		Folder	12/18/2011 5:59 PM
Janine-Warner		Folder	12/4/2011 5:04 PM
negocios		Folder	12/4/2011 5:04 PM
New Design		Folder	12/4/2011 5:04 PM
templates		Folder	12/4/2011 5:04 PM
writing		Folder	12/4/2011 5:04 PM
bio-Janine.html	8KB	HTML Do...	12/18/2011 11:46 PM
bio.html	11KB	HTML Do...	12/4/2011 1:12 AM
contact.html	5KB	HTML Do...	12/4/2011 12:26 AM
favicon.gif	0KB	GIF image	6/8/2009 12:00 AM

Log...

Figure 4-11: The row of icons across the top control FTP functions.

4. **To upload a file, select the file from the Local View panel and click the Put Files icon (the up arrow) in the Files panel.**

The Local View panel displays the files on your hard drive.

The files are copied automatically from your hard drive to your web server when you transfer them. You can select multiple files or folders to be transferred simultaneously.

After you upload files to your server, test your work by using a web browser to view them online. Sometimes things that look and work fine on your computer (such as links) won't work on the server.

5. **To download files or folders, select the files or folders from the Remote View panel and click the Get Files icon (the down arrow) in the Files panel.**

   The Remote View panel displays the files on your server.

   The files are copied automatically from your web server to your hard drive when you transfer them.

   Be aware that when you copy files to or from your server, the files you're transferring overwrite the files already at the destination. Dreamweaver notifies you about the overwriting if it notices you're replacing a newer file with an older one, but it can't always correctly assess the proper time differences. Take note of these warnings, but keep in mind that you can get warnings that aren't always accurate when they're based on the age of a file, especially if you use more than one computer to work on your website.

   When the transfer is complete, you can open the files on your hard drive.

6. **To close this dual-panel dialog box and return to Dreamweaver's main workspace, simply click the Expand/Collapse icon again.**

Synchronizing local and remote sites

One of the most valuable features in Dreamweaver's FTP options is the capability to automatically synchronize the files on your hard drive with the files on your server. This cool feature helps you keep track of which pages you've edited and ensures that they've been updated on the server. This capability may not matter much to you the first time you upload your site, or if you have only a few pages in your site. But if you have a large site and make frequent updates, this feature is a wonderful way to make sure you upload all the changes you make to your server. Dreamweaver also confirms which files are updated after you complete the synchronization.

Follow these steps to synchronize your website:

1. **Make sure the site you want to work on is selected and displayed in the Files panel.**

2. **Click the Connects to Remote Host icon, in the top left of the Files panel, to log on to your remote site.**

3. **Click the Expand/Collapse icon (labeled in Figure 4-11) to expand the dialog box and view the remote and local sites simultaneously.**

   The Site dialog box displays both the remote and local views of the site. (To collapse this dialog box, click the Expand/Collapse icon again.)

4. **Choose Site⇨Synchronize.**

   The Synchronize Files dialog box appears.

Downloading an existing website

If you want to work on an existing website and you don't already have a copy of it on your computer's hard drive, you can use Dreamweaver to download any or all files in any website (that you have the login information to access). Then you can edit the existing pages, add new pages, or use any of Dreamweaver's other features to check links and manage the site's further development. The first step is to get a copy of the site onto your computer by downloading it from the server.

To download an existing website, follow these steps:

1. **Create a new folder on your computer to store the existing site.**

2. **Use Dreamweaver's site setup features to specify this folder as the local site folder.**

   Follow the instructions at the beginning of Chapter 2 to set up a site, if you're not sure how to do this yet.

3. **Enter the FTP settings in the Basic server dialog box (refer to Figure 4-10).**

   I explain how to do this in the "Setting up Dreamweaver's FTP features" section.

4. **Connect to the remote site by clicking the tiny Connects to Remote Host icon, which looks like the ends of two cables, in the Files panel.**

5. **Click the Get Files icon, which looks like a down arrow, to download the entire site to your local drive.**

Sometimes your web host has files on the remote server that you don't need to download. If you want to download only specific files or folders from the site, select only those files or folders in the Remote Site pane of the Files panel and click the Get Files icon. (See the sidebar "Why can't I see my files on the Server?" to find the folder on your web server that corresponds to the local site folder on your hard drive.) Re-creating the folder structure on your local computer is important because Dreamweaver needs to know the relative location of all the files in your site to set links properly. The safest option is to download the entire site; but if you're working on a large web project, downloading part of the structure will enable you to work on a section of the site without downloading it all.

If you're working on only one page or section of a site, I recommend that you choose to include *dependent files,* meaning any files linked from those pages, as you download them. Choosing this option ensures that the links are set properly when you make changes and that all related files are downloaded to your hard drive.

6. **After you download the site or specific files or folders, you can edit them as you do any other file in Dreamweaver.**

5. In the Synchronize drop-down list, choose whether to synchronize the Entire Site or Selected Files Only.

6. In the Direction drop-down list, choose which option you want to use to copy the files:

   • **Put Newer Files to Remote:** This option copies the most recently modified files from your local site to the remote site. Select the

Delete Remote Files Not on Local Drive option *only* if you're sure you want those files removed from your web server.

- **Get Newer Files from Remote:** This option copies the most recently modified files from your remote site to the local site. If you want to remove those files from your local copy, select the Delete Local Files Not on Remote Server box.

- **Get and Put Newer Files:** This option updates both the local and remote sites with the most recent versions of all the files.

Be careful of the Delete Remote Files Not on Local Drive feature when using Get or Put. As a general rule, I recommend that you leave it deselected because you may have folders and files on the server, such as log files, that don't exist on your hard drive, and you don't want to delete them inadvertently.

7. Click the Preview button.

The Site FTP dialog box displays the files that are about to be changed.

Now you have the option to verify the files you want to delete, put, and get. If you don't want Dreamweaver to alter a file, deselect it from the Site FTP dialog box now or forever live with the consequences.

8. Click OK.

All approved changes are automatically made, and Dreamweaver updates the Site FTP dialog box with the status.

9. When the synchronization finishes, you can choose to save or not save the verification information to a local file.

I recommend that you save the verification information because it can be handy if you want to review your changes after synchronization is complete.

Setting cloaking options

The Dreamweaver Cloaking option enables you to exclude folders or files from site-publishing features, meaning they won't be uploaded to the live site when you're synchronizing or uploading a batch of files to the server. If you're wondering why you might want to prevent files from uploading to your web server, consider this: The Cloaking feature is a handy way to prevent large graphics, such as Photoshop files, from being uploaded and taking up room on your server, while still storing your high-resolution graphics in your local site folder so you can easily keep track of them. This capability is useful, for example, if you have a layered .psd or .tiff file that you want to store near the optimized JPEG versions you use in your site. (You find information about converting images into JPEG and other web-friendly formats in Chapter 3.)

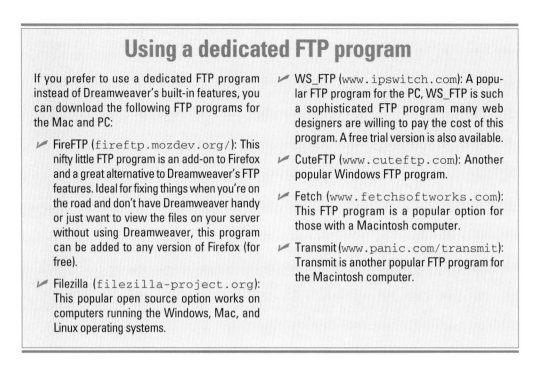

Using a dedicated FTP program

If you prefer to use a dedicated FTP program instead of Dreamweaver's built-in features, you can download the following FTP programs for the Mac and PC:

✔ FireFTP (fireftp.mozdev.org/): This nifty little FTP program is an add-on to Firefox and a great alternative to Dreamweaver's FTP features. Ideal for fixing things when you're on the road and don't have Dreamweaver handy or just want to view the files on your server without using Dreamweaver, this program can be added to any version of Firefox (for free).

✔ Filezilla (filezilla-project.org): This popular open source option works on computers running the Windows, Mac, and Linux operating systems.

✔ WS_FTP (www.ipswitch.com): A popular FTP program for the PC, WS_FTP is such a sophisticated FTP program many web designers are willing to pay the cost of this program. A free trial version is also available.

✔ CuteFTP (www.cuteftp.com): Another popular Windows FTP program.

✔ Fetch (www.fetchsoftworks.com): This FTP program is a popular option for those with a Macintosh computer.

✔ Transmit (www.panic.com/transmit): Transmit is another popular FTP program for the Macintosh computer.

You can use the Cloaking feature to save any type of files in your local site folder, with the assurance that no one can accidentally publish the files with Dreamweaver until you uncloak them and publish them. This feature is best used for large files you don't want on your web server, such as .psd, .tiff, .avi, and other high-resolution image or video formats.

Using Design Notes to Keep in Touch

If you sometimes forget the details of your work or neglect to tell your colleagues about updates to pages in your website, the Dreamweaver Design Notes feature may save you some grief. If you're the only person working on a website, you probably don't need the features described in this section because they're intended for use on sites developed by a team of people who need to communicate with each other and make sure they don't overwrite each other's work.

Design Notes are ideal if you want to hide sensitive information from visitors, such as pricing structures or creative strategies, but make that information available to members of your development team. Comments, instructions, and other text saved as a Design Note in Dreamweaver can travel with any HTML file or image, even if the file transfers from one website to another or from Fireworks to Dreamweaver.

Essentially, Design Notes enable you to record information (such as a message to another designer on your team) and associate it with a file or folder. Design Notes work a lot like the *comment tag* (HTML code that enables you to embed in a page text that won't appear in a browser) but with a bit more privacy. Unlike the comment tag, which is embedded directly in the HTML code of a page (and can be seen if someone views the source code behind a page on the web), Design Notes are never visible to your visitors. The only way for a visitor to view Design Notes is to deliberately type the path to your notes subdirectory and view the notes files directly. You can even explicitly block this from being allowed, but only if you have administrative access to your server. To be even more secure, you can keep the notes on your hard drive and prevent them from ever being uploaded to your server — though, of course, your team members won't see your witty remarks.

To access the Design Notes page, choose Design Notes in the Category list in the Site Setup dialog box. The settings on this page enable you to control how Dreamweaver uses Design Notes:

- ✓ **Maintain Design Notes:** Select this option to ensure that the Design Note remains attached to the file when you upload, copy, or move it.

- ✓ **Upload Design Notes for Sharing:** Choose this option to include Design Notes when you send files to the server by using FTP.

- ✓ **Clean Up:** Use the Clean Up button to delete Design Notes that are not associated with any files in the site.

When you create graphics in Adobe Fireworks, you can save a Design Note for each image file that is also available in Dreamweaver. To use this integrated feature, create a Design Note in Fireworks and associate it with the image. Then when you save the Fireworks image to your local website folder, the Design Note goes with it. When you open the file in Dreamweaver, the Design Note appears when you right-click the image (Control+click on the Mac). This feature is a great way for graphic designers to communicate with other members of the web development team.

Part II
Creating Page Designs with Style

The 5th Wave   By Rich Tennant

HORNER BROS.
MAKERS OF PREMIUM
BELLS & WHISTLES

"As a website designer I never thought I'd say this, but I don't think your site has enough bells and whistles."

*T*oday, the best way to design websites is with Cascading Style Sheets (CSS). This part introduces you to the power and advantages of CSS, with two chapters on creating and using styles, and goes on to show you the latest design techniques made possible by CSS3.

In Chapter 5, you find an introduction to CSS and a review of all the great CSS features in Dreamweaver. In Chapter 6, you move on to creating CSS layouts, by combining `<div>` tags and other HTML elements with styles to create accessible, flexible designs that work well across the most popular web browsers. In Chapter 7, you discover how CSS3, the latest version of CSS, makes it possible to add drop shadows, gradients, and other advanced design features.

In Chapter 8, you discover how Dreamweaver templates can make creating web pages faster and easier — and best of all, how templates can save you time by making it possible to update and make design changes to multiple pages at once. In Chapter 9, you find out how to create tables, split and merge cells, and use table attributes. You also find tips about when it's best to use HTML tables and when CSS is the preferred option.

5

Introducing Cascading Style Sheets

*W*ant to add a little style to your pages? *Cascading Style Sheets (CSS)* are all the rage on the web, and with good reason: CSS is *the* way to create websites today if you want to follow the latest standards and develop sites that are accessible, flexible, and designed to work on a wide range of screen sizes and devices.

Unfortunately, most people find working with styles far more complicated and confusing than previous approaches to web design. In my experience, this confusion fades after you learn the basics and start working with styles. Indeed, with the addition of advanced design features, including drop shadows and gradients in CSS3, the advantages of CSS make it well worth the time it takes to master the techniques. This chapter explains how styles work, the different kinds of styles (and what they're best used for), and how to use the features in Dreamweaver that are designed for creating and editing CSS. In Chapter 6, you apply these basic skills to creating CSS layouts, and in Chapter 7, you discover how the latest CSS3 features have been integrated into Dreamweaver CS6.

The concept of creating styles has been around since long before the web. Desktop publishing programs, such as Adobe InDesign, and even word processing programs, such as Microsoft Word, have long used styles to manage the formatting and editing of text on printed pages. In a word processor, you can create and save styles for common features, such as headlines and captions. In print design, styles are great timesavers because they enable you to combine a collection of formatting options, such as Arial, bold, and italic, and then apply all those options at once to any selected text in your document using a single style. You also have the advantage that if you change a style, you can apply the change automatically — and everywhere you've used that style in a document.

On the web, you can do all that and more with CSS because you can use style sheets for more than just text formatting. For example, you can use CSS to create styles that align images to the left or right side of a page, add margin and padding space around text and images, and change background and link colors. For all these reasons (and more), CSS has quickly become the preferred method of designing web pages among professional web designers.

Introducing Cascading Style Sheets

CSS is a powerful tool because you can use it to make global style changes across an entire website. Suppose, for example, that you create a style for your headlines by redefining the `<h1>` tag to create large, blue, bold headlines. Then one fine day, you decide that all your headlines should be red instead of blue. If you aren't using CSS, changing all your headlines could be a huge undertaking — a matter of opening every web page in your site to make changes to the font tags around your headlines. But if you're using CSS in an external style sheet, you can simply change the style that controls the headline in the style sheet and — voilá — your headlines all turn red automatically.

If you ever have to redesign your site (and believe me, every good site goes through periodic redesigns), you can save hours or even days of work if you've created your design with CSS.

Understanding the basics of styles

Many people find CSS confusing at first because it's such a different approach to design than what they may be used to if they've worked in print. The following are four of the more confusing aspects of CSS for beginners:

- ✔ **Getting used to thinking about the styles on your site separate from your text, images, and other content:** For example, you want to avoid simply applying formatting directly to a heading to make it bold, green, and 24 point. In CSS, you create a style for your heading that includes bold, green, and 24 point; save that style in a separate place in your document or in a separate file called an external style sheet; and then apply the style to the heading text. As a result, if you want to change the way your headline looks later, you don't go to the headline text in your page to make the change. Instead, you edit the style in the style sheet, and it automatically changes any heading text formatted with that style.

✓ **Understanding all the different kinds of style selectors you can choose from, such as class, ID, and tag selectors:** No matter how you create your styles, each style definition, or *rule,* contains a selector and a declaration. The *selector* identifies the name and type of style, for example, #container or .caption. The *declaration* defines the style and describes its properties, such as bold, blue, or 300 pixels wide. If that doesn't mean much to you yet, don't worry. Dreamweaver's four selector types are described in detail later in this chapter, and as you discover how styles work, new terms such as selectors and declarations begin to make a lot more sense.

✓ **Understanding when it's best to create external style sheets, internal style sheets, or inline styles:** External style sheets offer the greatest advantages because they enable you to use the same styles across any or all pages in a website. Sometimes, however, internal style sheets are useful, such as when you want to apply a style to only a single page. The section "Using internal versus external style sheets" explains how best to use the different types of style sheets.

✓ **Understanding how you combine CSS and HTML to create web pages:** For example, you can create a class style, such as .caption and apply it to the paragraph tag to change the appearance of text only when it appears under your images, or you can redefine a tag, such as the <h1> tag, to change the way all headlines look on a page.

If you're starting to feel baffled already, hang in there. I'm just giving you an overview before I take you further and further down the rabbit hole. CSS is a topic that's hard to grasp until you learn a number of basic concepts. Even if you're not quite sure you understand everything I've described, keep reading. As you make your way through these three chapters on CSS, it should all start making more and more sense.

Combining CSS and HTML

Most professional web designers today recommend creating web page designs by combing HTML and CSS. Here's the simplified version of how the two work together:

1. Use HTML to create the structure of a page with tags, such as division (<div>), heading (<h1>, <h2>, and so on), and paragraph (<p>).

2. Create styles in CSS that specify the size of these elements, where they appear on a page, and a variety of other formatting options.

Similarly, you use HTML to insert images and create links, and then add styles to change formatting options, such as removing the underline from your links or changing the color that appears when someone rolls a cursor over a link.

Understanding style selectors

When you create new styles, you first have to choose which selector to use for which job. The selector corresponds to the kind of style you create. Each selector option has different naming conventions, restrictions, and uses. If you're completely new to working with styles, this may not make much sense yet, but understanding the basics of selectors is a fundamental part of working with styles. I encourage you to read through all these descriptions of selectors so you can appreciate your options before you move on.

 Don't feel you have to memorize all this. Instead, consider folding down the corner on this page so you can refer to this list of selectors as you create and edit styles later.

The following sections offer descriptions of each of the four selection types, which are available from the New CSS Rule dialog box when you create styles.

Class selectors

The class selector is the most versatile selector option. *Class styles* can format any element (from text to images to multimedia), and you can use them as many times as you like on any page in a website.

Class style names always begin with a period (often called a "dot"). You can create class styles with any name as long as you don't use spaces or special characters. (Hyphens and dashes are okay.) Thus, if you create a style called *caption* for the text that appears under your pictures, it should be written like this with the dot followed by the name:

```
.caption
```

Dreamweaver helps you with the opening dot. If you choose class as the selector type and forget to include a dot at the beginning of the name, Dreamweaver adds one for you. Just don't include any space between the dot and the style name.

However, the dot appears only in your style sheet code. When you *apply* a class style to text or another element, the dot doesn't appear with the name in your HTML code. If you think that's inconsistent, you're not alone. A class style is indicated by a dot in the CSS style sheet but by the word *class* in

HTML code. Thus, if you applied the `.caption` style to a paragraph tag to format the text under an image, the HTML code would look like this:

```
<p class="caption">This photo of a family of Fallow deer was
              taken in Northern California.</p>
```

Class styles must be applied to an element, such as the paragraph tag shown in this example. Class tags can also be used in combination with other styles, making it possible to apply more than one style to an element.

When you create a class style in Dreamweaver, the style is displayed in the CSS Styles panel on the right side of the workspace, shown in Figure 5-1. You can apply class styles by using the CSS drop-down list, also shown in the figure.

For more details and step-by-step instructions for creating and applying styles with class selectors, see Chapter 6.

Photos by Ken Riddick

Figure 5-1: Styles created with class selectors are available from the CSS drop-down list.

ID selectors

Think of *ID styles* as the building blocks of most CSS page layouts. ID styles, unlike other styles, must be unique, so they can be used only once per page. This characteristic makes them well suited to formatting <div> tags and other block-level elements that are used to create distinct sections, such as a sidebar or the header or footer of a page. You can create as many ID styles as you want for each page, but you can use each one only once on each page.

ID styles must begin with a pound character (#). Similar to class styles, Dreamweaver adds # to the beginning of the style name automatically if you forget to include it. And, as with a class style, don't include a space between # and the style name.

Being unable to use ID styles more than once per page has some advantages, especially when you are creating complex websites with many compound styles. But this limitation is also the reason why many designers use the ID style sparingly, opting instead to create most styles with the class selector.

Similar to class styles, you can name ID styles anything you like as long as you don't use spaces or special characters (again, hyphens and underscores are okay). An ID style used to identify the sidebar section of a page could look like this:

```
#sidebar
```

Similar to class styles, # isn't used in the HTML code. When a style is applied to an element, such as a <div> tag, the HTML code looks like this:

```
<div id="sidebar">Between these tags with the sidebar ID
          style, you would include any headlines, text, or
          other elements in your sidebar.</div>
```

In the predesigned CSS layouts included in Dreamweaver, all the designs are created by combining a series of <div> tags with ID styles using names such as #container, #header, and #footer to identify the main sections of the design. In Figure 5-2, you can see how a collection of ID and compound styles are displayed in the CSS Styles panel.

Tag selectors

The tag selector is used to redefine existing HTML tags. Select this option if you want to change the appearance of an existing HTML tag, such as the <h1> (heading 1) tag or the <ul> (unordered list) tag.

Photos by Ken Riddick

Figure 5-2: Styles created with the ID selector are used only once per page and are ideal for creating a CSS layout with <div> tags.

In many cases, redefining existing HTML tags with your desired formatting using CSS has advantages over creating new styles. For example, content formatted with the heading 1 tag is well recognized on the web as the most important text on a page. For that reason, many search engines give priority to text formatted with the heading 1 tag. Similarly, the hierarchical structure of the <h1>–<h6> tags helps ensure that, even if visitors to your site change the text size in their web browser, text formatted with the heading 1 tag is still larger relative to text formatted with a heading 2 tag, which is larger than text formatted with the heading 3 tag, and so on.

When you use the tag selector, the style definition is applied automatically to any text or other element that's been formatted with the corresponding tag. Thus, if you've formatted a heading with an <h1> tag and then create a new <h1> style, the formatting you used to define the style will apply automatically to the heading as soon as the style is created.

When you choose the tag selector type, all HTML tags become visible in a drop-down list in the New CSS Rule dialog box. You simply choose the tag style you want to create, as shown in Figure 5-3, where I've selected h1.

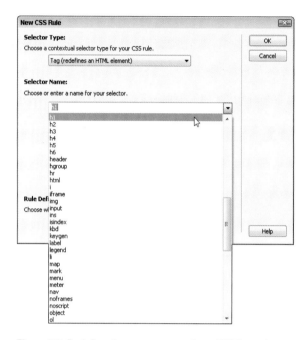

Figure 5-3: Redefine the appearance of any HTML tag by creating a style with a tag selector.

Creating compound styles

The *compound selector* can be used to combine two or more style rules to create a style definition that is displayed only when one style is contained within another. Compound styles are useful, for example, when you want to use the heading 1 tag multiple times to format headlines in different ways on the same web page. For example, you could create one style for headlines that appear in the main story area of a page and another style for headlines that appear in the sidebar on the page but use the heading 1 tag to format both.

Compound styles are created by combining ID, class, or tag styles. Following is an example:

```
#sidebar h1
```

See Figure 5-4 for an example of how an <h1> style defined like this within a #sidebar ID style looks in the New CSS Rule dialog box. For a compound style, you must

   ✔ Include a space between each name or tag in a compound style

   ✔ Not include the brackets around the tag in a style name

In this example, the style definition will apply only to <h1> tags that appear within another element, such as a <div> tag with an ID style #sidebar.

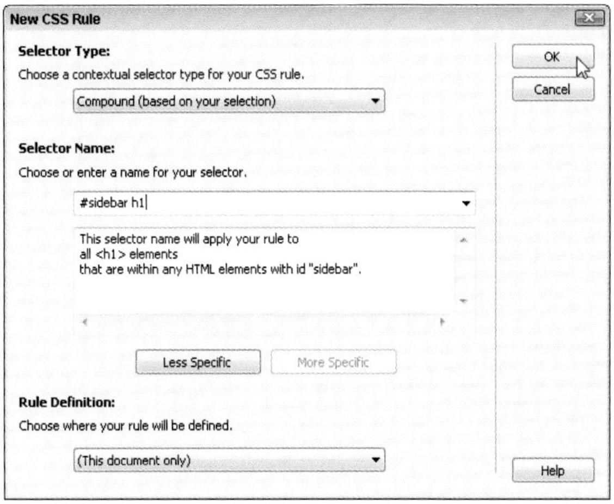

Figure 5-4: Use the compound style selector to combine styles.

If a compound style combines more than one tag, it's written like this:

```
#sidebar h1 a:link
```

Again, you must include a space between each name or tag. In this example, you see a style that defines the appearance of the active link tag only when the link is located inside an element formatted with the <h1> tag that's also inside an element formatted with the #sidebar ID. A compound style like this enables you to create links in a sidebar headline that look different than links in another part of the sidebar.

After you figure out the differences among these style selector options and when they're best used, you're well on your way to mastering the art of creating and applying styles in Dreamweaver, which is covered in Chapter 6.

Using internal versus external style sheets

In CSS, you have the option of creating internal, external, or inline styles. You can even use a combination of these options, or attach multiple external style sheets to the same web page. Here's an explanation of these options:

- ✔ **Internal styles:** If you create internal styles, the CSS code is stored in the `<head>` area at the top of the HTML page, and you can apply the styles on only that page. If you're just creating a one-page website or styles used on only one page, an internal style sheet is fine, but for most sites, external style sheets offer many advantages.

- ✔ **External styles:** If you save your styles in an external style sheet, they're stored in a separate file with a `.css` extension. You can attach external style sheets to any or all pages in a website in much the same way that you can insert the same image into multiple pages. You can also attach multiple external style sheets to the same page. For example, you can create one style sheet for styles that format text and another for layout styles. You can also create external style sheets for different purposes, such as one for print and one for screen display. For a web designer, external style sheets offer two big advantages: They enable you to create new pages faster and more easily and to update styles across many pages at once.

- ✔ **Inline styles:** Inline styles are created within a document at the place that a style is used and apply only to the element to which they're attached in the document. Inline styles are generally considered the least useful of the three style sheet options because to change the defined style you must change the code that contains the element, which means you lose the benefits of making global updates and creating clean, fast-loading code. For example, creating one style for all your headlines and saving it in an external style sheet is more efficient than applying the style formatting options to each headline separately.

At the bottom of the New CSS Rule dialog box, shown in Figure 5-5, you find a Rule Definition drop-down list. Use this list to specify where and how you want to save each new style that you define. The options are

- ✔ **This Document Only:** Create an internal style for the open document only.

- ✔ **New Style Sheet file:** Create the new style in an external style sheet and create a new external style sheet simultaneously.

✔ **An existing external style sheet:** Choose any existing external style sheet attached to the page by selecting the name of the style sheet from the Rule Definition drop-down list. In Figure 5-5, I am selecting an existing style sheet with the name `style.css`.

Rule Definition:

Choose where your rule will be defined.

```
style.css
(This document only)
(New Style Sheet File)
style.css
```

Figure 5-5: Save a new CSS rule in an internal or external style sheet.

If you're creating a style that you're likely to use on more than one page in your site, saving the style to a new or an existing external style sheet is your best choice. If you save a style in an internal style sheet and later want to add it to an external style sheet, you can move the style by clicking and dragging the style into the external style sheet list in the CSS Styles panel.

Looking at the code behind the scenes

Even if you *prefer* not to look at the code behind your web pages, it's helpful to have at least some familiarity with different kinds of tags, CSS, and other code that Dreamweaver creates for you when you design web pages. The following examples show what the CSS code in an internal or external style sheet would look like in Dreamweaver for the following styles:

✔ An ID style created with the ID selector, named `#container`, and defined as 780 pixels wide with the left and right margins set to auto (a cool trick for centering a CSS design, covered in Chapter 6).

✔ A style created with a class selector, named `.caption`, and defined as Verdana, Arial, Helvetica, sans serif, small, italic, and bold.

✔ A style created with a tag selector to redefine the HTML tag `<h1>` as follows: Arial, Helvetica, sans serif, large, and bold. (***Note:*** Because the heading tags already include bold formatting, it's not necessary to include bold in the style definition.)

```
#container {
          width: 780px;
          margin-right: auto;
          margin-left: auto;
}
.caption {
          font-family:  Verdana, Geneva, sans-serif;
          font-size: small;
          font-style: italic;
          font-weight: bold;
}
h1 {
          font-family: Arial, Helvetica, sans-serif;
          font-size: large;
}
```

Comparing CSS Rule Options

After you determine what selector type is best for your style — and decide whether you want to save it in an external or internal style — you're done with the New CSS Rule dialog box (described in the previous sections). You are ready to move on to the CSS Rule Definition dialog box and define the formatting and other options you want to include in your style. You find step-by-step instructions for creating new style rules later in this chapter. This section continues the overview to help you better understand your choices before you start creating a new style.

The CSS Rule Definition dialog box includes eight categories, each with multiple options. All these choices can seem a bit daunting at first, which is why I've included in this section a general overview of the options in each category. Again, don't feel you have to memorize all these options; you can always refer to this section when you're creating new styles.

Before you get overwhelmed by all the options, here's a tip. You don't *have* to specify any of the settings in the dialog boxes that follow when you create a new style in Dreamweaver. When you leave an option blank, you let the default browser settings (or other styles) already applied to the page take control. For example, if you don't specify a text color in a class style named .caption, the text formatted with the style remains black — the default color in most web browsers, unless another style contains formatting instructions for the color of that text. (You find instructions for changing the text color for an entire page in Chapter 6.)

In most cases, you select only a few options from one or two categories for each new style you create. I've included the full list here so you can appreciate all the options.

Not all the options in the CSS Rule Definition dialog box are supported by all the web browsers in use today, so the way styles are displayed on a web page can vary depending on the browser. Similarly, some CSS options aren't included in Dreamweaver because they're not commonly supported. The following section describes the options in each of the categories offered in the CSS Rule Definition dialog box.

The Type category

The Type category features a collection of options that control the display of (you guessed it) the text in your pages. With the Type category selected (see Figure 5-6), you have the following formatting options:

✔ **Font-Family:** Specifies a font, a font family, or a series of families. You can add fonts to the list by choosing Edit Font List in the drop-down list. (For an explanation of why Dreamweaver includes font collections — and a look at how to create new ones — see the upcoming section, "Why so many fonts?")

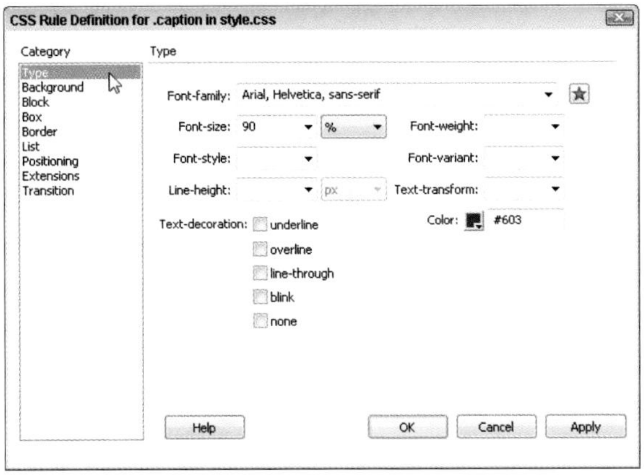

Figure 5-6: The Type category in the CSS Rule Definition dialog box.

✔ **Font-Size:** Defines the size of the text. You can choose a specific numeric size or a relative size. Use the drop-down arrow to select from a list of options that includes ems and percentages. (For more on these options, see the upcoming section, "Understanding CSS size options.")

✔ **Font-Style:** Enables you to choose whether the text appears as normal, italic, or oblique. (Italic and oblique are rarely different in a web browser, so stick with italic unless you have a specific reason not to.)

✔ **Line-Height:** Enables you to specify the height of a line on which the text is placed (graphic designers usually call this *leading*). You can specify line height in a variety of ways, including pixels, picas, and percentages. (For more on these options, see the upcoming section, "Understanding CSS size options.")

✔ **Text-Decoration:** Enables you to specify whether text is underlined, *overlined* (a line appears over the text), displayed with a strikethrough, or displayed with the *blink effect* (which makes text appear to flash on and off). You can also choose None, which removes all decorative effects.

The None option removes the underline from linked text. And please, use the other decoration options sparingly, if at all. Links are underlined automatically; if you underline text that isn't a link, you risk confusing viewers. Overlined and strikethrough text can be hard to read. Use these options only if they enhance your design. And by all means, resist the blink effect; it's distracting and can make the screen difficult to read.

- **Font-Weight:** Enables you to control how bold the text appears by using a specific or relative boldness option.

- **Font-Variant:** Enables you to select small caps. Unfortunately, this attribute isn't supported by most browsers.

- **Font-Transform:** Enables you to globally change the case of selected words, making them all uppercase, all lowercase, with initial caps, or with no capitalization.

- **Color:** Defines the color of the text. You can use the color well (the square icon) to open a web-safe color palette in which you can select predefined colors or create custom colors. You can also enter any hexadecimal code in this field; just make sure to include the pound sign (#) at the beginning. For example, you would enter #ffffff for white.

After you select the Type options for your style sheet, click Apply to apply them, and click OK to save the settings and close the CSS Rule Definition dialog box.

Why so many fonts?

You may have heard that you can now use any font you want on your web pages, thanks to CSS3. This statement is mostly true (at least for anyone using the latest web browsers) but with some limitations: You must have the legal right to publish the font, and the font must be hosted on a web server. In Chapter 7, you find detailed instructions for using the @font-face options, as well as a list of websites that make it easier to link to fonts without having to worry about copyright issues.

Whether you use the most common fonts, which are included in font collections in Dreamweaver (covered in this section) or you use a hosted font with the @font-face rule (covered in Chapter 7), you need to include the name of the font in a style using the font-family rule in your style sheet. In this section, you learn how to use the CSS Style Definition dialog box option to define a font-family rule using the font collections included in Dreamweaver.

When you use the font-family rule in a style to format text on your web pages, you don't have complete control over how that font appears on your visitor's computer. Unless you use the @font-face rule covered in Chapter 7, the browser has to be able to find the font on the hard drive of the computer that displays the web page.

To help ensure that your text appears as you intend, Dreamweaver includes collections of the most common fonts on Windows and Macintosh computers (the ones that your visitors are most likely to have), grouped together in families, such as

- Arial, Helvetica, sans serif
- Georgia, Times New Roman, Times, and serif

When you apply a collection of fonts, the browser displays the formatted text in the first font available in the list. For example, if you choose the font collection that starts with Georgia and your visitors have Georgia on their hard drives, they see your text in Georgia. If they don't have Georgia, the text is displayed in the next font on the list that your visitors do have — in this case, Times New Roman. If they don't have that font either, the text is displayed in Times. And if they don't even have Times (which would be very unusual), the browser looks for any serif font. (*Serif* describes fonts, such as Times, that have those little curly things on the edges of letters; *sans serif* means no curly things, which is what you get with a font such as Arial.)

You can create your own font collections by selecting the Edit Font List option from the bottom of the Font-Family drop-down list in the Property inspector or in the Type category of the CSS Rule Definition dialog box. In the Edit Font List dialog box, shown in Figure 5-7, you can do the following:

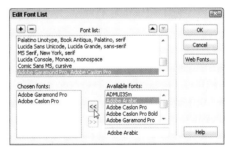

- **Add or remove a font collection** by using the plus and minus buttons at the top of the Edit Font List dialog box.

- **Add individual fonts to a collection** by selecting the font name from the bottom right of the dialog box and using the double–left arrows to add it to a font list.

Figure 5-7: The Edit Font List dialog box.

- **Remove a font from a collection** by using the double–right arrows.

The only way to ensure that text appears in the font you want is to create the text as a graphic in a program, such as Photoshop or Fireworks, and then insert the graphic with the text into your page. That's not a bad option for special text, such as banners or logos; but it's usually not a good option for all your text because graphics take longer to download than text and are harder to update later.

Understanding CSS size options

With CSS, you can specify sizes for fonts and other elements in so many ways that confusion can set in. You might have heard of point sizes and pixel sizes, but these aren't necessarily the best options when you're designing for the Internet. On the web, where display windows can vary from giant monitors to tiny cell phone screens, using relative sizes can help you create more flexible and adaptable designs, something you can't do as well with fixed pixel or point sizes. As you work in Dreamweaver to create web pages, be sure to get familiar with the following sizing options:

- **Small, medium, and large relative sizes:** Although these relative sizes were popular in the early days of the web, most web designers today prefer to use ems or percentages.

- **Percent-based relative sizes:** Use percentages to make text larger or smaller, relative to that base size. For example, you could define the text in a caption style as 90 percent and your caption text would appear at 90 percent of the size of the rest of the text on the page. You could then make headlines 150 percent (for example) and subheads 125 percent.

- **Em:** The most popular option among designers who follow standards on the web, the *em* size is based on the amount of space taken up by a capital letter *M* in the font face specified in a style. Expressing the size of your text using ems may seem complex (especially when you're new to web design), but this option is ideal on the web because the size is adjusted relative to the displayed text size. Em and ex (covered in the next bullet) work much like percentages but they adapt even better to different user settings and monitor sizes.

- **Ex:** Similar to em, the *ex* option is based on the size of a lowercase *x* in the specified font face. The *em* size is generally preferred.

The Background category

Using the Background category in the CSS Rule Definition dialog box (see Figure 5-8), you can specify a background color or image for a style — and control how the background is displayed on the page. You can use background style settings for any element of your web page that can display a background — including `<div>` tags and heading tags. For example, you could alter the `<body>` tag to include background settings that apply to the entire page, or you could create an ID style with a background setting that would add a background color only to an individual `<div>` tag. By including the background in the ID style of a `<div>` tag, you can limit the background to appear on-screen only where the `<div>` tag is used.

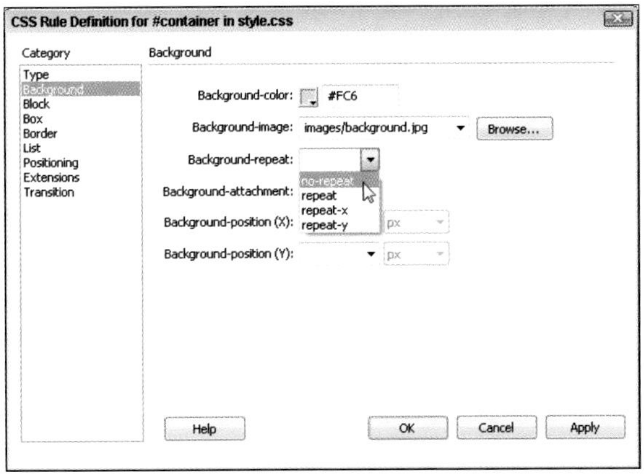

Figure 5-8: The Background category in the CSS Rule Definition dialog box.

In the example shown in Figure 5-8, I've defined the rule for an ID style named `#container` to include a background image, which I'm further defining with the No-Repeat option. Another advantage of CSS is that it includes more precise control of background images than is possible with HTML — which, by default, repeats a background image across and down a page.

You can choose from these Background options:

✓ **Background-Color:** Specifies the background color of a defined style. You can use the color well to open a web-safe color palette in which you can select predefined colors or create custom colors. You can also enter a hexadecimal color code; just make sure to include the #, as in #000000 for the color black.

✓ **Background-Image:** Enables you to select a background image as part of the style definition. Click the Browse button to select the image.

✓ **Background-Repeat:** Determines how and whether the background image tiles across and down the page. In all cases, the image is cropped if it doesn't fit behind the element to which the style is applied. The Repeat options are

  • **No-Repeat:** The background is displayed once at the top left of the element.

  • **Repeat:** The background image repeats vertically and horizontally in the background of the element.

  • **Repeat-X:** The background repeats horizontally, but not vertically, in the background of the element.

  • **Repeat-Y:** The background repeats vertically, but not horizontally, in the background of the element.

✔ **Background-Attachment:** This property determines how the background behaves when the page is scrolled. The options are

• **Fixed:** The background remains glued to one place in the viewing area and doesn't scroll out of sight, even when the web page is scrolled.

• **Scroll:** The background scrolls along with the web page.

✔ **Background-Position (X):** Enables you to align the image left, center, or right, or to set a numeric value to determine the precise horizontal placement of the background. You can use horizontal positioning with only No-Repeat or Repeat-Y.

✔ **Background-Position (Y):** Enables you to align the image top, center, or bottom, or to set a numeric value to determine the precise vertical placement of the background. You can use vertical positioning with only No-Repeat or Repeat-X.

The Block category

The Block category (see Figure 5-9) defines the spacing and alignment settings and is commonly used for styles that will define the display of text on a web page.

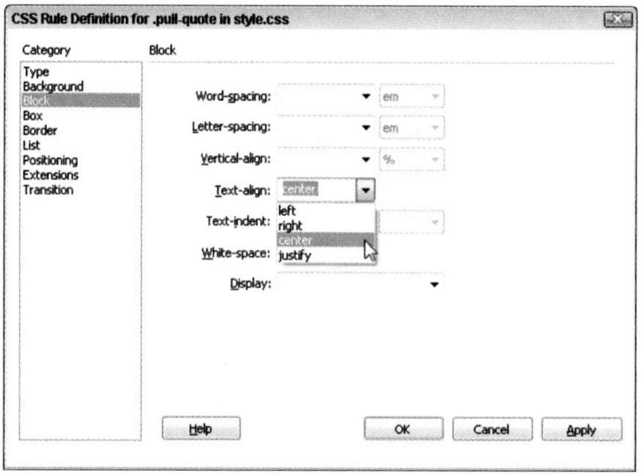

Figure 5-9: The Block category in the CSS Rule Definition dialog box.

You can choose from these Block category options:

✔ **Word-Spacing:** Defines the amount of white space inserted between words in points, millimeters (mm), centimeters (cm), picas, inches, pixels, ems, and exs. (See the previous section "Understanding CSS size options.")

✐ **Letter-Spacing:** Defines the amount of white space inserted between letters in points, millimeters (mm), centimeters (cm), picas, inches, pixels, ems, and exs.

✐ **Vertical-Align:** Aligns inline elements, such as text and images, in relation to the elements that surround them. Your options are Baseline, Sub, Super, Top, Text-Top, Middle, Bottom, and Text-Bottom, or you can set a numeric value.

✐ **Text-Align:** Enables you to left, right, center, or justify your text. You can use this setting, for example, as part of the definition of an ID style when you want to align the contents of a <div> tag, as when you center the text in a footer. (You can find details about styling <div> tags in Chapter 6.)

✐ **Text-Indent:** Specifies how far the first line of text is indented. Negative numbers are allowed if you want the first line to begin outdented. However, be careful that your text doesn't end up so far outdented that it's off the page.

✐ **White-Space:** Tells the browser how to handle line breaks and spaces within a block of text. Your options are Normal, Pre (for preformatted), and Nowrap, which prevents elements from being separated if they must wrap to fit within a browser window or other container.

✐ **Display:** Indicates how to render an element in the browser. For example, you can hide an element by choosing None and change the positioning of an unordered list from horizontal to vertical by choosing Inline.

The Box category

The Box category (see Figure 5-10) defines settings for positioning and spacing. As you can read in Chapter 6, these settings are ideal for creating page layouts with ID styles to position <div> tags.

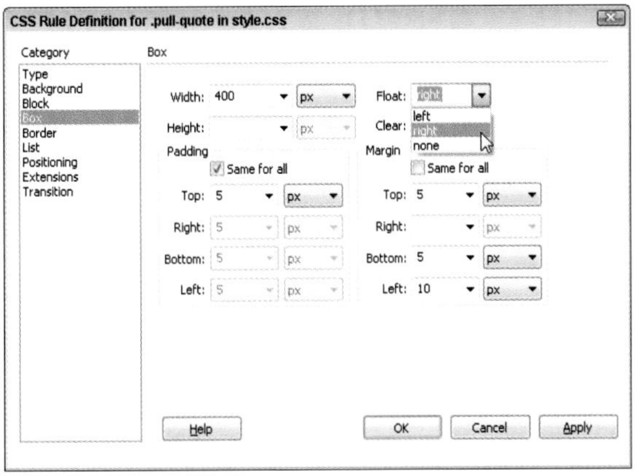

Figure 5-10: The Box category in the CSS Rule Definition dialog box.

You can use the Box category properties to set these values:

- **Width:** Enables you to specify a width for any element that can have its dimensions specified, such as a `<div>` tag. You can use pixels, points, inches, centimeters, millimeters, picas, ems, exs, or percentages for your measurements. (See "Understanding CSS size options" earlier in this chapter for the basics of sizing with ems, exs, and percentages on the web.)

- **Height:** Enables you to specify a height for any element that can have its dimensions specified.

  The Height field is often left empty to enable elements (such as `<div>` tags) to expand to fit their contents.

- **Padding:** Sets the amount of space within the borders of an element. For example, you can use padding to create space between the borders of a `<div>` tag and its contents. You can set padding separately for the top, right, bottom, and left. Padding is measured in pixels, points, inches, centimeters, millimeters, picas, ems, exs, and percentages.

- **Float:** Enables you to align elements, such as images and `<div>` tags, to the left or right of a page or other container causing text or other elements wrap around it.

- **Clear:** Prevents floating content from overlapping an area to the left or right, or to both sides of an element. This option is useful for preventing overlapping of elements, especially when the Float option is used.

- **Margin:** Sets the amount of space around an element. Margins can be used to create space between the edge of an element and other elements on the page, such as between an image and text or between two `<div>` tags. You can set the margin separately for the top, right, bottom, and left. Padding is measured in pixels, points, inches, centimeters, millimeters, picas, ems, exs, and percentages.

Setting padding and margin spacing can be tricky because they add to the overall size of your image, `<div>` tag, or other element. For help on setting these options to best fit your design, see Chapter 6.

The Border category

The Border category defines settings such as Width, Color, and Style and is commonly used to define borders around images, tables, and `<div>` tags. As shown in Figure 5-11, you can specify border settings on all four sides of an element or create borders on only one, two, or three sides of an element. With this technique, you can use the border settings to create dividing lines between `<div>` tags that create columns or add separating lines above or below elements.

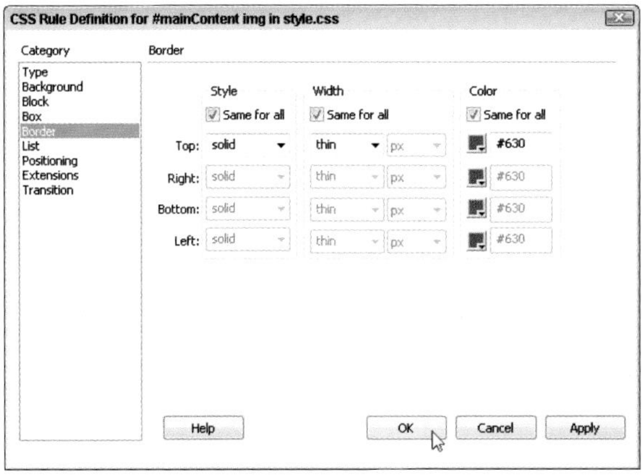

Figure 5-11: The Border category in the CSS Rule Definition dialog box.

The List category

The List category defines settings such as the size and type of bullets for list tags. You can specify whether bullets are Disc, Circle, Square, Decimal, Lower-Roman, Upper-Roman, Lower-Alpha, Upper-Alpha, or None (see Figure 5-12). Choose None if you want to use the list tag with no bullet. If you want to use a custom bullet, you can use the Browse button to insert an image to be used as the bullet. You can also control the location of the list bullet in relation to the list item. In Chapter 6, you find instructions for redefining the unordered list tag to create rollover effects for links, a popular option for creating navigation rows and other collections, or lists, of links.

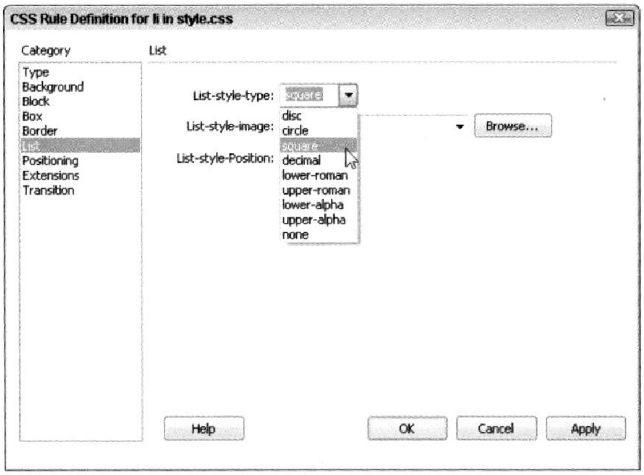

Figure 5-12: The List category in the CSS Rule Definition dialog box.

The Positioning category

The Positioning category (see Figure 5-13) enables you to alter the way elements are positioned on a page. As you can read in Chapter 6, positioning can dramatically change the way block-level elements appear in a browser. *Block-level elements* include table, list, header, paragraph, and `<div>` tags. For example, AP Divs in Dreamweaver are simply `<div>` tags that use absolute positioning to place elements in a specific part of a page.

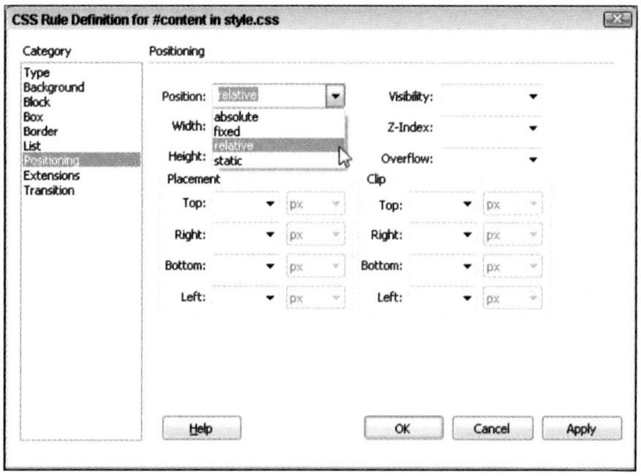

Figure 5-13: The Positioning category in the CSS Rule Definition dialog box.

Positioning is always determined relative to something else, such as another element on the page or the browser window. How you set up positioning depends on where your element is on the page — and on whether the element is inside another element (such as a `<div>` tag). Here are the Positioning options:

- **Position:** Enables you to specify the position of an element, such as a `<div>` tag. Options include

    - **Absolute:** Uses the top and left coordinates to control the position of an element relative to the upper-left corner of the browser window or the upper-left corner of an element that contains the element. (For example, the positioning of an AP Div contained within another AP Div is based on the position of the first AP Div.)

    - **Fixed:** Positions an element relative to the top-left corner of the browser. The content of an element using fixed positioning remains constant even if the user scrolls down or across the page.

- **Relative:** Uses a position relative to the point where you insert the element into the page or relative to its container.

- **Static:** Places the content at its location within the flow of the document. By default, all HTML elements that *can* be positioned are static.

✔ **Width** and **Height:** Enables you to specify a width and height that you can use in styles you apply to images, `<div>` tags, or any other element that can have its dimensions specified. These settings serve the same function as the Width and Height in the Box category. Entering a value in either category causes the same value to appear in the other.

✔ **Placement:** Defines the size and location of an element within its containing element. For example, you can set the right edge of the element to line up with the right edge of the element that contains it. You can specify the Top, Right, Bottom, and Left options separately and you can use pixels, points, inches, centimeters, millimeters, picas, ems, exs, or percentages for your measurements. (See "Understanding CSS size options," earlier in this chapter, for basics about ems, exs, and percentages.)

✔ **Visibility:** Enables you to control whether the browser displays the element. You can use this feature with a scripting language (such as JavaScript) to change the display of elements dynamically. For example, you can cause an element to appear on a page only when a user clicks a button — and then make the element disappear when the button is clicked again. The Visibility options are

  - **Inherit:** The element has the visibility of the element in which it's contained. This is the default.

  - **Visible:** The element is displayed.

  - **Hidden:** The element isn't displayed.

✔ **Z-Index:** Controls the position of an element, such as an AP Div, on the Z-coordinate, which controls the stacking order in relation to other elements on the page. Higher-numbered elements overlap lower-numbered elements. (Note: This setting only works on elements that use absolute or relative positioning settings.)

✔ **Overflow:** Tells the browser how to display the contents of an element if the container, such as a `<div>` tag, can't fit the element's entire size.

  - **Visible:** Keeps content, such as an image or text, visible, even if it expands beyond the defined height or width of a container.

  - **Hidden:** Cuts off the contents if they exceed the size of the container. This option doesn't provide scroll bars.

- **Scroll:** Adds scroll bars to the container regardless of whether the contents exceed the element's size.

- **Auto:** Makes scroll bars appear only when a container's contents exceed its boundaries.

✔ **Clip:** Specifies which part of an element is visible (by controlling which part of the element is cropped) if the content of an element overflows the space allotted and you set the Overflow property to Scroll or Auto.

The Extensions category

Extensions (see Figure 5-14) include filters and cursor options:

✔ **Page-Break:** Inserts a point in a page — either before or after an element — where a printer sees a page break. This option enables you to better control the way a page is printed.

✔ **Cursor:** Defines the type of cursor that appears when a user moves the cursor over an element.

✔ **Filter:** Enables you to apply special effects, such as drop shadows and motion blurs.

Filters are visible only in Microsoft Internet Explorer, which is now used by a minority of the web audience, so most web designers avoid these options.

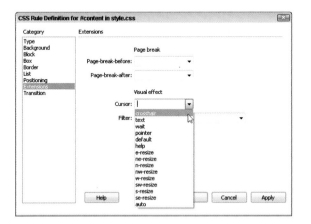

Figure 5-14: The Extensions category in the CSS Rule Definition dialog box.

The Transition category

The Transition category, shown in Figure 5-15, provides a new set of options added in version CS6. The Transition category is designed to help you create and manage CSS3 *transitions*, which can be used to create interactive effects by gradually changing the style of an element from one property to another. CSS3 transitions are covered in Chapter 7.

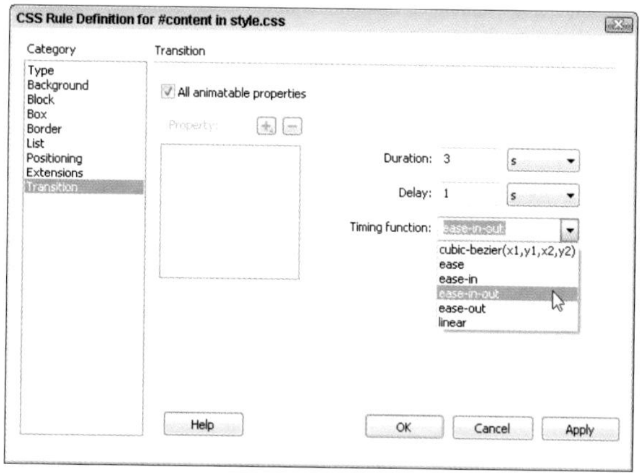

Figure 5-15: The Transition category in the CSS Rule Definition dialog box.

The Transition category has the following options:

- **All Animatable Properties:** Select this box if you want the transition rule to apply to all the elements on the page that can be animated.

- **Property:** Enables you to specify which CSS property you are targeting with the effect. Click the plus sign (+) to add a property or the minus sign (–) to remove one.

- **Duration:** Defines the length of time the transition will take to complete.

- **Delay:** Specifies a time delay between when a page loads and when the transition begins.

- **Timing Function:** Enables you to choose the type of transition you want from the drop-down list (as shown in Figure 5-15).

Switching between CSS and HTML Mode in the Property Inspector

The Property inspector is split into two sections: HTML and CSS. In Figure 5-18, you see the HTML mode of the Property inspector; Figure 5-19 shows the CSS mode. Note that buttons on the left side of the Property inspector make switching between these two modes easy.

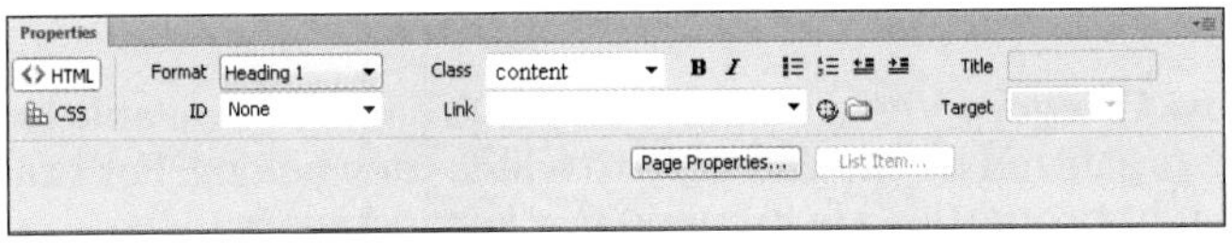

Figure 5-18: The HTML mode of the Property inspector.

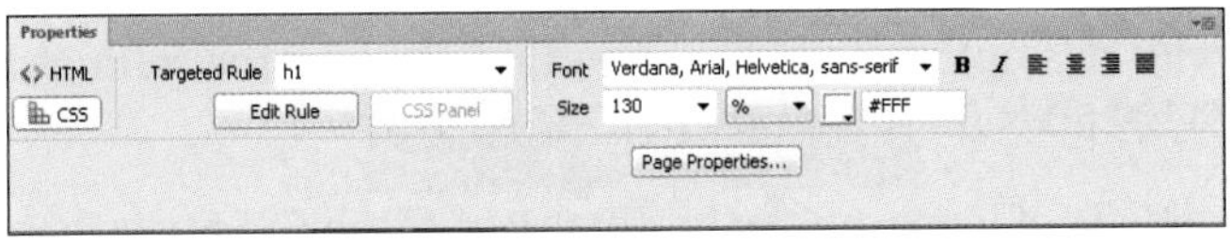

Figure 5-19: The CSS mode of the Property inspector.

If you're new to CSS and HTML, understanding the differences between these two modes can be a little confusing. Essentially, if you use the formatting icons, such as bold and italic, in HTML mode, Dreamweaver adds HTML tags and attributes. If you use these same icons in CSS mode, Dreamweaver launches the New CSS Rule dialog box so you can create a style that includes these formatting options.

In CSS mode, you can also choose to edit existing styles to add new formatting options to styles that are already applied to text, images, or other elements on a page. Thus, you can edit existing styles by simply selecting the style in the Targeted Rule drop-down list and then using the Font, Size, and other fields in the Property inspector to make changes or additions.

Whenever you edit an existing style that has already been applied to elements on a page, the changes you make to the style are applied automatically anywhere the style is used. This feature is wonderful when you want to change several things at once but can be problematic if you want to make a heading appear one way on one page and another way somewhere else.

Anytime you want to create or edit a style, use the Property inspector in CSS mode. On the other hand, if you want to apply an existing style to an element on the page, make sure you're in HTML mode. For example, if you want to align an image with a class style or apply an ID style to a <div> tag, you need to be in HTML mode. To apply a style in HTML mode, select the image, text, or other element in the page where you want to apply the style and then use the Class or ID drop-down lists to select the style; Dreamweaver automatically applies it.

Similarly, if you want to apply an HTML tag, such as the <h1> tag, you want to be in HTML mode, but if you want to create or edit a CSS rule for the <h1> tag, you want to do that from the CSS mode. Of course, you don't have to create or edit styles with the Property inspector. Consider this a shortcut method; you may still prefer to use the CSS Rule Definition dialog box (covered in the previous section) to make significant changes to a style.

Organizing Style Sheets

External style sheets (or *linked style sheets*) offer the greatest advantages with CSS, but you also need to manage these style sheets separately from your HTML web page. The following sections introduce you to the external style sheets that come with Dreamweaver, as well as tips for attaching, moving, copying, and editing styles in external style sheets.

Attaching an external style sheet to a page

After you've created an external style sheet, you can attach it to any web page. In the step-by-step instructions that follow, you can use any of the style sheets included in Dreamweaver (covered in the previous section), or you can use these instructions to attach any style sheet you create. (You find detailed instructions for creating your own style sheets in Chapter 6.) Begin by opening the page to which you want to attach the style sheet and then follow these steps:

1. **Choose Window⇨CSS Styles.**

   The CSS Styles panel appears.

2. **Click the Attach Style Sheet icon in the CSS Styles panel (the first button in the lower-right area).**

   The Attach External Style Sheet dialog box appears, as shown in Figure 5-20.

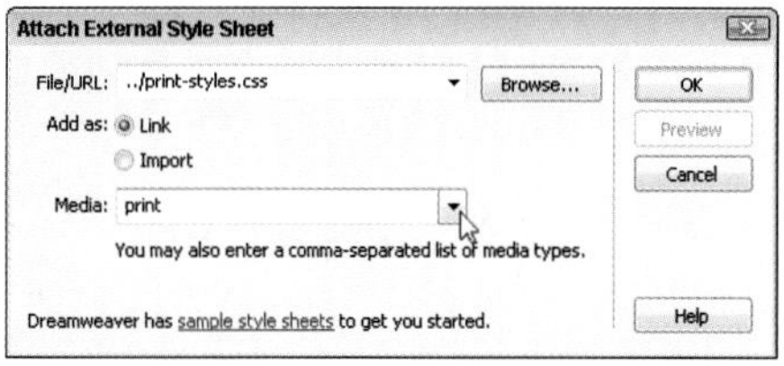

Figure 5-20: The Attach External Style Sheet dialog box.

3. **Click the Browse button and locate the CSS file in your local site folder.**

You can also enter a URL if you want to use a remote CSS file located on another website, but it's most common to use a style sheet contained in the website you're working on. Either way, Dreamweaver sets the link to the style sheet automatically, includes the code for the style sheet's link at the top of the HTML file, and lists all the styles in the external style sheet in the CSS Styles panel.

4. **Select the Link or Import option.**

If you're attaching a style sheet to an HTML file, your best choice is almost always to choose Link, which is the default option. Choose Import if you want to create one master external style sheet that contains references to other style sheets, an advanced option that enables one style sheet to refer to another.

5. **In the Media drop-down list, choose an option.**

With the Media drop-down list, you can specify the intended use for the style sheet. For example, if you've created a style sheet that formats your page for printing, choose the Print option. You can leave this option blank if you're attaching a style sheet to control the way the page appears in a browser.

6. **Click OK.**

The dialog box closes, and the external CSS file is automatically linked to the page. Any styles you've defined in the external style sheet appear in the CSS Styles panel, listed under the name of the style sheet, and all the styles automatically become available for use on the page.

You can attach multiple style sheets to the same HTML page. For example, you can save all your text styles in one style sheet, save all your layout styles in another, and then attach both to the same document — which makes all the defined styles available to the page. Similarly, you create different style sheets for different purposes, such as one for printing the file and another for browser display.

Moving, copying, and editing styles

After you attach an external style sheet to a document, you can move, copy, and edit styles as follows:

- **Moving styles:** Move any internal styles into the external style sheet by simply clicking the name of a style in an internal style sheet in the CSS Styles panel and dragging it onto the name of an external style sheet. In Figure 5-21, you can see that I'm moving a body style from the internal style sheet, which by default is `<style>`, into the external style sheet `text-styles.css`. If you have attached more than one external style sheet to a document, you can also move styles from one external style sheet to another using click and drag.

✏ **Copying styles:** You can copy styles from one document to another by right-clicking (Control-clicking on a Mac) a style name in the CSS Styles panel and choosing Copy. Then open the document where you want to add the style, right-click (Control-click on a Mac) the name of an internal or external style sheet in the CSS Styles panel, and choose Paste.

Figure 5-21: Drag styles from an internal to an external style sheet.

✏ **Editing styles:** You edit styles in an external style sheet the same way you edit styles in an internal style sheet — by clicking or double-clicking the style name in the CSS Styles panel. (For more detailed instructions, see the sections in Chapter 6 about editing class styles and editing styles in Dreamweaver's CSS layouts.) Any changes you make to a style in an external style sheet are applied automatically to all the files to which the external style sheet is attached. (Remember that you must upload the style sheet to your web server for the changes to take effect on the published version of the site.)

If you want to edit a remote CSS file, download the file to your hard drive before you open it in Dreamweaver. In Dreamweaver, you open .css files by double-clicking them or choosing File➪Open, both of which open the style sheet in Code view. Code view is the only view available for CSS files because they're text files and have no layout components. When you view an external style sheet this way, you can still use the CSS Styles panel to edit any defined styles — even if the style sheet isn't linked to an HTML page. Be sure to save the CSS file when you finish editing it!

If you prefer, you can also edit the code by hand directly in Code view. Figure 5-22 shows an example of a style sheet opened directly in Dreamweaver. Note that the CSS Styles panel displays all relevant style information and gives you access to the CSS editing tools.

When you edit an external style sheet, you must upload it to your server before the style changes will be applied to your page on your live website.

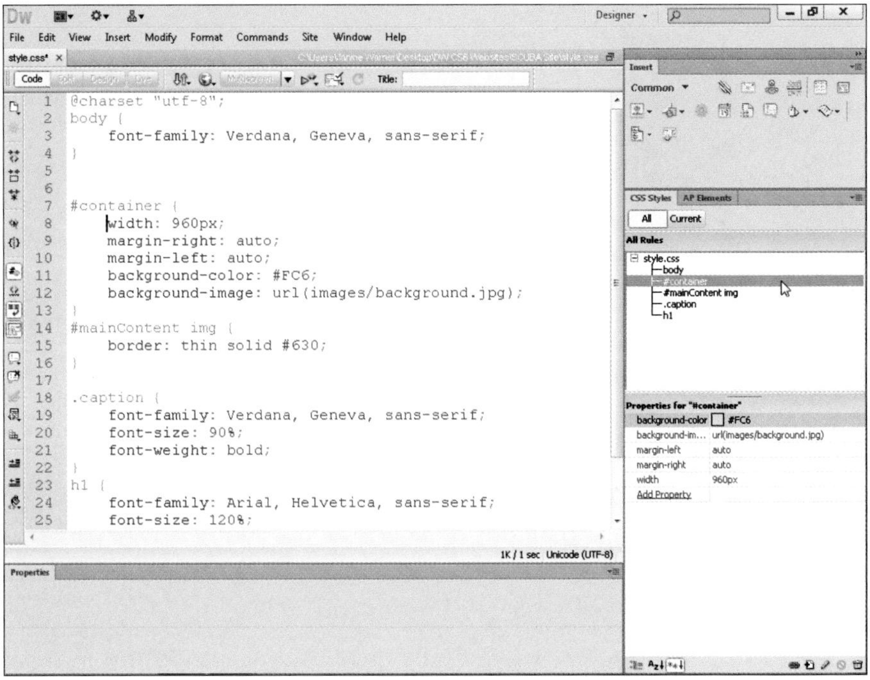

Figure 5-22: You can edit external style sheets (files with a .css extension) by opening them as you would any other document.

6

Creating and Editing CSS Styles

*W*hether you're new to CSS or you've been struggling (I mean *designing*) with styles for years, Dreamweaver's many CSS features offer welcome assistance. This chapter walks you through the process of creating and applying styles using the class, tag, and ID selectors. You also find instructions for customizing the CSS layouts included with Dreamweaver. And you discover not only how to create styles for text, but also how to position and align images, text, and other elements on a web page (even how to center text and other elements, which is not as easy as you might imagine with CSS). Finally, you discover how Dreamweaver makes it easy to edit, rename, and even remove styles.

If you're new to CSS or Dreamweaver, I recommend that before you start this chapter you at least skim through Chapter 5, where you find an introduction to CSS and a review of the many panels, dialog boxes, and inspectors you can use to create, apply, and edit styles in Dreamweaver.

Brace yourself: You're getting into some of the most complex web design features that Dreamweaver offers, but I think you'll find the power and precision of these options well worth the effort. If you want to design web pages that can be edited and maintained efficiently, look good in a variety of screen sizes, and meet the latest web standards, CSS is clearly your best option.

Creating Styles with Class and Tag Selectors

Get ready to create your first styles. I start out with the class and tag selectors because they are among the easiest to understand.

As you go through the steps to create a new style in Dreamweaver, you may be surprised by the number of options in the many panels and dialog boxes available for creating CSS. However, you use only a few of the available options to create most styles.

You can always refer to Chapter 5 for more detailed descriptions of the different selector types as well as the many options in the New CSS Rule and CSS Rule Definition dialog boxes, which you can use when you create or edit styles.

Creating styles with the class selector

The class selector can be used to create styles that you can apply to any element on a page and as many times as you like on the same page. Thus, class styles are ideal for defining the formatting of elements such as photo captions, which may appear in many places in a website.

Using styles created with the class selector is a relatively straightforward process. First, you create a new style using the class selector and give it a name; then you apply the style to an element on the page by selecting that style name from the Class drop-down list in the Property inspector.

In this section, you find step-by-step instructions for creating a style with the class selector. In the next section, you see how to format text by applying a style created with the class selector. These same instructions can be used to create and apply any class style in Dreamweaver.

To define a new class style, create a new document or open an existing file, and then follow these steps:

1. **Choose Format⇨CSS Styles⇨New.**

   Alternatively, you can click the New CSS Rule icon at the bottom of the CSS Styles panel.

The New CSS Rule dialog box appears, as shown in Figure 6-1.

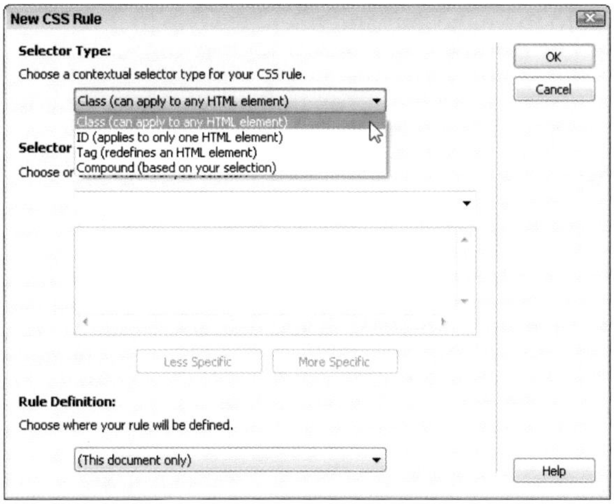

Figure 6-1: The New CSS Rule dialog box.

2. **Choose a selector type.**

   To create a class style, choose (you guessed it) Class from the Selector Type drop-down list.

3. **In the Selector Name field, type a new name for the style beginning with a dot (.).**

   For this example, I type *.caption*.

   You can name a class style anything you like, as long as you don't use spaces or punctuation and you begin the class style names with a dot (.). If you choose the Class option and neglect to enter a dot at the beginning of the name, Dreamweaver adds one for you when you click OK.

4. **From the Rule Definition drop-down list, choose where you want to create the selector.**

   Choose This Document Only (which is what I choose in this example) to create the new style in an internal style sheet. An internal style sheet applies only to the current page, which means the style can be used to format elements only in the document you have open in Dreamweaver. When you select this option, the style is created and added to the top of the open HTML page in the <head> section.

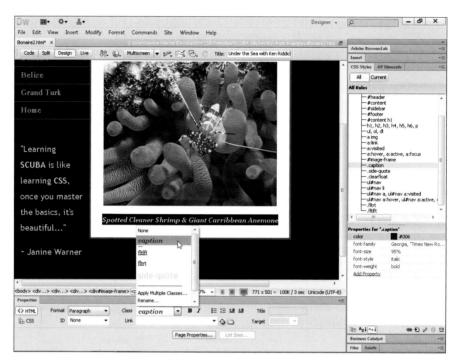

Figure 6-3: To apply a class style, select an element in the main workspace, and then choose the style from the Class list.

Creating styles with the CSS tag selector

In addition to creating new class styles, you can create styles that add or alter the rules of existing HTML tags. These styles are created using the *tag selector,* which is also known as the *element selector.* When you create a style in the New CSS Rule dialog box using the tag selector option, you can alter the appearance, position, and other features of an existing HTML tag.

Many HTML tags already include formatting options. For example, the heading tags include formatting to style text in large and bold. So, when you create a style with a tag selector, you have to consider the formatting options already associated with that tag. Any options you specify in the CSS Rule Definition dialog box will be added to the existing formatting or will override the formatting. For example, in the steps that follow, I create a CSS rule for the <h1> tag by changing the font to Georgia, which will take the place of the default font Times — but I don't need to include bold in the style definition to make the text bold because bold is in the default style of the <h1> HTML tag.

When you create a style for an existing HTML tag, you don't need to apply the style for the formatting to change the way you do with class styles. Wherever you've used the HTML tag, the style definition settings are applied automatically. Thus, when you create a style and define the font for the <h1> tag as Georgia, any text formatted with the <h1> tag will change to Georgia.

You may ask, "Why would I redefine the <h1> tag instead of just creating a new headline style as a class style?" Although you can define a new class style instead of redefining an HTML tag, sometimes using an existing HTML tag is better. Heading styles are especially important on the web because text formatted in an <h1> tag is well recognized as the most important text on a page. Among other things, text formatted in an <h1> tag may get special consideration from search engines.

To redefine an HTML tag (such as the <h1> tag) with the tag selector, create a new file or open an existing one and then follow these steps:

1. **Choose Format⇨CSS Styles⇨New.**

   Alternatively, you can right-click (Control-click on a Mac) anywhere in the CSS Styles panel and choose New, or you can click the New CSS Rule icon at the bottom right of the CSS Styles panel. The icon looks like a small plus sign (+).

   The New CSS Rule dialog box opens.

2. **Choose Tag from the Selector Type drop-down list.**

3. **Choose the HTML tag you want to redefine from the Selector Name drop-down list.**

   You can also type to enter the name of a tag into the Selector Name field. In this example, shown in Figure 6-4, I typed *h1* to redefine the <h1> heading tag.

4. **From the Rule Definition drop-down list, choose to add the style to an internal or external style sheet.**

   In this example, I choose to add the new style to an external style sheet named `styles.css` that I've already attached to this page, so it's easy to add the new style. You can choose the New Style Sheet File option to create a new external style sheet as you create the style, or you can select This Document Only to add the new style to an internal style sheet.

   You can attach an external style sheet to any or all pages in a website. When you choose an external style sheet, the new style is added to a separate CSS file as it's created. When you create or edit a style in an external style sheet, any changes you make are applied to all pages to which that style sheet is attached.

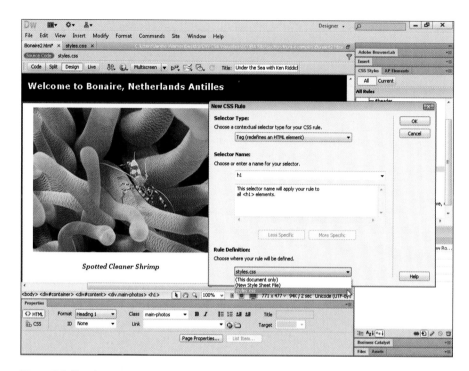

Figure 6-4: Use the tag selector to redefine an existing HTML tag and to save the new style to an external style sheet.

5. Click OK.

The CSS Rule Definition dialog box opens.

6. Choose a category and specify the options you want to use to redefine the new tag style.

For this example, I redefined the `<h1>` tag to use the Georgia font instead of the default browser font, changed the size to extra large, and changed the text color to dark green.

7. Click OK.

Any text or other element you've formatted with the HTML tag immediately changes to reflect the formatting in the new definition of the tag's style.

If you want the ability to use the same HTML tag with different formatting in different parts of the same page, you can create compound styles, as described in Chapter 5. This works well, for example, if you want text formatted with the `<h2>` tag to look different in the main part of your page than it does in a sidebar.

Resetting HTML elements with CSS

Because not all browsers interpret HTML and CSS in the same way, many web designers begin designing pages by creating styles that remove any border, padding, or margins included in an HTML tag by defining a style that sets those values to 0 (as you see in the following example).

Resetting common HTML tags to remove any padding or margins means that all your tags start with the same blank slate. In this way, you help ensure that any styles you create will be displayed more consistently across different web browsers.

In the CSS layouts included in Dreamweaver, you find styles that reset common tags, including the heading and list tags. In this example, I've set the border, padding, and margins to 0 to ensure a more consistent display across different web browsers:

```
h1, h2, h3, h4, h5, h6, p, ul, ol, li, {
border:0; margin:0; padding:0;
```

Creating Layouts with CSS and Div Tags

The key to understanding how CSS works in a page layout is to think in terms of designing with a series of infinitely adjustable containers, or *boxes*. Indeed, this approach to web design is commonly called the *box model*.

Think of the box model this way: First you use HTML tags, such as the <div> (*div*ision) tag or <p> (*paragraph*) tag, to create boxes around each section of your content. Then you use CSS to style each box, using CSS rules to control the position and alignment of each box by specifying such settings as Margin, Padding, Float, and Border. The combined effect is one beautiful page, created by combining CSS styles with HTML tags.

Although you can use any HTML tag as part of your page layout, the <div> tag is used most often to create the boxes for main sections of a page, such as the banner area, commonly used at the top of a page, the main content area, sidebars, and footer. Think of <div> tags as generic containers designed to contain text, images, or other content. Essentially, <div> tags create divisions on the page, separating one section of content from another. Unlike other HTML tags, <div> has no inherent formatting features. Unless CSS is applied to a <div> tag, it's invisible on a page when viewed in most web browsers; yet the tag has a powerful purpose because you can easily format with CSS any content surrounded by opening and closing <div> tags.

Splitting the view

If you're creating a series of `<div>` tags to position content on a web page, you may find it easier to keep track of the `<div>` tags if you use Dreamweaver's Split view, as shown in the figure. Split view enables you to see Code view and Design view simultaneously. To split the workspace area, choose View⇨Code and Design or click the Split View button, located just under the Insert panel at the top of the workspace.

If you select an image, text, or another element on a page in Design view, it's highlighted automatically in Code view — a great feature that makes it easier to find your place in the code when you're trying to troubleshoot what's happening behind the scenes. I like to use Split view to keep an eye on the code as I create page designs — especially when I'm inserting `<div>` tags. When you're using only Design view, keeping track of how `<div>` tags are arranged and nested can be hard.

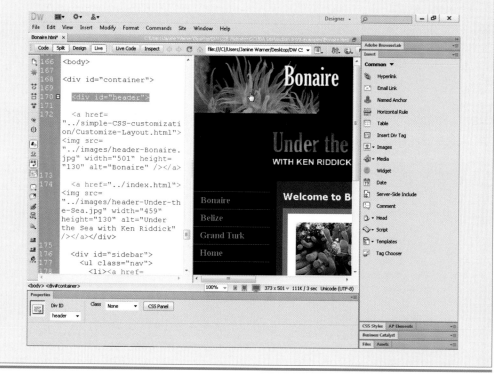

Adobe uses the box model to create all the CSS layouts included in Dreamweaver. In these layouts, each `<div>` tag in the page has a corresponding style. As a result, to change the size or positioning of the header, footer, or any of the other main areas of the page separated by `<div>` tags, you need to edit the corresponding style. You find detailed instructions for how to identify and edit these styles in the sections that follow.

Using Dreamweaver's CSS Layouts

Dreamweaver includes a collection of CSS layouts you can customize to create a seemingly infinite variety of page designs. These layouts give you a head start when you create a new page; they're designed to work well in a variety of web browsers, so they can help you avoid common problems caused by the different ways web browsers display CSS. For all these reasons, I almost always recommend starting your design work in Dreamweaver with a CSS layout chosen in the New Document window.

One of the challenges with CSS is that it's still a relatively new addition to the world of web design, and it continues to change. Unfortunately, browser support — which can make the difference between a beautiful web page and a jumbled, unreadable design — hasn't always kept up, and the companies that make browsers haven't always agreed on how to display CSS. (You find more about browser differences and testing in Chapter 4.)

To help you get around the problems caused by browser differences, Adobe dedicated the equivalent of decades of time (at least in Internet years) to designing a collection of CSS layouts designed to display well in many different web browsers. Whether you're creating a simple XHTML page, using Dreamweaver's templates, or designing advanced database-driven sites with PHP, you're sure to appreciate the benefits of starting your page designs with one of Dreamweaver's prestyled layouts.

Before you rush off to check out all the cool CSS layouts included in Dreamweaver, let me warn you: They're not much to look at when you first open them. They're intentionally designed with the most basic of formatting options and a dull color scheme — but fortunately color styles are some of the easiest styles to alter in CSS.

No matter what your experience level, the following sections are designed to help you appreciate how Dreamweaver's CSS layouts work and to help you create your own page designs by customizing the layouts step by step. You find out how to change the width of columns, the formatting styles for text, and the alignment of any element on the page in one of Dreamweaver's layouts. If you're new to CSS, altering one of these layouts may seem confusing at first; trust me, altering an existing layout is much easier than creating a design from scratch. (If you haven't read Chapter 5 yet, you can skim that chapter to get a handle on the basics before you begin working with Dreamweaver's CSS layouts.)

Comparing CSS layout options

Dreamweaver includes a variety of CSS layouts, designed with two distinct approaches to CSS. When you create a new page with one of these layouts, the first thing you must do is decide which type of layout you want to use. Essentially, you have two options:

- **Liquid layouts** are designed to expand and contract depending on the size of the browser window.

- **Fixed layouts** are centered within the browser and set to a width of 960 pixels. (As you discover in the next section, you can change the width by editing the corresponding style.) In the upcoming examples, I selected a design that creates a two-column, fixed layout, with a left sidebar, header, and footer.

In general, fixed layouts give you greater control over your design and are an easier option to start with because the positioning of elements on a page is more predictable. Liquid layouts are designed to be flexible, so they adapt to fit many screen sizes. However, the elements in the design can move around and the design can change considerably from a small screen to a large one.

Creating a new page with a CSS layout

To create a new page using one of Dreamweaver's CSS layouts, follow these instructions:

1. **Choose File➪New.**

   The New Document dialog box appears.

2. **Choose Blank Page from the left column and HTML from the Page Type column in the middle.**

   Alternatively, you can choose an option in the bottom part of the Page Type section that corresponds to the programming language used on your site, such as ASP.NET, PHP, or ColdFusion, and then progress to Step 3. (If you're not familiar with these programming options, stick with HTML.)

3. **Select any of the CSS layouts listed in the Layout section.**

   For this example, I chose 2 Column Fixed, Left Sidebar, Header and Footer. In Figure 6-5, note that when you select a CSS layout, a preview of the layout is displayed at the top right of the dialog box.

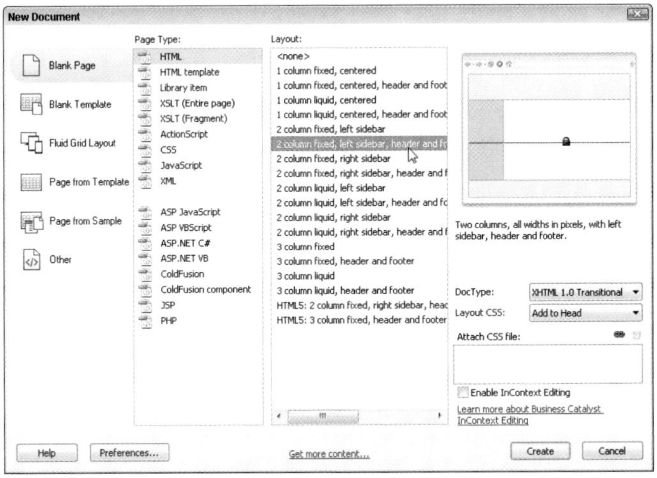

Photo by Ken Riddick

Figure 6-5: When you select the name of a CSS layout, a preview appears in the top-right corner.

4. **From the Layout CSS drop-down list, choose the type of style sheet you want to create as you design the page:**

   - **Add to Head** creates an internal style sheet and includes all the styles for the layout in the Head area of the new document.

   - **Create New File** creates a new external style sheet with all the page styles as you create the new document with the design.

   - **Link to Existing File** adds the style sheet information for the new document to an existing external style sheet.

   Note: You can always change how the style sheet is set up later by moving styles from an internal style sheet to an external one or from one external style sheet to another. (You can find instructions for creating external style sheets and moving styles at the end of Chapter 5.)

5. **Click Create.**

   The new page is created and opened in the main workspace.

6. **Choose File➪Save to save the page and styles.**

   If you saved the styles in an external style sheet, a second box prompts you to save the style sheet separately. If the styles are contained in an internal style sheet, they're saved automatically when you save the page.

   Save all the pages of a website, including external styles sheets, in your local site folder. (For more about defining a website and specifying a local site folder in Dreamweaver, see Chapter 2.)

Why Dreamweaver's CSS layouts use class styles instead of ID styles with <div> tags

Although there's no hard and fast rule, the common practice is to combine ID styles with <div> tags to create the main sections of a page when you create a layout using CSS. The differences among style selectors are covered in more detail in Chapter 5, but essentially, ID styles are best used for elements that will appear only once per page, such as the main sections of a page, which are commonly identified as the container, header, and footer of a page.

In contrast, class styles can be used multiple times on each page, so they are more versatile and ideal for styles you want to use over and over, such as a style for the caption under a photo, or a style that adds alignment to elements.

If you study the code behind web pages on the Internet (you can do this by choosing

View⇨Page Source in Firefox or View⇨Source in Internet Explorer), you'll quickly discover that web pages are created in many, many different ways; not everyone follows the same rules. The designer who created the CSS layouts in Dreamweaver decided that it was simpler and more versatile to create these layouts using class styles, so you won't see ID styles in the style sheets at all.

Again, it's not wrong to use only class styles, but that approach is different from the one many people use on websites these days. To help you appreciate both approaches, this chapter shows you how to edit the class styles used for the main content areas in the Dreamweaver CSS layouts and how to use ID styles for this purpose when you create a custom CSS layout.

Editing the styles in a CSS layout

After you create a new page with a CSS layout, you have a seemingly infinite number of options for editing it, but first you have to determine which styles in the style sheet correspond to the elements you want to edit.

In this example, I've chosen a fixed-width layout, so I know I need a style that specifies the fixed width for the entire layout. Following a common practice of using <div> tags to contain elements on a page and using styles to describe how they should be displayed, every CSS layout in Dreamweaver includes a <div> tag with a style named .container. To change the width of a design, change the corresponding .container style, as shown in this section.

The steps in the following sections explain how to edit the overall design of a page created with a Dreamweaver CSS layout. I've broken the process into several step lists to help you follow along more easily. ***Note:*** The steps assume you're proceeding through the sections in order.

As you can probably imagine, you can edit the styles in a CSS layout in many ways to create your own designs, but the process I explain in the following sections should serve you well as you get started with any of these layouts.

After you adjust the existing styles to get the basic page design the way you want it, you can create as many additional styles as you desire. For example, in my example in this section, I deleted the sidebar's <div> tags and styles, which are included in this layout to create a row of vertical links. Instead, I want links across the top of the page, just under the banner (which you find out how to create in the section "Creating a Navigation Bar from an Unordered List of Links," later in this chapter).

Checking out the available styles and making basic edits

You can use these same basic instructions with any CSS layout included in Dreamweaver. To edit styles in a CSS layout, follow these steps:

1. **Open a page file that's based in a Dreamweaver CSS layout, and choose Window⇨CSS Styles (or click the CSS Styles button to expand the panel).**

   The CSS Styles panel opens or expands.

2. **Click the plus sign (or triangle on a Mac) next to the style sheet name to open the list of styles.**

   All the styles associated with the new page are listed, as shown in Figure 6-6.

   To change any element in the design of this page, you edit the corresponding style.

3. **Select the name of any style listed in the CSS Styles panel.**

   The corresponding CSS rules defined for the style are displayed in the Properties pane at the bottom of the CSS Styles panel, as shown in Figure 6-6. Clicking through the list of styles and reviewing their corresponding rules is a good way to get a quick overview of the design and to see where the various page-formatting options are stored.

The styles named `.container`, `.header`, `.sidebar1`, `.content`, and `.footer` control the main sections of the page. For example, the `.header` style, which is shown in Figure 6-6, includes a rule that makes the background color black. Thus, to change the color of the header area at the top of the page, you change the background color setting in the `.header` rule. (You find detailed instructions for editing the `.container` and other main styles in this CSS layout in the "Customizing content areas" section, later in this chapter.) As explained in the nearby sidebar "Why Dreamweaver's CSS layouts use class styles instead of ID styles with <div> tags," Dreamweaver CS6 does not include ID styles in the CSS layouts.

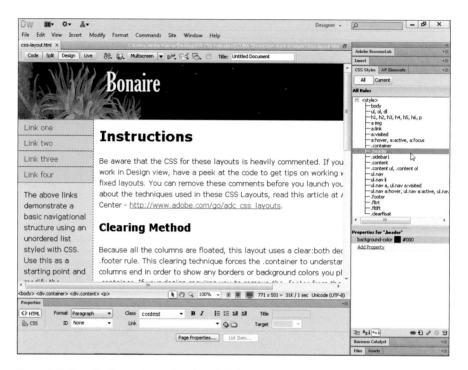

Figure 6-6: Alter the formatting options in a CSS layout by editing the corresponding style definition in the CSS Styles panel.

Editing page-wide settings

To edit page-wide settings — such as the background color of the page, or the main font face, size, and color of the text used throughout the page — follow these steps:

1. **Double-click the style for the `<body>` tag in the CSS Styles panel.**

   The CSS Rule Definition dialog box opens, displaying the rules for the `<body>` tag style, as shown in Figure 6-7.

2. **Select the Type category from the options at the left in the dialog box, and change or add your desired Font settings.**

   You can change the font face, size, style, and weight. To change the space between lines of text, change the line height.

3. **Select the Background category and use the color well in the Background-Color field to specify a color for the entire background of the page.**

Alternatively, you can enter any hexadecimal color code in the Background-Color field. To add a background image, click the Browse button to the right of the Background-Image field and select the image you want to serve as the background. Use the Background-Repeat drop-down list to specify how the background image should repeat (if at all) on the page.

4. **Click the Apply button to preview your changes and then click OK to save the changes and close the dialog box.**

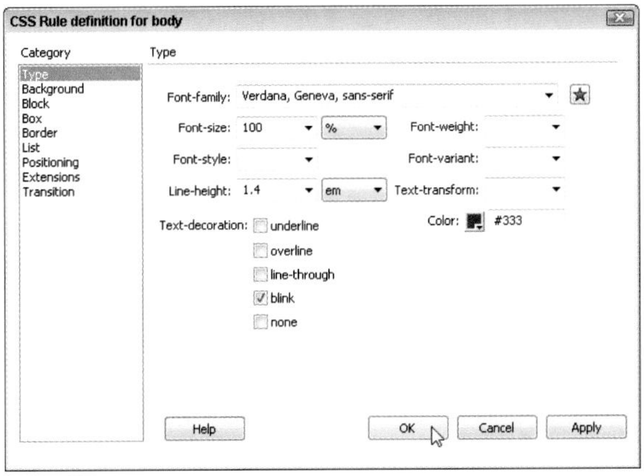

Figure 6-7: Define page-wide settings in the style for the <body> tag.

Customizing content areas

To change the width or other settings of the main content areas, which control the overall size of the page and the header, footer, and sidebar, follow these steps:

1. **To change the width of the entire main design area, double-click the .container style in the CSS Styles panel.**

   You open the .container style in the CSS Rule Definition dialog box. If you click once to select a style (such as the .container style), your choice's style definition appears in the Properties pane (refer to Figure 6-6), where you can also edit the style.

2. **Select the Box category on the left of the CSS Rule Definition dialog box.**

   The box settings open in the dialog box, as shown in Figure 6-8.

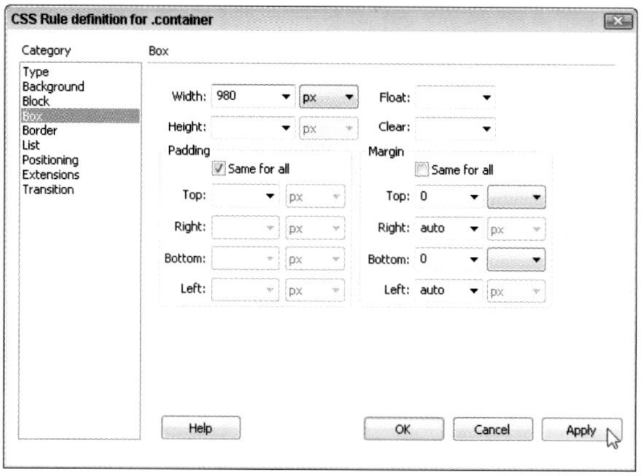

Figure 6-8: Change the width of the design by using the Box category to the edit the .container style.

3. **Select a size in the width field or type a new number for your desired page width.**

   In this example, I changed the width to 980. When you alter the width of the .container style, as I did here, you change the width of the entire design because all the other <div> tags are contained in the <div> formatted with the .container style — and they're all set to expand to fill the .container <div>. (For more on the best width for a web page, see the sidebar "How wide should I make my web page's design?")

4. **Click Apply to preview the changes. Click OK to save the changes and close the dialog box.**

   The new size is applied automatically to the .container <div> — and the page layout changes.

   Reducing the width of the .container <div> causes the .content <div> to drop below the sidebar because the .content <div> is now too wide for the space created by the .container. This problem is common; when you change one style, you often affect elements controlled by other styles. The next step explains how to fix the problem.

5. **To alter the size of the content area of the page, edit the style name** .content.

   a. **Double-click the** .content **style in the CSS Styles panel.**

      The .content style opens in the CSS Rule Definition dialog box.

   b. **Choose the Box category.**

   c. **Reduce the width of the** .content **style.**

6. **To change the background color of any style on the page, double-click the corresponding style and select the Background category in the CSS Rule Definition dialog box.**

   In the CSS layout I'm using in this example, the sidebar is defined in a style named `.sidebar1`. Thus, to change the background color, I double-clicked `.sidebar1` in the CSS Styles panel to open `.sidebar1` in the CSS Rule Definition dialog box. Then I selected the Background category and clicked the color well (as shown in Figure 6-9) to change the color. (***Note:*** Changing the background color of the sidebar will not change the color of the links at the top of the sidebar in this layout. Move on to the next step to find out how to edit those.)

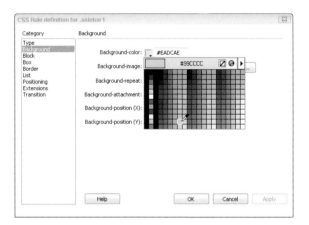

Figure 6-9: Change the background color by opening the corresponding style, selecting Background, and choosing a color from the color well.

7. **Change the links in the top of the left sidebar:**

   a. **Double-click the compound style** `ul.nav a, ul.nav a:visited` **to open it in the CSS Rule Definition dialog box.**

   b. **Select the Background category and use the color well to change the color.**

   c. **Select the Box category and change the width or adjust the padding.**

   (See "Comparing Margins and Padding in CSS," later in this chapter, for more on these design elements.)

8. **Edit the section at the top of the page:**

   a. **Double-click the** `header` **style in the CSS Styles panel.**

   b. Select the Background category and use the color well to change the color.

   c. Select the Box category to change the width or adjust the padding.

9. **Add an image to the banner:**

   a. **Delete the placeholder image labeled Insert Logo.**

   b. **Choose Insert ⇨ Image and select an image using the Select Image Source dialog box.**

10. **Replace text and insert images in the sidebar and main content areas.**

   You can add or replace text and insert images in any page created from a CSS layout, just as you would in any other web page, by using the Select Image Source dialog, shown in Figure 6-10.

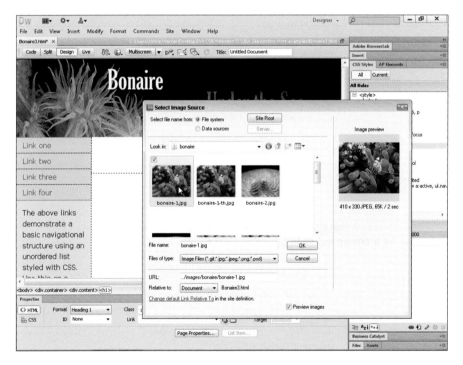

Figure 6-10: The Select Image Source dialog box.

11. Choose File⇨Save to save the page and styles.

If you saved the styles in an external style sheet, you're prompted by a second dialog box to save the style sheet separately. If the styles are contained in an internal style sheet, they're saved automatically when you save the page.

You can combine CSS layouts with Dreamweaver's template features to create a *template* — a page design you can use to create additional pages without repeating all the steps to customize the styles for each page. (As you discover in Chapter 7, Dreamweaver's template features offer many advantages when you're designing a site with more than a few pages; for example, you can make changes that affect many pages at once.)

Here's a related tip: If you intend to use the design as a template, make sure you save your styles in an external style sheet so you can edit the style rules outside the template. (Find instructions for creating external style sheets and for moving internal styles into an external style sheet in Chapter 5.)

Creating compound styles

Compound styles make it possible to create more specific styles. Of the many uses for compound styles, one of my favorites is the capability to create tag styles that appear differently in different parts of the same page.

When you redefine a tag (as with the unordered list and link tags), the new style applies to all uses of that tag within a page, unless you define the tag as a compound style by including the name of its container in the style name.

For example, in the "Creating a Navigation Bar from an Unordered List of Links" section, instead of creating a new tag style with just the name of the `<ul>` tag, I created a compound style called `#navbar ul` to redefine the `<ul>` tag *only* when it's contained within a `<div>` tag with an ID of `navbar`.

When you create compound styles like this, make sure you separate each style name by a single space. In this example, I also created styles for the `<li>` and `<link>` tags in the same way, creating styles with the names `#navbar a:link`, `#navbar a:hover`, and `#navbar ul li`. You can create compound styles with multiple tags and style names to create more specific CSS rules.

Creating a Navigation Bar from an Unordered List of Links

Here's a great CSS trick for turning a bulleted list (or unordered list) into a navigation bar with a simple rollover effect. Using a bulleted list for navigation bars is a well-accepted convention for websites that meet current accessibility standards. A bulleted list is a logical choice for navigation elements; even if the style rules are removed, the links still stand out from the rest of the elements on the page and are clearly grouped together in a list.

In Figures 6-11 and 6-12, you see how the same page appears with and without the styles applied to the content. In Figure 6-11, you see links contained in an unordered list. In Figure 6-12, those same links are still contained in the unordered list, but the CSS styles change their appearance dramatically.

To see how any web page looks without its styles applied when using the Firefox web browser, as shown in Figures 6-11, choose View⇨Page Style⇨No Style.

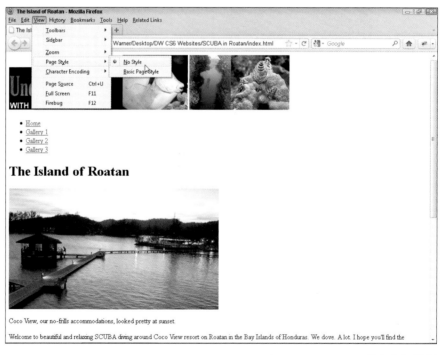

Photos by Ken Riddick

Figure 6-11: The same web page shown in Figure 6-12 with the No Style option selected in the Firefox browser.

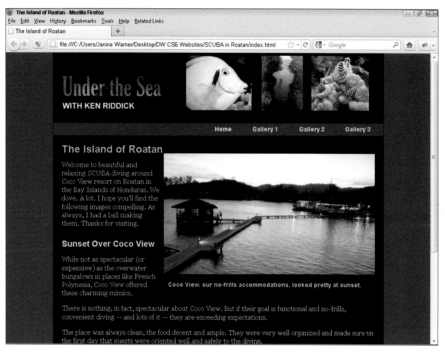

Photos by Ken Riddick

Figure 6-12: The same page shown in Figure 6-11 but with styles turned on.

Thanks to CSS, you can gain the benefits of styling a list of links with the unordered list tag and still format your links with any style you choose. That way you don't have to keep those boring bullets and can align your links horizontally or vertically. Using CSS instead of images to create a rollover effect (like the one featured in the following steps) not only makes your page more accessible but also helps your page load faster.

As you figure out different design tricks, such as the navigation bar I explain in this section, you may find it helpful to see other pages without the styles applied, as you do in Figure 6-11. In Firefox, you can turn off the styles on any page that uses CSS by choosing View⇨Page Style⇨No Style. As you see in Figure 6-11, when the styles are turned off, the page looks very different. In Figure 6-12, you see how the styles cause the `<div>` tags to align so that the three photos appear side-by-side in three columns. Similarly, the styles make the navigation links appear as a horizontal row instead of an unordered list.

You can use the following steps to add a list of links to any CSS layout included in Dreamweaver, as well as to any custom CSS layout you create yourself.

To create a navigation bar using CSS to redefine the unordered list and link tags, follow these steps:

1. **Click to place your cursor where you want to create your navigation bar in the page.**

   When you're creating a list of links to serve as your navigation bar, it's good practice to position those links at the top or side of the page, where visitors to your site can find them easily.

2. **Enter the text you want to serve as the links, separated by paragraph returns.**

   Be sure you use a paragraph return to separate each text block that you want to link; each link will be on a separate line and easy to format as an unordered list.

   You can type any text you want, but it's generally recommended that you keep the main navigation links in your site very short. For example, use a single word when possible (such as *Home*) instead of something longer (such as *The front page of the site*).

3. **Create links by selecting each piece of text in turn, clicking the Hyperlink icon in the Common Insert panel, and then selecting the page you want to link to, or entering any URL.**

   Essentially, you set these links as you would set any other links in your site. (You find detailed instructions for creating a variety of different types of links, including links to other websites and e-mail links, in Chapter 2.)

4. **Click and drag to select the entire set of links, and then click the Unordered List icon in the Property inspector, as shown in Figure 6-13.**

   A bullet point appears at the beginning of each link. If any link isn't set off with a separate bullet, click to delete the space between it and the link before it, and then press Return or Enter to separate the links with a paragraph return (which will be automatically converted into a bullet in the unordered list).

5. **To add a `<div>` tag around a list of links (or any other content that is already on a page), click to select the content and then click the Insert Div Tag icon in the Common Insert panel.**

   The Insert Div Tag dialog box opens.

   Adding a `<div>` tag around the unordered list of links is helpful if you want to add formatting, such as the background color that fills the entire navigation row in this example.

Figure 6-13: Formatting a collection of links as an unordered list.

6. **Choose Wrap Around Selection from the Insert drop-down list, as shown in Figure 6-14.**

   For more precise control over where you add a new <div> tag, you can choose options from the Insert drop-down list at the top of the Insert Div Tag dialog box. Choosing the Wrap Around Selection option, for example, adds open and close <div> tags to the code before and after the selected content, in this case, the bulleted list of links.

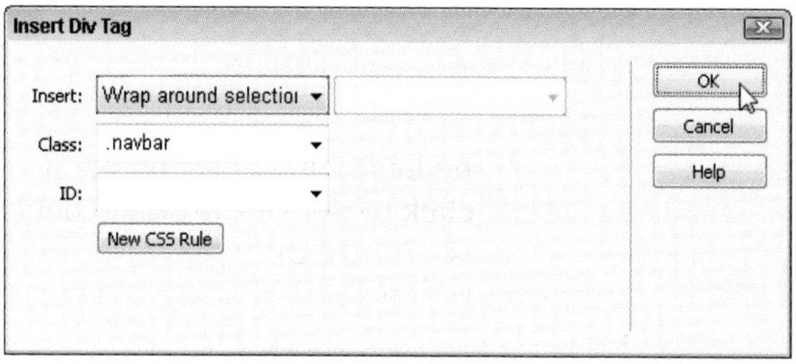

Figure 6-14: Adding a <div> tag around content to create a class style.

7. **Enter a name in the Class field or the ID field and click OK.**

   A <div> tag with the class or ID name you entered is added automatically to the page surrounding the list of links.

   In this example, I chose to create a class style with the name .navbar (as shown in Figure 6-14).

You can create a class or ID style to format the `<div>` tag that surrounds your list of links. If you plan to have only one navigation bar on the page, an ID style is a good option. If you plan to repeat the navigation bar in more than one place (as I did in this example by adding a navigation bar to the top and bottom of the page), create a class style so you can use it twice on the same page. (One of the advantages of creating a class style is that it can be used more than once on a page, so you can apply the same style to both navigation bars and they will be formatted with the same rules.)

8. **Click the New CSS Rule button at the bottom of the CSS Styles panel to define the new style name you entered when you added the `<div>` tag.**

   The New CSS Rule dialog box opens.

9. **Choose the option from the Selector Type drop-down list that corresponds with the type of style you want to create.**

   In this example, I'm creating a class style to go with the class name I gave to the new `<div>` tag (`.navbar`). If I had chosen to add an ID instead of a class in Step 7, I would choose ID from the drop-down list to create a corresponding style.

10. **Enter the name of the style and click OK.**

    The CSS Rule Definition dialog box opens.

    Note: You must enter the name exactly as you typed it when you created the `<div>` tag. In this example, I entered *.navbar*.

    If your cursor was in the `<div>` when you clicked the New CSS Rule button (in Step 8), the name will be entered already in the Selector Name field. Unless you want to be very specific with this style, I suggest you delete any other code that might appear and enter only the name of the style: *.navbar* for a class style or *#navbar* for an ID style.

11. **Specify your desired settings for color, background, size, margins, and padding.**

    For the `.navbar` style shown in this example, I set the font size to small and the background color to dark blue. I also added 5 pixels of padding to the top and bottom so the dark blue background would extend above and below the links.

12. **Click Apply to preview the style. Click OK to save the style and close the dialog box.**

    The formatting options you specified are applied automatically to the `<div>` tag around the links.

13. **To create a style that will affect only this unordered list, create a compound style that includes the class name** `.navbar`:

   a. **Choose Format⇨CSS Styles⇨New.**

   b. **Under Selector Type, choose Compound.**

   c. **In the Selector Name field, enter** .navbar ul, **as shown in Figure 6-15, and then click OK.**

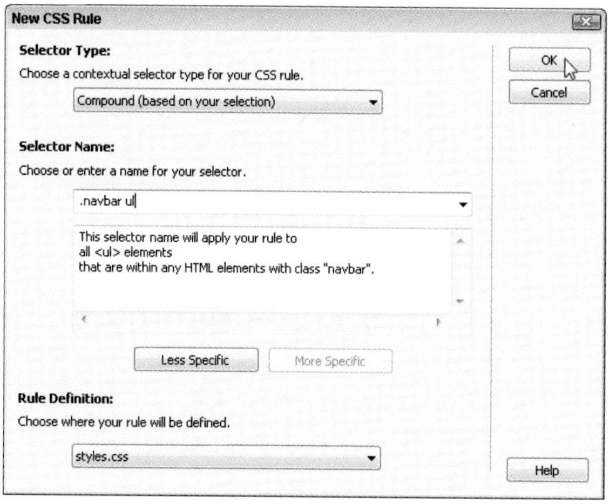

Figure 6-15: Use compound styles to redefine the same HTML tag in multiple ways.

   d. **In the CSS Rule Definition dialog box, choose the Box category and set margins and padding to** 0.

   e. **Select the Same for All check box for both margins and padding to remove the margins and padding included in the** `<ul>` **HTML tag.**

   f. **Click OK to save the style and close the dialog box.**

   The spacing around the list of links that was formatted as an unordered list disappears.

14. **Create a new compound style to redefine the list item tag s:**

   a. **Choose Format⇨CSS Styles⇨New.**

   b. **Under Selector Type, choose Compound.**

    c. In the Selector Name field, enter .navbar ul li **(make sure to include spaces between each name) and then click OK.**

    d. In the CSS Rule Definition dialog box, select the Block category and set Display to Inline.

    This step changes the style of the <li> tag from vertical to horizontal.

    e. Select the List category and set Type to None to remove the bullet.

    f. Select the Box category and set margins left and right to 20 pixels.

    This step separates the list items from one another in the horizontal list. You can change the setting to create the amount of space between links that best fits your design.

    g. Click OK to save these settings and close the dialog box.

15. **Create a new style to redefine the link tag:**

    a. Choose Format⇨CSS Styles⇨New.

    b. Under Selector Type, choose Compound.

    c. In the Tag field, enter .navbar a:link **and then click OK.**

    You can make this style as specific as you choose. For example, the style .navbar a:link will change the appearance of any links in the .navbar <div>. However, if you create the style .navbar ul li a:link, that style will apply only to links that appear in the .navbar <div> and inside the unordered list tags. Because these are the only links I use in the .navbar <div>, I don't need to be so specific; both styles will work the same in this example.

    d. In the CSS Rule Definition dialog box, select the Type category and set Text-decoration to None.

    This step removes the underline from linked text.

    e. Still in the Type category, choose a color from the color well to specify the color of links when they're loaded on a page.

    Here I set the text color to an off-white.

    f. Click OK to save these settings and close the dialog box.

16. **Create a new style to redefine the hover-link tag so that the link color will change when a user rolls a cursor over the link:**

    a. Choose Format⇨CSS Styles⇨New.

    b. Under Selector Type, choose Compound.

    c. In the Tag field, enter .navbar a:hover **and then click OK.**

Again, I could create a more specific compound link by entering *.navbar ul li a:hover*, but it's not necessary here.

d. In the CSS Rule Definition dialog box, select the Type category and set Text-decoration to None.

This step removes the underline from linked text. If you prefer to have the underline appear when a user rolls a cursor over a link, select Underline.

e. Still in the Type category, choose a color from the color well to specify the link's color when users roll their cursor over the link.

I set the text color to a bright yellow. The more dramatic the color difference between the a:link and a:hover colors, the more dramatic the rollover effect.

f. Click OK to save these settings and close the dialog box.

17. **Create a new style to redefine the visited link tag so the link color changes after a user clicks a link:**

a. Choose Format⇨CSS Styles⇨New.

b. Under Selector Type, choose Compound.

c. In the Tag field, enter .navbar a:visited **and then click OK.**

d. In the CSS Rule Definition dialog box, choose the Type category and set Text-decoration to None.

e. Still in the Type category, choose a color from the color well to specify the link's color after it's been visited.

Here I set the text color to a light gray. If you want the color to remain the same, set the a:visited link to the same color as the a:link.

f. Click OK to save these settings and close the dialog box.

18. **Click the Live View button at the top of the workspace or click the Preview button to view the page in a browser to see the effect of the link styles, as shown in Figure 6-16.**

Photos by Ken Riddick

Figure 6-16: Click Live View to preview your links.

Comparing block and inline elements

As a general rule, HTML tags can be divided into block elements and inline elements. *Block elements,* such as the `<div>` tag, interrupt the flow of the page, creating a box or block around which other page elements align. In HTML, block elements include the paragraph (`<p>`) tag, which creates a line break before and after it's used and doesn't allow anything to appear alongside it. Heading tags, such as `<h1>`, `<h2>`, and `<h3>`, and list tags, such as `<ul>` and `<ol>`, are also block elements.

In contrast, *inline elements* follow the flow with text. For example, the `<strong>` and `<em>`

tags, which apply bold and italics, respectively, are inline elements. You can place these elements one after another, and a new line break doesn't appear between each element. They simply flow with the text. For that reason, the `<span>` tag, which is an inline element, is a good choice for applying styles that you want to affect a small amount of text within a block, such as when you want to add a little color to text contained within `<p>` tags. Dreamweaver often adds `<span>` tags when you apply a class style to text in the middle of a paragraph.

Comparing Margins and Padding in CSS

When creating or editing CSS styles, new web designers are often confused by how and when to use margins and padding. Both settings add space between elements — for example, a margin between text and an image or a little padding between the border of a `<div>` tag and its contents. Here's how margins and padding work:

 ✓ **Padding** adds space inside an element. Think of padding as a way to add a cushion around the inside of a box so your content doesn't bump into the sides of your box.

 ✓ **Margins** add space outside an element. Think of margins as a way to add space between boxes, on the sides of images, or around any other element on a page, so things don't bump into each other.

Figure 6-17 shows a `<div>` tag with a corresponding ID style that creates the thin black border around the `<div>` tag and defines it as follows:

500 pixels wide

25 pixels of padding inside the `<div>` tag border

50 pixels of margin spacing outside the `<div>` tag border

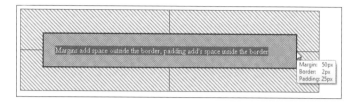

Figure 6-17: Padding is added to the inside of an element; margins are added to the outside.

Here's the confusing part:

- **Padding adds to the specified width.** If you specify a width for a <div> tag (or any other box element) — as I have in Figure 6-17 — the padding increases the total width. In my example, the <div> tag will fill 550 pixels of space on the page: 500 pixels for the width plus 25 pixels on each side of padding.

- **Margins add to the total space taken up by an element in a page.** The margins of the <div> tag style are set to 50 pixels, so the <div> tag is positioned 50 pixels from the top and left of the page and no other element will appear on-screen closer than 50 pixels on the right or at the bottom. Adding margin space prevents elements from bumping up against each other, but you need to remember, that the <div> tag will then effectively take up all that space on the page — the combined width, plus padding, plus margins.

- **Borders add to the specified element width.** The ID style for the <div> tag also includes border settings, which cause the dark border to surround the <div> tag. In this example, I created a 4-pixel border, which adds 8 pixels to the width. If you choose the thin border setting, it adds 2 pixels to each side of the <div> tag (4 pixels total).

How wide should I make my web page's design?

Although you can set the width of your web page's design to any size, most web designers create pages that are 960 pixels wide. That size is based on the most common screen resolution on most computer desks. If you want your web pages to look good on computers with monitors set to 1024 by 768, design your pages to be 960 pixels wide (to leave room for the borders of a web browser). When you design pages that are 960 pixels wide, they display well also on the iPad 1 and 2.

3. **Enter a name for the style.**

   You can name ID styles anything you like, just don't use spaces or special characters. Also ID style names must begin with the pound sign (#). If you don't enter # before the name, Dreamweaver adds one for you as it creates the new ID style. In this example, I named the style `#container`.

4. **Select a style sheet option from the Rule Definition drop-down list.**

   To add the style to an internal style sheet, which makes the style available only to the page you have open, choose This Document Only.

   To add the style to any existing external style sheet in the site, choose the name of the style sheet from the drop-down list.

   To create a new external style sheet as you create the style, choose New Style Sheet File.

5. **Click OK.**

   The New CSS Rule dialog box closes and the CSS Rule Definition dialog box opens. The name you entered appears at the top of the CSS Rule Definition dialog box.

6. **Choose the Box category from the left of the dialog box and then specify the formatting settings.**

   As shown in Figure 6-18, for the container `<div>` tag in this example, I set the width to 960 pixels. Here's the trick to centering a `<div>` tag like this: Set the left and right margins to Auto. That way, a browser automatically adds an equal amount of margin space to each side of the `<div>` tag, effectively centering it on the page.

7. **Click the Apply button to preview the style and then click OK to close the CSS Rule Definition dialog box and save the style.**

8. **Click to select the ID that surrounds all the content on the page.**

   To make sure you've selected the right `<div>` tag, click to place your cursor anywhere in the main part of the page, then click the `<div>` tag listed to the farthest left in the Quick Tag Selector at the bottom of the workspace. The outline of the `<div>` tag and all its contents will be highlighted.

9. **With the `<div>` tag selected, click to select the name of the style you created from the ID drop-down list in the Property inspector.**

   The style rules you defined when you created the style are automatically applied to the `<div>` tag. In this example, the result is that the size of the `<div>` tag is changed to 780 pixels wide and the `<div>` tag and all its contents are centered on the page.

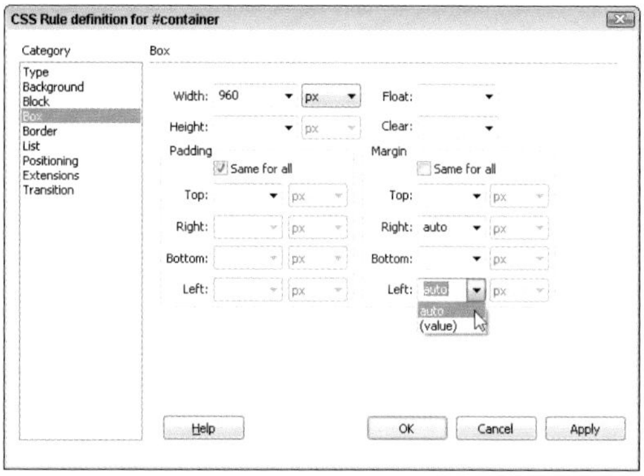

Figure 6-18: To center a <div> tag, set the left and right margins to Auto.

Aligning the contents of an element

If you want to align the contents of an element, you can use the Block category in the CSS Rule Definition dialog box. This technique is useful for centering the text in a <div> tag, for example, or for aligning a list of navigation links to the right side of a page. A common approach to using this option is to create an ID or a class style that you will apply to an entire <div> tag and include the text alignment option as part of the style rule. In Figure 6-19, I'm setting the Text-Align field to Center as part of an ID style named #footer that I plan to apply to the <div> tag at the bottom of the page to center the copyright information.

In this example, I also used the Type category to change the size and font of the text in the same style named #footer. Combining all these rules in one style enables me to apply multiple formatting options at once when I assign this ID to the <div> tag that surrounds the copyright information.

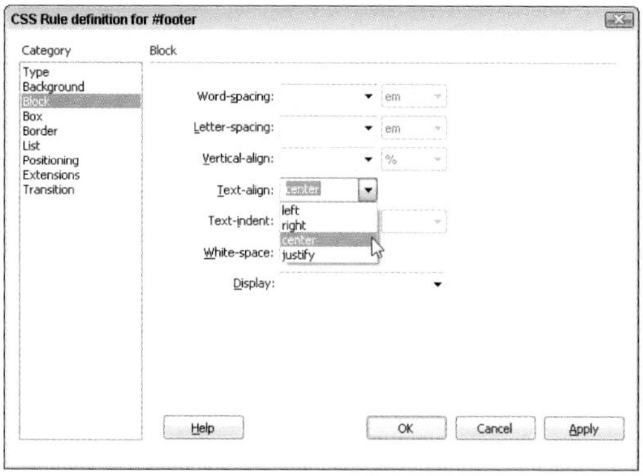

Figure 6-19: Use the Text-Align list in the Box category to center the contents of a <div> tag.

Aligning elements with floats

Designers often align an image, a `<div>` tag, or another element to the left or right of a web page and then wrap any text or other content around that element. In Figure 6-20, I've used a style to align the image to the right of the column so that the text wraps next to it on the left. In the steps that follow, you find out how to create styles like this one.

CSS offers many advantages when it comes to aligning elements like this, but the way you set up these styles is not as obvious as you might expect at first because you use the float option.

After you understand that you can float elements, such as images, to the left or right side of a page, it's pretty easy to create styles that accomplish this goal. In this exercise, you learn to create two styles that are ideal for aligning images to the left and right of a page, complete with a little margin just where you need it.

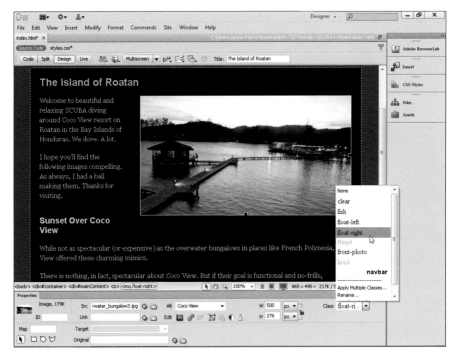

Photos by Ken Riddick

Figure 6-20: When you align an image to the left or right using floats, adjacent text wraps around the image.

To create two class styles that you can use to align images and other elements to the left and right of a page, follow these steps.

1. **Click the New CSS Rule icon (it looks like a small piece of paper with a plus sign over it) at the bottom of the CSS Styles panel.**

   Alternatively, you can choose Format➪CSS Styles➪New.

   The New CSS Rule dialog box opens.

2. **Choose Class from the Selector Type drop-down list.**

   In this case, the class selector is ideal because you're likely to use your alignment styles more than once on a page.

3. **Enter a name for the style.**

   You can name class styles anything you like; just don't use spaces or special characters. Class style names must begin with a dot (.). If you don't enter a dot before the name, Dreamweaver adds one for you as it creates the new class style.

   In this example, I named the style `.float-left`.

4. **Select a style sheet option from the Rule Definition drop-down list.**

   To add the style to an internal style sheet, which makes the style available only to the page you have open, choose This Document Only.

   To add the style to any existing external style sheet in the site, choose the name of the style sheet from the drop-down list.

   To create a new external style sheet as you create the style, choose New Style Sheet File.

5. **Click OK.**

   The New CSS Rule dialog box closes, and the CSS Rule Definition dialog box opens. The name you entered appears at the top of the CSS Rule Definition dialog box.

6. **Choose the Box category from the left side of the dialog box.**

   The Box options open.

7. **Choose an option from the Float drop-down list.**

   To create a style that will align images or other elements to the left of a page, chose Left from the Float drop-down list. To create a style that will align images or other elements to the right of a page, chose Right from the Float drop-down list.

In all my sites, I create two styles like this, one to align images and other elements to the left, and another to align to the right. ***Note:*** Most (but not all) CSS layouts included in Dreamweaver CS6 already have float styles that you can use to align elements to the right and left. These class styles are named `.fltlft` (for, you guessed it, float left) and `.fltrt` (for float right).

8. **Add margin space to create a margin around the floated element.**

   It's good practice to add margin space to the opposite side from the float setting. For example, if you are creating a style to float an image to the left, add 5 or 10 pixels of space to the Right margin field. Then, when you use the style to align an image to the left side of the page, a margin will also be created between the image and any text or other element that wraps next to the image.

9. **Click OK to close the CSS Rule Definition dialog box and save the style.**

   The style name and definition appear in the CSS Styles panel and become available in the Class drop-down list in the Property inspector.

10. **Click to select the image or other element you want to align in the page.**

11. **Click to select the name of the style you created from the Class drop-down in the Property inspector.**

    The style rules you defined when you created the style are automatically applied. If you had selected an image in a page of text, the image would move to the left side of the page and the text would wrap around it with a margin between the image and text.

12. **Repeat Steps 1–11, once with the float set to Right and 5 to 10 pixels of margin space in the Left margin field in the Box category, and again with the Float set to Left and 5 to 10 pixels of margin space in the Right margin field in the Box category.**

Editing, Renaming, and Removing Styles

After you create and apply a few styles, you're likely to want to go back and edit some of them. Fortunately, Dreamweaver makes it easy to rename, edit, and even remove styles, as you learn in the sections that follow.

Editing an existing style

You can change the attributes of any style after you create it by editing its style definition. This is where some of the biggest advantages of Cascading Style Sheets come into play. You can make global changes to a page (or even to an entire website) by changing a style; when you edit the style, the changes are applied automatically to every element that uses the style.

One of the reasons why external style sheets are so valuable is that you can create styles that are used on any *or* all pages in a site. Beware, however, that this capability can also lead to problems. If you decide to edit a style when you use it on a new page, don't forget that you'll be changing the formatting everywhere else you've already used that style.

You can create new styles by duplicating an existing style, giving it a new name, and then altering the style definitions. This time-saving trick is useful when you want to create a new style that's similar to an existing one.

To edit any existing style (whether it was created using the class, tag, or ID selector), follow these steps:

1. **Open the CSS Styles panel by choosing Window⇨CSS Styles.**

2. **Double-click the name of an existing style in the CSS Styles panel.**

   The style is opened in the CSS Rule Definition dialog box.

   Alternatively, you can click once to select any style in the CSS Styles panel and then edit that style in the Properties pane at the bottom of the panel, as shown in Figure 6-21.

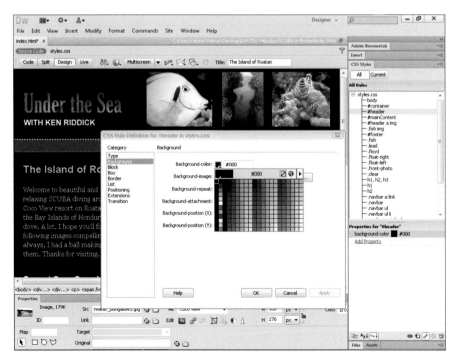

Photos by Ken Riddick

Figure 6-21: To edit a style, double-click its name in the CSS Styles panel.

3. **Edit the settings for the style to your liking.**

- **If you edit a style in the CSS Rule Definition dialog box,** changes are applied automatically when you click the Apply button or when you click OK.

- **If you edit a style definition in the Properties panel,** the changes are applied automatically as soon as you press the Return or Enter key or click outside the formatting field in the panel.

Renaming existing styles

You can rename a style in the CSS Styles panel in much the same way you'd rename a filename in the Files panel, by clicking to select the name and then typing a new name.

If you change a name in the CSS Styles panel, you must also change the name in the corresponding page code, or reapply the style using the Property inspector — which can get complicated if you've used the style in many places.

For example, let's say you create a class style and name it #footer and then apply it to the <div> tag that surrounds the content at the bottom of your web page using the Property inspector (as I did in the first exercises in this chapter). Then suppose you decide to change the name of the style to #copyright because you want to add another <div> that you'll use as the footer later. Changing the name from #footer to #copyright in the CSS Styles panel is easy enough, but then you have to make sure to update every place you've used that style in your site — either by reapplying the style using the Property inspector or by changing the name in the code wherever the style has been applied.

If you want to change the name of a class style, Dreamweaver includes a feature that updates the corresponding code automatically, but only for class styles and only if you change the name using the right-click (or Control-click) option described in the instructions that follow. If you change the name of an ID style, you must reset the style using the Property inspector, or change the corresponding references in the code manually using Code view or the Quick Tag Editor.

To rename a class style and update the style references in the code at the same time, open any page where the style is used and follow these instructions:

1. **Open the CSS Styles panel by choosing Window➪CSS Styles.**

2. **Right-click (Control-click) the name of the class style in the CSS Styles panel.**

3. **Choose Rename Class, as shown in Figure 6-22.**

   The Rename dialog box opens.

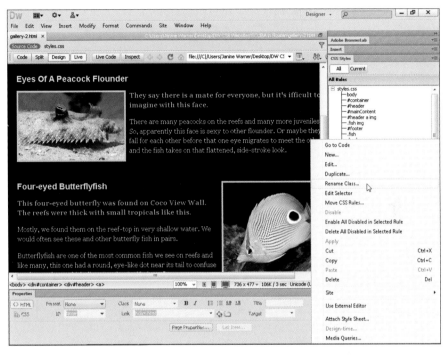

Figure 6-22: You can rename a class style and change the style name automatically in the page code.

4. **Type a new name in the New Name field and click OK.**

5. **If the style you want to rename is saved in an internal style sheet, you're finished!**

   The name will change automatically anywhere the style is applied in the code. Any changes appear in the Results panel, which opens automatically at the bottom of the workspace.

6. **If you've already applied the style and the style is saved in an external style sheet, do the following:**

   a. **Click Yes when the message appears, asking whether you want to "Use Find and Replace to fix the documents that use this style?"**

      The Find and Replace dialog box opens (see Figure 6-23) with the name of the style already filled in. Don't change these settings unless you know what you're doing with these advanced search strings and want to alter the way Dreamweaver renames the style.

   b. **Click Replace All to automatically update all references to the style in the code.**

Dreamweaver warns you that this operation can't be undone, but you can always rename the style again by repeating these steps if you change your mind.

c. Click Yes to update all references.

The name changes automatically anywhere the style is applied in the code. Any changes appear in the Results panel, which opens automatically at the bottom of the workspace.

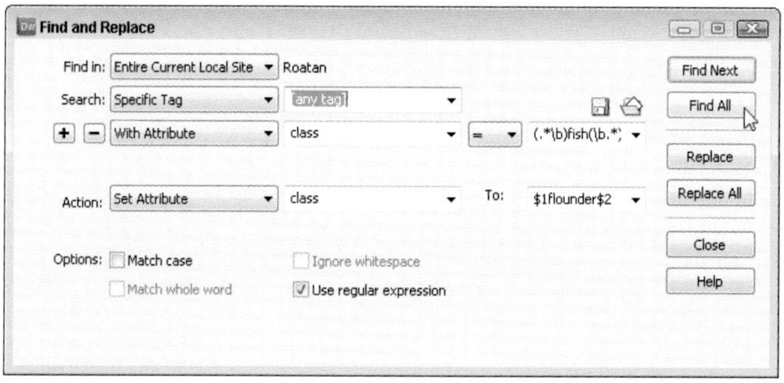

Figure 6-23: Dreamweaver sets up the needed search strings to rename class styles.

Removing or changing a style

If you want to remove or change a style applied to any text, image, or other element on your page, here are two options:

- Click to select the text, image, or other element. Then open the Class or ID drop-down lists in the Property inspector and choose None, as you see in Figure 6-24.

- Click to select the element, and then right-click (Control-click on a Mac) the tag the style is applied to in the Tag Selector at the very bottom of the workspace (just above the Properties inspector), as shown in Figure 6-25. When you right-click the name of a tag in the Tag Selector, a list opens with many options; choose the corresponding option for the selected style. In the example shown in Figure 6-25, I selected the <p> tag that surrounds the first paragraph and chose the Set Class option to open a list of all class styles in the site. To change or remove a style this way, simply select the style you want and it will replace any style that has already been applied.

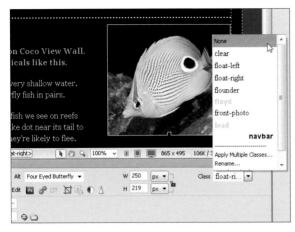

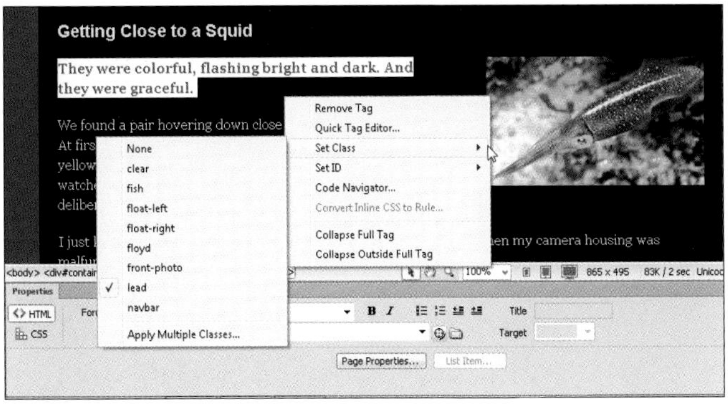

Photos by Ken Riddick

Figure 6-24: To remove a style, select any element and choose None from the Class drop-down list.

Figure 6-25: Use the Tag Selector to change or remove any style or HTML tag.

Photos by Ken Riddick

For a list of more advanced CSS training resources online and offline, visit www.DigitalFamily.com/dreamweaver and look for the article on "Where to learn advanced CSS tips and tricks."

7

Designing with CSS3

In This Chapter

▶ Comparing browser support for CSS3

▶ Adding text and drop shadows

▶ Making rounded corners

▶ Using almost any font you want

▶ Targeting style sheets with media queries

*W*hen most designers learn about the new features in CSS3, including drop shadows, gradients, and vastly improved font support, their reaction is: "It's about time!" These long-awaited design improvements provide a compelling reason to graduate to using CSS3 right away, even though older web browsers won't display all of these fancy new features. The good news is that if a browser doesn't support a new CSS rule, such as rounded corners, it simply ignores the style information. Visitors with older browsers may see square corners on the borders of your `<div>` tags instead of rounded ones, or common fonts such as Times or Arial in place of the more obscure fonts you may prefer to use in your page designs.

..we make stories respond to readers wi.. layouts that are as creative as you are.

I recommend you start using CSS3 style rules even if some of your visitors can't see them because CSS3 is clearly the wave of the future. As people update their web browsers and new computers replace old ones, CSS3 will become increasingly well supported. So why wait? Your most savvy visitors will appreciate the design enhancements and faster download time, today, and everyone else will come around before too long.

That said, you may not want to add every new CSS3 feature to your pages right away (some are better supported than others, even in the latest browsers). In this chapter, I introduce the most popular CSS3 features, including adding drop shadows to text and images, creating rounded corners on `<div>` tags, and using almost any font you want.

Comparing Browser Support for CSS3

To help you appreciate how a page designed with CSS3 looks in different web browsers, I used Adobe's BrowserLab to preview the page shown in Figures 7-1 and 7-2. Note that Figure 7-1 shows how the page looks in the latest version of Google Chrome, well known for its excellent support of CSS3. In contrast, Figure 7-2 shows how the page looks in Internet Explorer version 6.0 — an older version of Microsoft's browser that does not support CSS3 rules. Many web designers agree that it's okay to create web pages that don't look the same in all browsers, as long as the text is still readable by all your visitors.

The contrast between these two figures demonstrates the CSS rules and other features that are most problematic in very old web browsers. Note that in Figure 7-2, you don't see the text shadow on the main headline; the transparency in the PNG file in the image of the iPad; and the rounded corners and background color set to 50 percent opacity on the three `<div>` tags on the right side of the design.

Photo by Charlie Simpson

Figure 7-1: Google Chrome displays all CSS3 features used in this design.

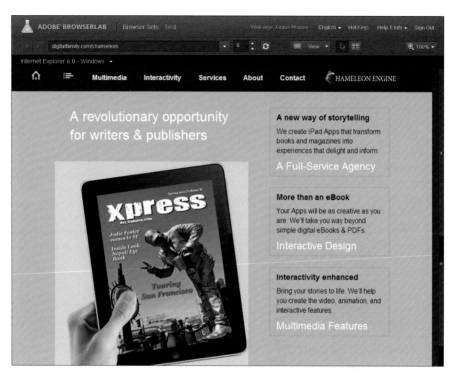

Figure 7-2: Internet Explorer version 6 can't display all CSS3 styles in this design.

Although Internet Explorer 6 does support background images, the big background image in the Chameleon Engine website is not displayed in Figure 7-2 because I set the background image width to 100%. This setting makes the background expand to fill the entire browser screen, whether small or large, but also prevents IE 6 from displaying the background image at all. To get around this problem in the final website (which you can view online at www.ChameleonEngine.com), I redesigned this page. Now the background image is inserted in a <div> tag, which makes the photo appear, even in IE6, although the photo no longer expands to fill the entire screen in such an old browser.

In Chapters 5 and 6, I cover the basics of CSS. If you're new to working with style sheets, I recommend that you start with the basics in those chapters before moving on to the more advanced CSS3 features covered in this chapter. In Chapter 4, you find more tips and resources for testing your web pages in different web browsers.

Adding drop shadows to images and divs

In addition to text shadows, CSS3 gives you the power to add shadows to images, boxes created using <div> tags, and other elements. In Figure 7-5, for example, I'm using the CSS Styles pane to define a rule that will add a drop shadow to all images in this page.

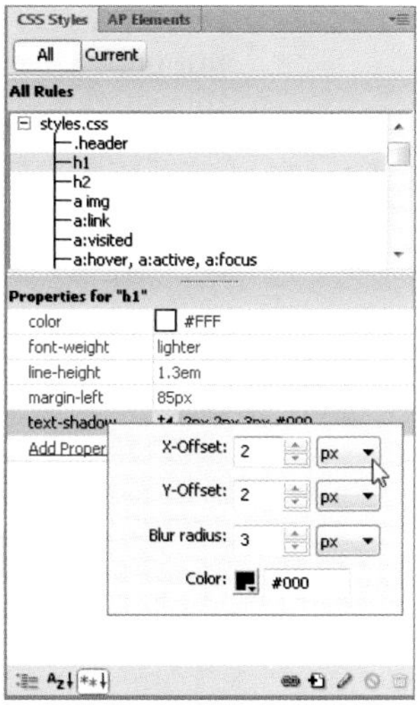

The following style adds a drop shadow to all images on a page:

```
img {box-shadow: 3px 3px 4px 5px #000;}
```

Much like the text shadow covered in the preceding section, the first two values specify how much the shadow extends on the x- and y-axis. The third value describes the amount of blur. The box-shadow rule includes a fourth setting that specifies the spread radius of the shadow. At the end of the list, the hexadecimal color code defines the color of the shadow.

Again, much like the text-shadow rule, you can use the Property pane at the bottom of the CSS Styles panel to add a box-shadow rule. Click the Add Property link on the left side of the CSS Styles Property pane and then enter **box-shadow**, or select the Box-Shadow style rule from the drop-down list. Then click the small arrow to open the options box shown in Figure 7-5.

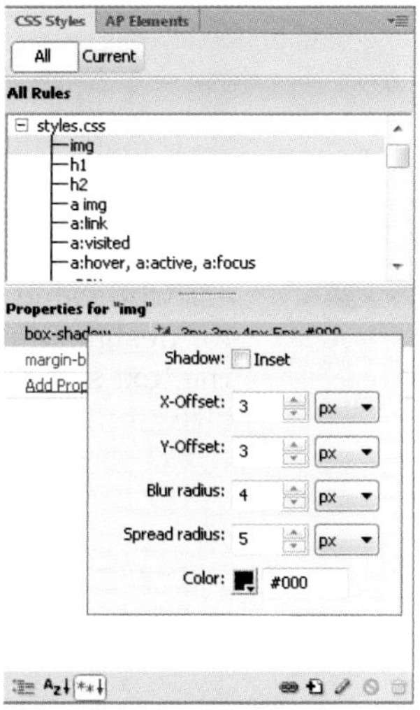

By default, drop shadows using the box-shadow rule in CSS3 appear to the right and below any element to which they are applied. However, if you add an inset rule, by selecting the Inset box shown in Figure 7-5, the shadow appears in the top left of an element.

Figure 7-4: You can add drop shadows to images, div tags, and other elements using CSS3.

Figure 7-5: Add drop shadows to images, div tags, and more by adding a box-shadow rule.

Softening Edges with Rounded Corners

Another popular CSS3 rule, border-radius, enables you to add rounded corners to the borders of <div> tags and other box elements. Using CSS3, you can specify how much corners are rounded, and you can apply the style to any or all corners of an element.

In Figure 7-6, you see a `<div>` tag with a border and a colored background, as well as the `border-radius` style rule applied to the top-left and bottom-right corners.

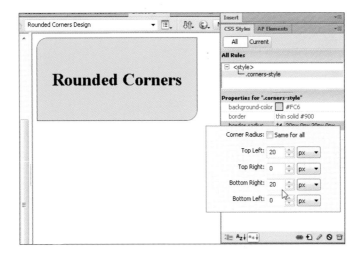

Figure 7-6: The radius of the rounded corner.

You can use the em measurement to design rounded corners that scale with the size of the text. The em measurement is a popular choice among designers who value creating pages that look good on small and large screens and for designs that adapt gracefully when a visitor to a site chooses to increase the text size to make a page more readable. For more on the em and other sizes in CSS, see Chapter 5.

Enhancing Your Site with Custom Fonts

The few fonts that come installed on most Windows and Mac computers are woefully inadequate. Serious designers spend hours searching for just the right font to convey the feeling they want to elicit in a design, which is why so many of us are excited that CSS3 offers a better solution.

The `@font-face` option, new in CSS3, enables you to link to any font available from a web server. Add a little drop shadow and other styling elements with CSS3, and you can create fantastic font effects without resorting to the old workaround: using images with styled text created in Photoshop. The

`@font-face` rule offers many advantages because using text instead of images on your pages means they load faster and are easier to update.

Using the `@font-face` rule requires two steps. First you link to a font hosted on a web server, and then you use that font in the `font-family` rule in your CSS styles, as you discover in this section.

Finding fonts online

Although you can upload any font to a server and link to the font to make it available to your web page, an online font repository offers many advantages. Online font repositories take care of licensing issues. Much like images and written materials, most fonts are protected by copyright law, so you must have permission before uploading a font and making it available on the web.

A further complication is that not all web browsers support the same types of fonts. Covering everything you need to know to host fonts on your own server is well beyond the scope of this book. However, let me simply suggest that you do what most web designers do: Get your fonts for your website from one of the font repositories online and let them take care of everything for you.

The following are the most popular font sites online today:

- **Google Web Fonts** (`www.google.com/webfonts`): The easiest site to use (as you see in the step-by-step instructions that follow), Google Web Fonts offers a limited collection of fonts but you can use all their fonts for free.

- **Typekit** (`www.typekit.com`): The one to watch, Typekit offers a wide range of professional-quality fonts and was recently acquired by Adobe. You can try this service for free, but if you get much traffic, want to use all their fonts, or want to use fonts on more than one website, you'll have to pay monthly subscription fee.

- **Fontspring** (`www.fontspring.com`): A clearing house that bundles the online and offline use of fonts, Fontspring provides a premium service with reasonably priced font collections that you can use across printed and digital materials.

- **Font Squirrel** (`www.fontsquirrel.com`): Font Squirrel features a collection of free fonts in font kits. You have to download the kits and then upload and host them on your own server, but the price is right — free. Font Squirrel also provides a font generator that you can use to create the four font types you need to support the most popular web browsers. This service is useful if you have the rights to a font and want to host it yourself.

Using custom fonts from the Google Web Fonts site

Follow these steps to add any of the fonts from the Google Web Fonts site to your pages:

1. **Open a web browser and visit** `www.google.com/webfonts`. **Click the big blue Start Choosing Fonts button.**

2. **Search through the fonts available on the site by selecting the type and style of font you're looking for, as shown in Figure 7-7.**

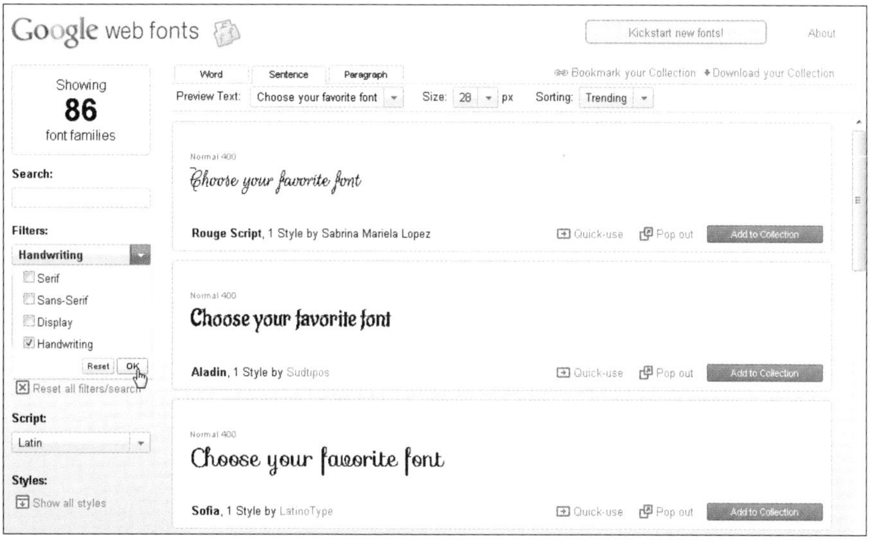

Figure 7-7: Search the Google Web Fonts collection of free fonts for your web pages.

3. **Find a font you like, and then click its Quick-Use link in the bottom-right corner.**

4. **Click the check boxes next to each of the font styles that you want to use on your web page.**

5. **Scroll down the page and select the Latin option (for English).**

   If you need the additional characters for another language, select the Latin Extended option instead.

6. **Scroll further down the page to the blue box with three tabs; click the first tab to link the font to your website.**

Google provides three options: Standard, @import, and Javascript. You find detailed descriptions of all three on the Google site.

7. **Copy the link from the Standard tab field on Google just as you would copy any other text or code from a web page.**

8. **In Dreamweaver, paste the link into the head area of your web page between the open** `<head>` **and close** `</head>` **tags.**

9. **Return to the Google Web Fonts site and at the bottom of the page, copy the name of the font family.**

You find the name of the font family in the Integrate the Fonts into Your CSS area.

10. **In Dreamweaver, paste the name of the font family into the CSS rule where you want to use the font.**

11. **Apply the rule to text in your web page.**

If you use the font in a Tag selector style, such as the `<h1>` tag, when you apply the tag to text, the font will be automatically applied as part of the rule. If you use the font in a class or ID style, the style must then be applied to a tag that surrounds the text, such as a `<p>` tag or a `<div>` tag. You discover more about class, ID, and tag styles in Chapter 5.

12. **Publish the page to a web server and then preview the page in a web browser to see the font.**

Note that you may not see the font displayed in Dreamweaver, even if you use the Live view option. To ensure that the font works on your page, you may need to transfer the page to a web server using FTP and preview the page after it's published online. You find out more about using Dreamweaver's FTP features in Chapter 4.

Using Media Queries to Target Devices

When you design web pages with CSS, you can create one style sheet that's used no matter which device a page is displayed on, or you can create multiple style collections designed specifically for each device. CSS3 adds the capability to use a *media query* to target your style sheets based on the device's screen resolution, aspect ratio, and other distinguishing factors. These additional options are especially useful when you're designing for mobile devices, including the iPhone and iPad.

The capability to target devices in CSS makes it possible to use different style sheets for different types of displays, including desktop and laptop monitors, iPad-size screens, or iPhone-size screens. If you don't use media queries to target your CSS, the iPhone and iPad automatically adjust your designs for you, shrinking or enlarging the page to best fit the screen.

If you truly care about designing for optimum display on the iPhone and iPad, finding out how to use media queries to target your style sheets to each device is a helpful strategy.

Media queries build on the CSS2 capability to target style sheets based on media type. *Media types* enable you to use one style sheet to control how a page appears on a computer monitor, for example, and a second one to change the appearance of that same page when it's sent to a printer. For example, in a print-specific style sheet, you might remove a busy background image or change the text color to give it more contrast on a white sheet of paper.

When you use a media query in CSS3, you can factor in more values than you can with just a media type. These additional values include screen resolution and aspect ratio, which are especially useful when you're designing for mobile devices, such as smartphones and tablets.

Specifying media types and features

A media query is made up of a media type, such as `screen` or `print` (the two most common) and an optional expression that checks for particular features, such as the height or width. The most commonly used media types are

- ✔ `all`: Suitable for all devices
- ✔ `print`: Designed for print preview and for display when a page is printed
- ✔ `screen`: For content displayed on any screen

The Handheld media type is best used only for cell phones and other devices with small screens, limited bandwidth, and monochrome displays that support only bitmapped graphics. iOS devices and most smartphones are categorized as `screen` media types.

Applying styles to your page designs

You can apply style sheets by linking them, importing them, or embedding them as internal styles into the head region of your page's HTML. You can even target devices using inline styles — a handy option if you want to apply a specific rule only to certain devices.

You can use a combination of these options, and you can import, or link, multiple external style sheets to the same web page. After you've defined the media type with the media features you want to target, you specify how the styles should be applied to the page. In the next section, you see an example of how this process works.

Targeting devices when linking external style sheets

The most common (and simplest) way to target devices with media queries is to link multiple external CSS style sheets to each HTML page. The code for the CSS and HTML are saved in separate files, and the `<link>` tag connects the two.

You can link multiple style sheets to one HTML page. For example, you can create one style sheet for styles that format text and another for layout styles. You can also create external style sheets for different purposes, such as one for print and one for screen display. Two big advantages of external style sheets are that they make creating new pages faster and easier and enable you to update styles across many pages at once. *Note:* You can attach more than one external style sheet to the same Web page.

Include the `<link>` tag within the open `<head>` and close `</head>` tags at the top of the HTML code of a web page. The following example includes two style sheets — one designed for a computer screen and the other designed for print:

```
<link rel="stylesheet" type="text/css" media="screen"
      href="screenstyles.css">
<link rel="stylesheet" type="text/css" media="print"
      href="printer.css">
```

You can use a similar technique to target mobile devices, such as the iPhone and iPad. This example links four separate style sheets to the same web page, each designed for optimal display in the iPhone or iPad in landscape and portrait modes. To target other mobile devices, simply change the size to match the device.

```
<!--iPad portrait -->
<link href="css/ipadportrait.css" rel="stylesheet"
      media="only screen and (min-device-width: 768px)
      and (max-device-width: 1024px) and (orientation:
      portrait)">

<!--iPad landscape -->
<link href="css/ipadlandscape.css" rel="stylesheet"
      media="only screen and (min-device-width: 768px)
      and (max-device-width: 1024px) and (orientation:
      landscape)">
```

```
<!--iPhone portrait -->
<link href="css/iphoneportrait.css" rel="stylesheet"
        media="only screen and (min-device-width: 320px)
        and (max-device-width: 480px) and (orientation:
        portrait)">

<!--iPhone landscape -->
<link href="css/iphonelandscape.css" rel="stylesheet"
        media="only screen and (min-device-width: 320px)
        and (max-device-width: 480px) and (orientation:
        landscape)">
```

The comment tags are optional and are included only to make the code easier for humans to read. When you comment code in HTML, you use these tags:

```
<!-- comment here --!>
```

Many browsers now have built-in testing tools, generally called *add-ons* or *extensions,* that you can install, that indicate which CSS rules apply to each element in a web page. These tools and add-ons make testing CSS a lot easier. I recommend the popular, free Firebug add-on, which you can download at www.getfirebug.com.

For a detailed list of CSS selectors and other resources, visit www. DigitalFamily.com/dreamweaver.

8

Saving Time with Templates and More

In This Chapter

▷ Creating pages quickly with a template

▷ Using templates to change to multiple pages automatically

▷ Using the Library for frequently used elements

▷ Designing a web page with the Tracing Image feature

Strive for consistency in all your designs — except when you're trying to be unpredictable. A little surprise here and there can keep your website lively. But most websites work best and are easiest to navigate when they follow a consistent design theme. Case in point: Most readers take for granted that books don't change their designs from page to page and that newspapers don't change headline fonts and logos every day.

Publishers of books and newspapers want to make life easier for their readers, and consistency is one of the primary tools for making sure readers find publications familiar. That doesn't mean you should limit modern web design to what's possible in print, but it does mean we can all learn a thing or two from hundreds of years of print design.

Dreamweaver offers several features to help you develop and maintain a consistent look and feel across your site. In this chapter, you discover three of my favorite Dreamweaver features: templates, Library items, and the Tracing Image feature.

Both the Templates and Library item features help you work more efficiently and make changes to a site faster and easier. These features work well with CSS, and as you discover in this chapter, you can work even more efficiently by combining CSS with templates and library items. After you discover how these features make creating and managing websites faster and easier, you're well on your way to simplifying your work even before you start.

Templates in Dreamweaver make it easy to not only create pages with consistent design elements but also update those pages later when things change — and things always change on the web.

Tracing images are handy design tools, which you can insert into the background of a page to guide your design work. As you discover at the end of this chapter, tracing images aren't displayed in a web browser, but they are useful if you like to create your designs in a program such as Fireworks or Photoshop before you build your web pages in Dreamweaver.

Templating Your Pages

You can choose from many kinds of templates to create websites; and you can find many places on the web where you can buy templates or even download them for free. At its simplest, a *template* is a ready-made page design, usually created in a way that makes it easy to add your own text and images and to create pages based on the template. Some templates are easily customizable so that you can change design elements, such as colors, images, or fonts; others are harder to edit or change.

Not all templates are created equal. Keep in mind that templates designed for a program such as WordPress or Flash won't work in Dreamweaver — you need the right program for each kind of template. (See Chapter 1 for more about the different kinds of templates you can use in all sorts of different websites.)

In this chapter, I focus on Dreamweaver's .dwt templates, which you can use to create pages quickly as well as to make global changes across all the pages created from a template.

Dreamweaver templates are best used in the following scenarios:

✔ **Templates are definitely the way to go when you're creating a number of pages that share the same characteristics, such as the same background color, navigation links, or logo.** I recommend that you use a template anytime you create a site with more than a few pages. For example, you might create a template that includes your logo, a row of links at the top and bottom of each page, and styles for the site's main text colors and fonts, such as the template shown in Figure 8-1. After you create a template with all these features, you can use it as the basis for all the other pages in your site, such as the page shown in Figure 8-2. This approach enables you to quickly and easily create a series of pages that share the same navigation, logo, and so on. Best of all, if you ever decide to change one of these elements, such as your logo, you can change it once in the template and automatically update all the pages created from the template in your site.

✔ **If you want to use different design elements in different sections, you can create more than one template for a site.** For example, if you're creating a website for a bed-and-breakfast inn, you might create one template for all the pages where you want to show off the rooms in the inn and another for a collection of pages that feature great places to hike in the area.

When creating multiple templates for a website, you may want to use a *nested* template, a template whose design and editable regions are based on another template. For example, you can create a main template for elements that appear on every page across an entire site, such as navigation bar. Then add to the main template several secondary nested templates that have design variations for each section of a site.

✔ **Templates are valuable when you're working with a team of people with varying skill levels.** Say you're building a site for a pet store and want to let the employees update their own pet stories without messing up the page design. The fact that templates have locked regions can protect the most important elements of a page, making it easy for sales staff to add new information without accidentally breaking navigation elements or other consistent features. You can also design templates that work with Adobe Contribute, a much simpler and less expensive program, to make it easier for people who are not web designers to update a website. (See the nearby sidebar, "Easily update Dreamweaver sites with Adobe Contribute.")

The most powerful aspect of Dreamweaver's template feature is the capability to make global changes to every page created from a template. Even if you're working alone on a site, this aspect of templates can save hours (or even days) of time as the site grows and changes over time.

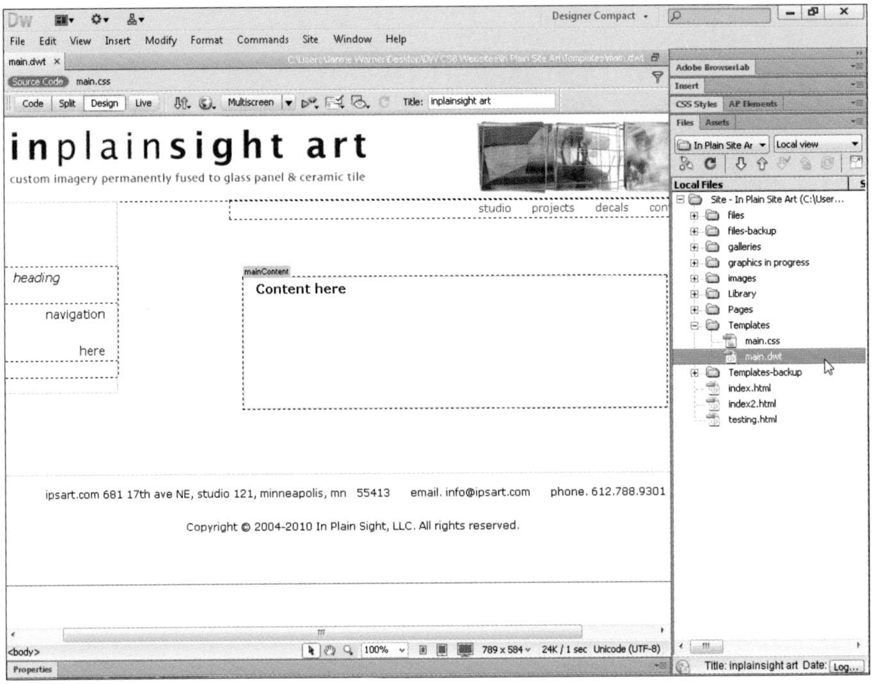

Artwork by Amy Baur, inplainsightart.com

Figure 8-1: You can create a simple template page, such as this one, and then use it to create many similar pages, such as the one shown in Figure 8-2.

Easily update Dreamweaver sites with Adobe Contribute

Adobe Contribute is a program that was created so that people who don't know much about web design can easily *contribute* to a website. Contribute works well not as a standalone program but as a kind of assistant to Dreamweaver, or better said, as the ideal tool for an assistant, such as your client's assistant who may need to update the website after it's built in Dreamweaver. Adobe has carefully integrated a number of features in Contribute that can be set up in Dreamweaver to make that collaboration work smoothly.

For example, using Dreamweaver's .dwt template features, you can designate areas of each page that can be edited by users of Contribute. You can also lock sections of a page so that they can't be edited in Contribute, which is a great way to protect elements you don't want changed, such as logos and navigation links, while making it easy for contributors to edit text and images in designated areas.

If you're working with other developers of a site who use Contribute, make sure you select the Enable Contribute Compatibility check box in the Contribute category of the Site Setup dialog box, covered in Chapter 4.

Figure 8-2: Consistent elements, such as the logo and navigation links, should remain the same while the main area of the page can vary dramatically from page to page.

Creating Templates

Creating a template is as easy as creating any other file in Dreamweaver. You can create an HTML Template page much as you would any other page by using the New Document dialog box. You can also turn any existing page into a template by choosing File⇨Save As and saving the file in the Templates folder.

Dreamweaver templates are distinguished by the extension .dwt (Dreamweaver Web Template), and by their location in the directory structure. Dreamweaver template files must be stored in a special folder named Templates (with a capital *T*) at the root level of the site.

When you create a template for the first time in a website, Dreamweaver automatically creates a Templates folder in your local site folder and stores all your .dwt template files in this folder. Templates must be kept in this common Templates folder and the folder must be kept at the top level or root level of your website (meaning you can't move the Templates folder into another folder) for the automated features in Dreamweaver to work properly.

Creating a new Dreamweaver template

You create a new template in Dreamweaver using the same New Document dialog box you use to create any other type of page. To create a Dreamweaver template, follow these steps:

1. **Choose File⇨New.**

   The New Document dialog box opens.

2. **In the list on the left, click the Blank Template option, as shown in Figure 8-3.**

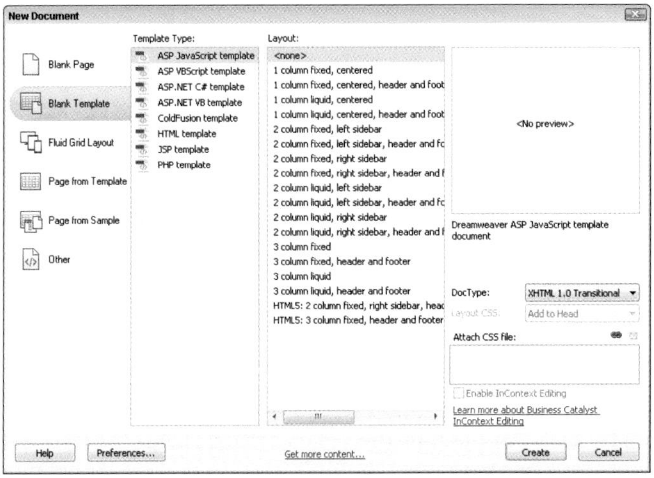

Figure 8-3: The Blank Template panel displays all the types of templates you can create.

3. **In the Template Type list, choose HTML Template.**

   In this example, I'm creating a new HTML page template, which will enable me to take advantage of template features without using the programming code required in the other template options. You can also choose from a variety of template options, including templates for ASP (Active Server Pages), ColdFusion, JSP (Java Server Pages), and PHP (a recursive acronym for Hypertext Preprocessor). These file types are used when creating dynamic websites and require more advanced programming than HTML.

4. **In the Layout area, choose <none> to create a blank page or select a predesigned CSS layout.**

   Dreamweaver's many CSS layout options, covered in Chapter 6, provide a great head start to creating a new page design. In this example, I selected a CSS layout as the basis for my page design.

5. Click the Create button.

A new blank template is created and opens in the main work area, and the New Document dialog box closes.

6. Choose File➪Save.

If you haven't disabled the warning (stating that the template doesn't have any editable regions and asking whether you really want to save it), click Yes to continue. You find instructions for creating editable regions in Step 10.

7. Click OK to save the page as is for now.

The Save window appears with the Templates folder open. If you don't already have a folder named Templates in your local site folder, Dreamweaver will create one for you when you create your first template.

To work properly, Dreamweaver templates must be saved in a folder named Templates in your local site folder. If you change the folder name or move the Templates folder into a subfolder, your templates will no longer work properly.

8. Create a design for the page by adding images, text, and other elements as you would in any other Dreamweaver file.

You find instructions for adding all these features to your pages throughout this book. Again, remember that you create a page design in a template just like you would in any other web page.

9. To create an editable region:

a. Select any image, text block, or content area.

Often the best option is to select an entire area of a page so that everything in that section becomes editable. If you've designed your pages with <div> tags and CSS, as covered in Chapter 6, a good option is to select the <div> tag for an entire section, such as the <div> tag styled with the mainContent class style that I've selected in this example.

A handy way to select a section surrounded by a <div> tag is to place your cursor anywhere in that area of the page, and then use the tag selector at the bottom of the workspace to select the <div> tag.

b. Choose Insert➪Template Objects➪Editable Region (as shown in Figure 8-4).

The New Editable Region dialog box opens.

c. Give the new editable region a name.

I recommend something that identifies the type of content it is, such as *headline* or *main-content*. The region you define as editable becomes an area that can be changed in any page created from the template. You can have multiple editable regions in one template.

Each editable region must have a different name; names can't use spaces or special characters, but underscores and hyphens are okay.

d. Click OK.

An aqua blue box (with an aqua blue tab at the top left of the box) surrounds the editable region (refer to Figure 8-1). The name you entered into the New Editable Region dialog box appears on the tab.

10. **When you finish designing the page and add all the editable regions you want, choose File⇨Save to save your template.**

When you save a new template page or you save an existing page as a template, Dreamweaver automatically adds the .dwt extension and saves the file into the Templates folder.

If you save a template before you specify any editable regions, Dreamweaver gives you a warning because templates aren't useful without editable regions. You don't have to create editable regions before you save a template, but you can't make any changes in any pages created from a template until you create one or more editable regions. You can always go back and add editable regions later. Saving your work before you create editable regions is generally good practice.

Figure 8-4: Make a selected element an editable region by using the Insert menu.

Saving any page as a template

Sometimes you get partway through designing a page before you realize that you'll probably want more pages that are similar. If you turn the page into a template, you can create the rest of the pages a lot more efficiently. Similarly, you may want to turn a page that someone else designed into a template that you can use throughout your website. No matter the page's origin, creating a template from an existing page is almost as easy as creating a template from scratch.

To save a page as a template, follow these steps:

1. **Open the page that you want to turn into a template.**

   Choose File➪Open and browse to find your file. Or open the site in the Files panel and double-click the file to open it.

2. **Choose File➪Save as Template, as shown in Figure 8-5.**

   The Save dialog box appears.

Artwork by Amy Baur, inplainsightart.com

Figure 8-5: You can save any HTML page as a template.

3. **In the Site drop-down list, choose a site.**

The menu lists all the sites you've set up in Dreamweaver. By default, the site you've set up and opened in the Files panel is selected when the dialog box opens. If you're working on a new site or haven't yet set up your site, flip to Chapter 2 for information on the site setup process.

You can use the Save as Template option to save a page as a template into any defined site, which makes it possible to save a page that you design for one site as a template in another site.

4. **In the Save As text box, type a name for the template.**

You don't have to add a description. However, if you're working on a big site with many templates, descriptions can help you keep track of which templates go with which sections of your site.

5. **Click the Save button.**

If you haven't disabled the warning (stating that the template doesn't have any editable regions and asking whether you really want to save it), click Yes to continue.

Note that the file now has the .dwt extension, indicating that it's a template.

6. **Click OK in the Dreamweaver dialog box that appears to update links in the template.**

Because your original file probably wasn't saved in the Templates folder, any links to other pages or images must be updated when the file is saved. After you click OK, Dreamweaver corrects any links in the file as it saves the file in the Templates folder.

7. **Make any changes that you want, and then choose File⇨Save.**

You edit a template just as you edit any other page in Dreamweaver.

8. **To create an editable region:**

a. **Select any content area, image, or text.**

b. **Choose Insert⇨Template Object⇨Editable Region (refer to Figure 8-4).**

The New Editable Region dialog box opens.

c. Give the new region a name.

You can name the region anything you like — just don't use spaces or punctuation. The region you define as editable becomes an area that can be changed in any page created from the template. You can create multiple editable regions in any template.

d. Click OK.

The editable region is enclosed in a highlighted area with a tab at the top left, identified by the name you gave the region.

9. **When you finish designing the page, choose File⊏Save to save your completed template.**

Making attributes editable

In addition to making any element in a page editable, you can also make the attributes of any element editable. This step is necessary only if you want to make an attribute editable when the tag itself is not editable (for example, when you want the ability to change the background image of a `<div>` tag but not the `<div>` tag itself).

Editable attributes are especially handy when you want to identify the open page of a site by changing the color of the link to that page. For example, suppose that all your links are blue in the navigation bar, but you want each page link to change to the color red when that page is open. By making only the color attribute of the link editable, you can change the blue color of, say, the About Us link to red when a visitor is on the corresponding About Us page.

To create editable attributes in a template, follow these steps:

1. **In any Dreamweaver template, select an item to which you want to give an editable attribute.**

   In the example shown in Figure 8-6, I selected the navigation link About Us and am in the process of making one of the its attributes editable.

   To make sure you've selected a link and not just the text, click anywhere in the linked text and then use the Tag Selector at the bottom of the workspace to select the `<a>` tag.

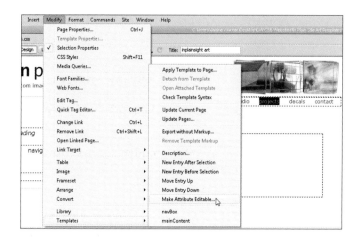

Figure 8-6: Select any link, image, or other tag and use the Modify menu to make the attributes of that tag editable.

2. **Choose Modify➪Templates➪Make Attribute Editable.**

   The Editable Tag Attributes dialog box appears, as shown in Figure 8-7.

3. **From the Attribute drop-down list, choose the attribute you want to make editable.**

   The attribute options vary depending on whether you select an image, a link, text, or another element on the page.

   In this example, I selected the HREF attribute to be able to change the color of the link, as shown in Figure 8-7. The link tag is one of the most confusing

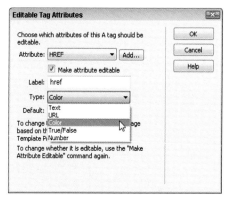

Figure 8-7: Identify which attributes you want to make editable.

HTML tags because it's known as the anchor tag and displayed as just an <a> in the Tag Selector. However, the full tag is <a href>, and in the Editable Tag Attributes dialog box, it's identified as HREF.

If the attribute you want isn't listed, click the Add button and then enter the name of the attribute.

4. **Click to select the Make Attribute Editable check box.**

   The options for that attribute become active in the bottom of the dialog box.

5. **In the Type drop-down list, select an attribute type.**

As shown in Figure 8-7, the link tag has several attributes. I selected Color in this example.

6. **Click OK to make the attribute editable and close the dialog box.**

To change an editable attribute in a page created from a template, follow these steps:

1. **Create a new page from the template, or open any page that was created with the template.**

2. **Choose Modify⇨Template properties.**

The Template Properties dialog box opens, listing any editable attributes.

3. **Select the attribute you want to edit to see your options in the bottom of the dialog box.**

To change the color of the link, which I set up as an editable attribute in the preceding steps, I selected href to display the Template properties. I then clicked the color swatch in the bottom left of the Template Properties dialog box and selected a color.

4. **Click OK to close the dialog box and save the setting.**

The new setting is applied when the dialog box closes. In this example, the color of the About Us link changed to the new color after the dialog box closed.

Creating a New Page from a Template

After you create a template, it's time to put it to use. You can use one template to create all the pages in your website or create different templates for different sections. For example, in the site featured in this chapter — at www.inplainsightart.com — I created two templates, one for the main pages and another for the gallery pages. Whether you create one template or a collection of templates for your site, creating a new page from a template is similar to creating any other page in Dreamweaver.

To use a template to create a new page, follow these steps:

1. **Choose File⇨New.**

The New Document window opens.

2. **In the list on the left, click the Page from Template option, as shown in Figure 8-8.**

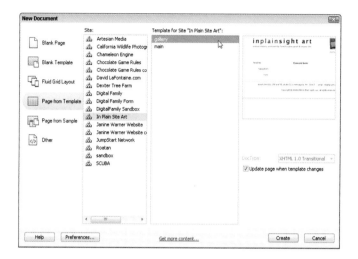

Figure 8-8: Preview and select any template saved in any defined website to create a new page.

3. **In the Site list in the middle of the page, choose the name of the site that contains a template you want to use.**

   The templates in the selected site appear in the Template for Site section just to the right of the Site list in the New Document window (refer to Figure 8-8).

4. **In the Template for Site list, select the template you want to use.**

   Note that when you click the name of a template, a preview of the selected template appears on the far right of the New Document window. In the example shown in Figure 8-8, I selected the gallery page template.

5. **Click the Create button.**

   A new page is created from the template and appears in the main work area.

6. **Edit any region of the page that's editable with Dreamweaver's regular editing features and save the file as you would save any other HTML page.**

When you create new pages from a template, you can change only the editable regions in each file created from the template. When you edit a template, only the regions that aren't defined as editable can be used to make global changes to all the pages created from the template. In the template shown in this example, only the main content area of the design can be edited in the page created from the template. The banner area at the top, the navigation on the left, and the footer with the copyright and address at the bottom are all locked regions that can be edited only in the template itself.

Making Global Changes with Templates

The great advantage of templates is that you can automatically apply changes to all the pages created with a template by altering the original template. For example, say the navigation links are an uneditable region in a template, and I decide to add a new section to the site. I can add a new navigation link to that section by editing the row of links at the top of the page in the template, and the new link is added to all the pages in the site created from that template.

To update files in a site that were created from a template, follow these steps:

1. **Open the template file.**

   Note that template files are distinguishable by the `.dwt` extension and are saved in the Templates folder.

   If you're not sure which template was used to create a page, its name appears in the top-right corner of the page (see the upcoming Figure 8-9). If you don't see the template name, choose View⇨Visual Aids⇨Invisible Elements to turn on the feature that displays the template name. Alternatively, you can open a template from any page created from a template, by following the steps in the next section.

2. **Use Dreamweaver's editing features to make any changes you want to the template.**

   Remember that only changes to uneditable regions are updated automatically. In this example, the logo and navigation elements are locked regions and can be edited to make global changes. Thus, if I add a new link to the row of links at the top of the page, it will be added to all the pages created from the template.

3. **Choose File⇨Save.**

   The Update Template Files dialog box appears, as shown in Figure 8-9, listing all the pages created from the template.

4. **Click the Update button to modify all pages listed in the Update Template Files dialog box.**

   (Click the Don't Update button to leave these pages unchanged.) If you click Update, Dreamweaver automatically changes all the pages listed in the Update Template Files dialog box to reflect any changes made to uneditable regions of the template.

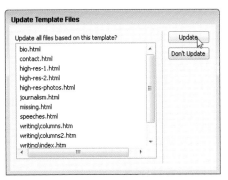

Figure 8-9: You can update all files created from a template automatically.

Opening a template from any page created from a template

If you're not sure which template was used to create a page, you can open the template while you have the page open, make changes to the template, and update all the pages created with it by following these steps:

1. **Open a document that uses the template that you want to change.**

2. **Choose Modify➪Templates➪Open Attached Template, as shown in Figure 8-10.**

   The template opens.

3. **Use Dreamweaver's regular editing functions to modify the template as you would edit any page or template.**

4. **Choose File➪Save.**

   The Update Template Files dialog box appears (refer to Figure 8-9).

Artwork by Amy Baur, inplainsightart.com

Figure 8-10: Open an attached template from within any page created from a template.

5. **Click the Update button to modify all the pages listed in the Update Template Files dialog box.**

    (Click the Don't Update button to leave these pages unchanged.) If you choose Update, Dreamweaver automatically changes all the pages listed in the Update Template Files dialog box.

    If you edit a template and have an open page that was created from that template, the changes are automatically applied to the open page but you need to save the page before closing it to save the changes.

    You can also apply changes to all the pages created from a template by using the Update Pages option. To do so, open the template, and then make and save your changes without applying those changes to pages created with the template. Anytime later, choose Modify⊏>Templates⊏>Update Pages to apply the update.

Reusing Elements with the Library Feature

The Library feature isn't a common feature in other web design programs, so the concept may be new to you even if you've been developing websites for a while. The Library feature is handy when you have a single element you want to reuse on many pages, such as a copyright statement you want to appear at the bottom of each page or even something as complex as a row of navigation links.

A *Library item* is a snippet of code that can contain almost anything, including images, videos, text, and links. You can't, however, use features created with Dreamweaver's Behaviors or Spry menu, which use JavaScript.

After you save a section of code in the Library, you can insert it into any page with drag-and-drop ease. If you ever need to change a Library item (by adding or changing a link, for example), simply edit the stored Library item, and Dreamweaver automatically updates the contents of the Library item on any or all pages where it appears throughout the site.

Like templates, Library items are a great way to store frequently used items and make global changes to those items if you need to update them in the future. You have more flexibility with Library items than templates because they're elements you can place anywhere on any page, even multiple times. Libraries aren't shared among sites the way templates are, but you can copy and paste the same Library item from one site into another.

Library items can't contain their own style sheets because the code for styles can appear only as part of the head area of an HTML file. You can, however, attach an external style sheet to a Library item to see how the styles affect the display of the Library item, but the same styles must be available on each page where the Library item is used for the styles to be applied. (For more on style sheets, see Chapters 5, 6, and 7.)

Creating and Using Library Items

The following sections show you the steps for creating a Library item, adding one to a page, and editing and updating a Library item across multiple pages. For these steps to work properly, you must do them in order. Before creating or using Library items, you must first set up the site and open it in the Files panel. (See Chapter 2 for instructions on setting up a site in Dreamweaver.)

Creating a Library item within an existing page works well because you can see how the item looks before you add it to the Library. You can edit an item after it's in the Library, but it may not look just as it will on a web page. For example, Library items don't include <body> tags when they're saved in the Library, so link colors are displayed as default blue when viewed in the Library, even if the link colors have been changed to, say, purple in the <body> tag of the page.

Creating a Library item

To create a Library item that you can use on multiple pages on your site, follow these steps:

1. **Open any existing file that has images, text, or other elements on the page that you want to save as a Library item.**

2. **From this page, select an element or collection of elements that you want to save as a Library item, such as the copyright information that appears at the bottom of this page.**

3. **Choose Modify⇨Library⇨Add Object to Library.**

   The Library Assets panel opens and displays any existing Library items. Your new Library item appears as *Untitled.*

4. **Click to select Untitled and replace it by typing a new name as you would name any file in Explorer on a PC or the Finder on a Mac.**

   When you create a Library item, Dreamweaver automatically saves it to the Library. Naming Library items makes them easier to identify when you want to use them. You can then easily apply Library items to any new or existing page in your site by following the steps in the next section.

Adding a Library item to a page

You can easily add elements from the Library to your pages by simply dragging them from the Assets panel to the page. When you add a Library item to a page, the content is inserted into the document and a connection is established between the content on the page and the item in the Library. This connection is important because it enables you to edit the Library item later and apply the changes to all pages where the item appears, but it also means that you can't edit the item on the page where it's inserted. You must edit Library items from within the Library, as you see shortly.

To add a Library item to a page, follow these steps:

1. **Create a new document in Dreamweaver or open any existing file.**

2. **From the Files panel, click the Assets tab, and then click the Library icon.**

   The Library opens in the Assets panel (see Figure 8-11).

3. **Drag an item from the Library to the Document window.**

   Alternatively, you can select an item in the Library and click the Insert button. The item automatically appears on the page. After you insert a Library item on a page, you can use any of Dreamweaver's formatting features to position it on the page.

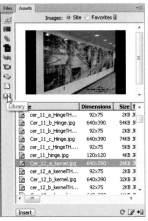

Artwork by Amy Baur, inplainsightart.com

Figure 8-11: The Assets panel provides access to the Library items list.

Highlighting Library items

Library items are highlighted to distinguish them from other elements on a page. In the Preferences dialog box, you can customize the highlight color for Library items as well as show or hide the highlight color. To change or hide Library highlighting, follow these steps:

1. **Choose Edit↷Preferences (Windows) or Dreamweaver↷ Preferences (Mac).**

   The Preferences dialog box appears.

2. **In the Category section on the left, select Highlighting.**

3. **Click the color box to select a color for Library items and then select the Show box to display the Library highlight color on your pages.**

   Leave the box blank if you don't want to display the highlight color.

4. **Click OK to close the Preferences dialog box.**

Making global changes with Library items

The Dreamweaver Library feature saves time because you can make changes to Library items and automatically apply those changes to any or all pages where the Library item appears. To edit a Library item, follow these steps:

1. **From the Files panel, click the Assets tab and then click the Library icon.**

   The Library opens in the Assets panel (refer to Figure 8-11).

2. **Double-click any item listed in the Library to open the item.**

   Dreamweaver opens a new window where you can edit the Library item.

   Because the Library item is just a snippet of code, it won't have a <body> tag in which to specify background, link, or text colors. Don't worry about this: The Library item acquires the right settings from the tags on the page where you insert it.

3. **Change the Library item as you would edit any element in Dreamweaver.**

   For example, you can change a link, edit the wording of text, change the font or size, and even add images, text, and other elements.

4. **Choose File⟳Save to save changes to the original item.**

   The Update Library Items dialog box opens, displaying a list of all the pages where the Library item appears.

5. **To apply the changes you made to the Library item on all listed pages, click the Update button. If you don't want to apply the changes to all the pages where the Library item appears, click the Don't Update button.**

   If you clicked the Update button, the Update Pages dialog box appears and shows the progress of the updating. You can stop the update from this dialog box, if necessary.

   If you want to create a new Library item based on an existing one without altering the original, follow Steps 1–3, and in place of Step 4, choose File⟳Save As and give the item a new name.

Editing one instance of a Library item

If you want to alter a Library item on a specific page or on a few pages, you can override the automated Library feature by detaching it, or breaking the link between the original item in the Library and the item inserted into the page.

After you break a connection, you can no longer update that page's Library item automatically.

To detach an instance of a Library item so that it can be edited independently, follow these steps:

1. **Open any file that contains a Library item and select the Library item.**

   The Property inspector displays the Library item options, as shown in Figure 8-12.

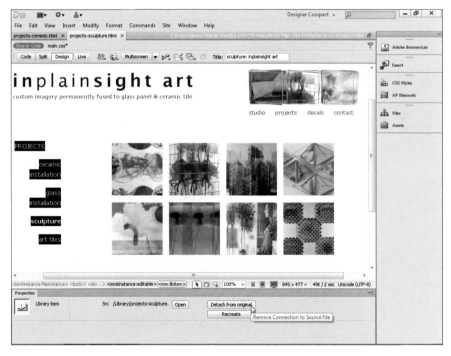

Artwork by Amy Baur, inplainsightart.com

Figure 8-12: You can detach a Library item in the Property inspector.

2. **Click the Detach from Original button.**

A warning message appears, letting you know that if you proceed with detaching the Library item from the original, you can no longer update this occurrence of it when the original is edited.

3. **Click OK to detach the Library item.**

Using a Tracing Image to Guide Your Design Work

The Tracing Image feature is especially popular among designers. The concept dates back to the earliest days of design. The Tracing Image feature enables you to use graphics as guides for your page designs, much as you might copy a cartoon through thin transparent paper.

The Tracing Image feature is ideal for people who like to first create a design in a program, such as Photoshop or Fireworks, and then model their web page after it. By using the Tracing Image feature, you can insert any web-ready image into the background of any Dreamweaver page. Then you can position `<div>` tags or insert tables or other elements on top of the tracing image, making it easier to re-create your design in Dreamweaver. You can use JPG, GIF, or PNG images as tracing images and you can create them in any graphics application that supports these formats.

Although the tracing image appears in the background of a page, it doesn't take the place of a background image and won't appear in a browser.

To add a tracing image to your page, follow these steps:

1. **Create a new page or open an existing page in Dreamweaver.**

2. **Choose View➪Tracing Image➪Load.**

The Select Image Source dialog box opens.

3. **Select a JPEG image you want to serve as your tracing image and click OK.**

The Page Properties dialog box opens with the Tracing Image options category selected, as shown in Figure 8-13.

4. **Click the Browse button to locate the image you want to use as a tracing image.**

The Select Image Source dialog box appears.

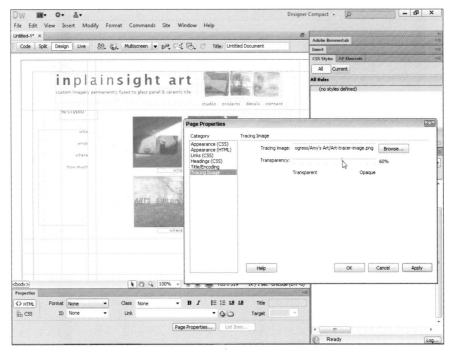

Artwork by Amy Baur, inplainsightart.com

Figure 8-13: The Page Properties dialog box lets you set the options for a tracing image, which you can use as a guide when designing your page.

5. **Click the image you want to trace from, and then click Apply to preview how the image looks behind the page.**

6. **Set the opacity for the tracing image with the Transparency slider.**

   Lowering the transparency level causes the tracing image to appear faded, which makes distinguishing between the tracing image and content on the page easy. You can set the transparency level to suit your preferences, but somewhere around 50 percent works well with most images.

7. **Click OK.**

   The tracing image appears in the Document window, and the dialog box closes.

You have a few other options with the Tracing Image feature. Choose View⇨Tracing Image to reveal the following options:

- ✔ **Show:** Hides the tracing image if you want to check your work without the image but don't want to remove it.

- ✔ **Align with Selection:** Enables you to automatically line up the tracing image with a selected element on a page.

- ✔ **Adjust Position:** Enables you to use the arrow keys or enter X, Y coordinates to control the position of the tracing image behind the page.

- ✔ **Reset Position:** Resets the tracing image to 0, 0 on the X, Y coordinates.

- ✔ **Load**: Enables you to add or replace a tracing image.

After you have the tracing image in place, you can use it as a guide while you design your page. Because the tracing image is behind the page, it won't interfere with your design work, and you can add any elements over the tracing image that you could add to any other web page. Use the tracing image as a reference as you insert and position <div> tags, images, and other elements.

9

Coming to the HTML Table

*1*n the early days of web design, HTML tables offered one of the only options for creating complex page layouts. By splitting and merging table cells and using them as containers for text and images, web developers could create intricate page designs despite the limits of HTML.

Using tables to create designs was far from ideal, and most of us found this solution frustrating. But because tables were all we had, we had to be clever, and we often resorted to imperfect tricks, such as

✔ Using a clear GIF to control spacing (see the sidebar "The transparent, or clear, GIF trick," later in this chapter).

✔ Using carefully designed background images to add graphic elements and the illusion of layers to specific parts of a page.

✔ Inserting tables within tables to create ever-more elaborate designs.

If you implemented all these tricks, you could use tables to position text, images, and other elements, anywhere you wanted on a page (well, almost anywhere). For example, you could use a table to align two columns of text side by side and then merge the cells at the top to create a wider space for a headline across the top to create a two-column layout like you might see in a newspaper or magazine. Because you could make the borders of a table invisible, you could use tables to create page designs without the table itself being visible on the page. Back in the day, we were all rather proud of ourselves for figuring out these clever work-arounds.

Today CSS has completely changed the way designers create web pages, and tables are no longer the recommended solution for creating page layouts, except when you need to format tabular data, such as a list of numbers you would display in columns and rows in a spreadsheet or data exported from a database.

Today, most professional designers use CSS to create overall page designs because pages designed with CSS download faster, are easier to update, and are more flexible and accessible than tables ever were. Chapters 5 and 6 are dedicated to showing you how to design web pages with CSS; Chapter 7 introduces you to the latest developments in web design with CSS3, which provides design options we only dreamed of back in the days when we created page layouts with tables.

In this chapter, you discover how to create and edit tables in Dreamweaver in the few cases where tables are still the best solution — when you need to format and sort tabular data in columns and rows. Even though tables are no longer *recommended* for creating page layouts, you may find this chapter helpful if you're working on a site that was designed the old-fashioned way.

Creating HTML Tables

Tables are made up of three basic elements: rows, columns, and cells. If you've ever worked with a spreadsheet program, you're probably familiar with tables. Working with tabular data in HTML tables is similar to working with a spreadsheet: In most cases, you'll want to create a row of headings along the side or top of a table and then create columns and rows that can be populated with text, images, and other data.

The code behind an HTML table is a complex series of `<tr>`, `<th>`, and `<td>` tags that indicate table rows, table header, and table data cells, respectively. Figuring out how to type those tags so that they create a series of little boxes on a web page was never an intuitive process. If you wanted to merge or split cells to create rows or columns with varying numbers of cells, you faced a truly complex challenge.

Thank the cybergurus at Adobe for Dreamweaver, which makes this process easy. With Dreamweaver, you can easily

✔ Create tables and modify both the appearance and the structure of a table by simply clicking and dragging its edges.

✔ Add any type of content to a cell, such as images, text, and multimedia files — even nested tables.

✔ Use the Property inspector to merge and split cells, add color to the background or borders, and change the vertical and horizontal alignment of elements within a cell.

You can create tables in Standard or Expanded mode in Dreamweaver:

✔ **Expanded mode,** shown in Figure 9-1, literally expands the borders and table cells. The added space makes editing content within tables easier because you can easily select inside and around tables. However, the added space also changes the way the table appears in Dreamweaver, which can be confusing because the space isn't visible when you view the page in a browser.

✔ **Standard mode,** as shown in Figure 9-2, is more consistent with how tables will appear in a browser. You should generally do most of your table editing, especially resizing and moving tables, in this mode.

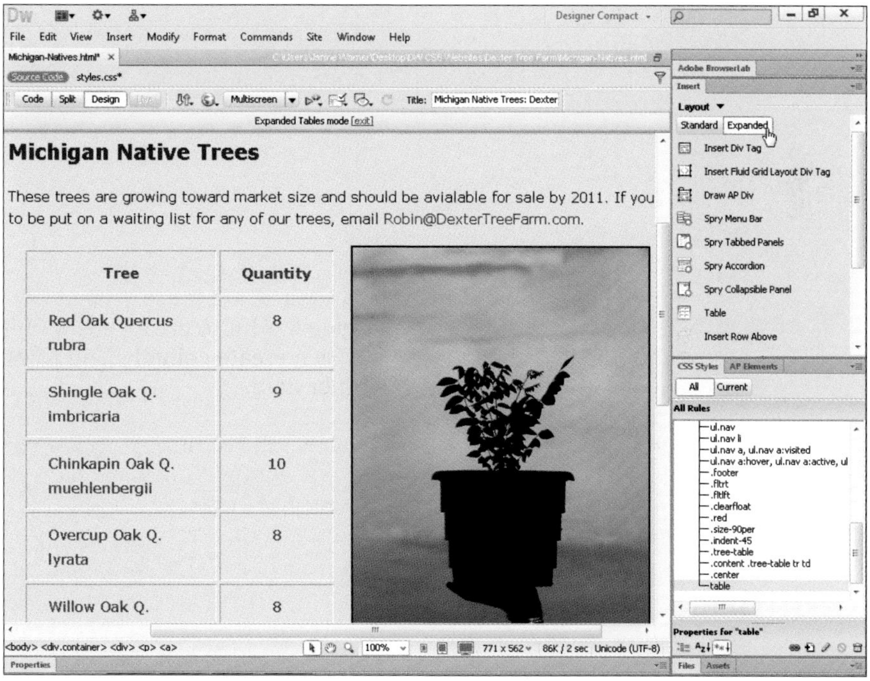

Photo by Janine Warner

Figure 9-1: In Expanded mode, Dreamweaver adds space around table cells, making it easier to select and edit the content within a table.

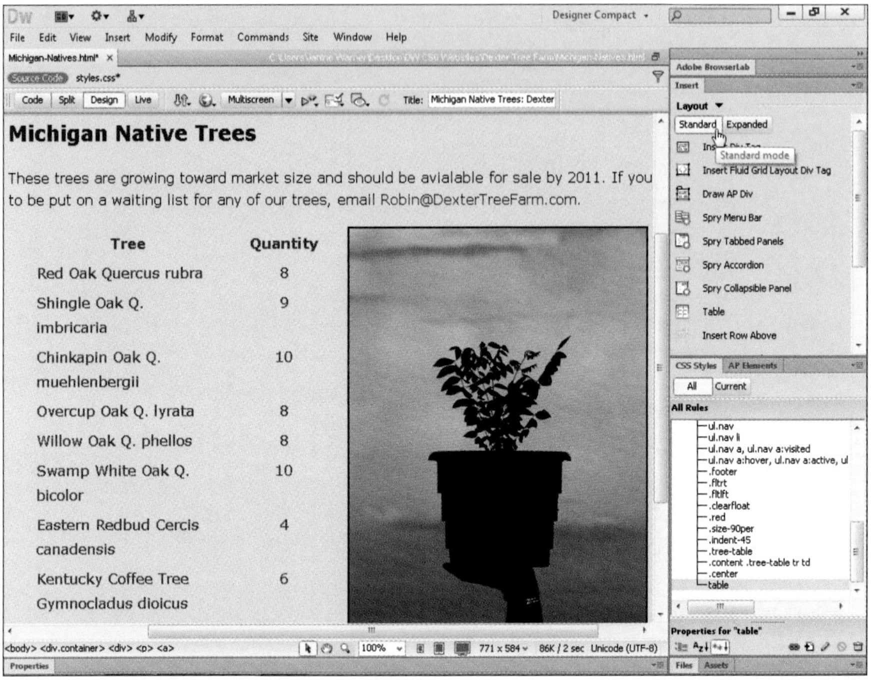

Figure 9-2: In Standard mode, Dreamweaver's table display is more consistent with how the layout will look in a web browser.

You can switch between these two modes by clicking the Standard and Expanded mode buttons in the Layout menu bar at the top of the work area, as shown in Figures 9-1 and 9-2. Alternatively, you can switch between modes by choosing Choose View➪Table Mode➪Standard Mode or Choose View➪Table Mode➪Expanded Tables Mode.

Creating Tables in Standard Mode

Although Expanded mode is useful for selecting and editing the contents of a table, Standard mode is best for creating tables and editing table properties, such as the width of cells and the borders that surround them. The following tips can help you create a table, and the sections that follow explain how to further refine it:

✔ **You can insert a table by choosing Insert➪Table or by clicking the Table icon in the Common or Layout Insert panel.**

✔ **When you insert a new table, the Table dialog box, as shown in Figure 9-3, makes it easy to specify many table settings at once.** For example,

I selected the Top option under Header to create a row of Header cells across the top of my table. Don't worry about perfecting the settings; you can always change these options later.

✔ **You can edit all the table options, except the Accessibility options, in the Property inspector.** When you select a table or cell, the attributes appear in the Property inspector at the bottom of the work area. Click the border of any table to select the entire table, and the Property inspector displays the table options, as shown in Figure 9-4. To view all the options, click the expander arrow in the lower-right corner of the Property inspector. (All these options are described in the next section.)

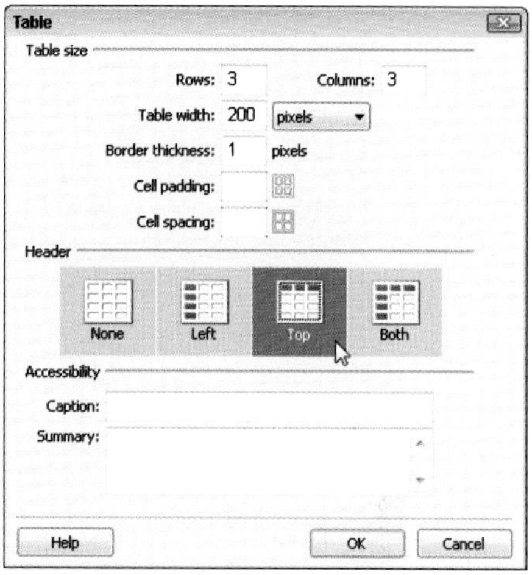

Figure 9-3: When you insert a table into a web page, specify the table's settings here.

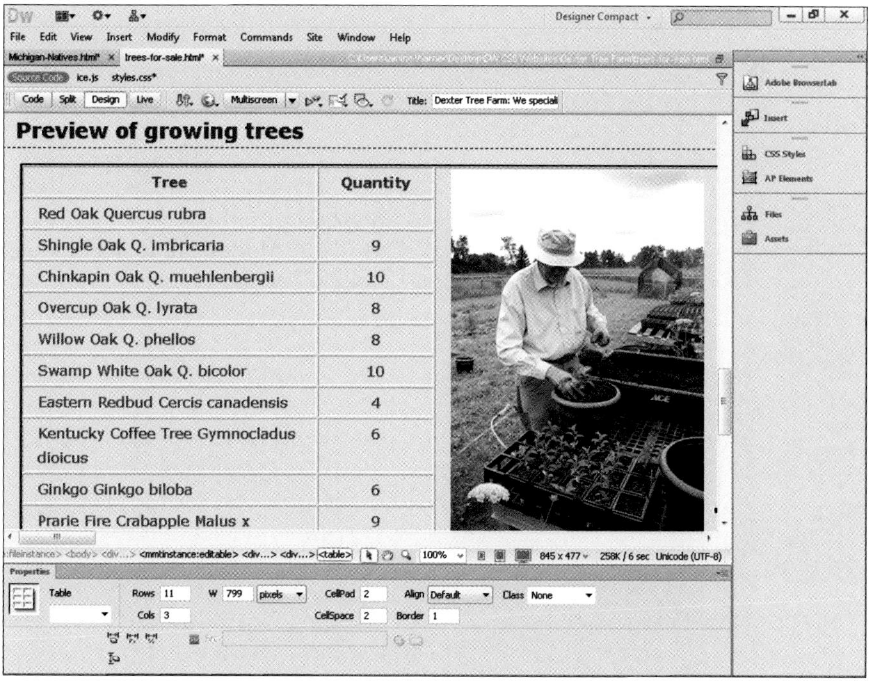

Photo by Janine Warner

Figure 9-4: The Property inspector displays Table properties when a table is selected.

✔ **Select a table with the Select Table command.** Sometimes selecting the entire table and not just an individual cell is tricky. If you're having trouble selecting the table, simply place your cursor anywhere in the table and choose Modify➪Table➪Select Table.

To create tables without missing any important steps, check out "Following a workflow for creating tables," at the end of this section. The steps there give you a framework for using Dreamweaver's table options from start to finish.

Choosing your table's appearance

When you select a table in Dreamweaver, the Property inspector gives you access to the following options for customizing your table's appearance:

✔ **Table:** Provides a text area where you can enter a name for a table. This name, or ID, is useful for targeting the table in scripts.

✔ **Rows:** Displays the number of rows in the table. You can alter the size of the table by changing the number. Be careful, though: If you enter a number that is smaller than the number of rows in your table, Dreamweaver deletes the bottom rows — contents and all.

✔ **Cols:** Displays the number of columns in the table. You can alter the size of the table by changing the number. Again, if you enter a number less than the number of columns in your table, Dreamweaver deletes the columns on the right side of the table — contents and all.

✔ **W (width):** Displays the width of the table. You can alter the width by changing the number. You can specify the width as a percentage or a value in pixels. Values expressed as a percentage increase or decrease the table's size relative to the size of the user's browser window or any enclosing container, such as another table or a `<div>` tag.

Table dimensions expressed as a percentage enable you to create a table that changes in size when the browser window is resized. For example, if you want a table to always take up 75 percent of the browser window, no matter how big the user's monitor or display area, set the size as a percentage. If you want a table to always be the same size regardless of the browser window size, choose pixels rather than percentages for your table width. See the nearby sidebar "How wide should you make a table?" for more help selecting a width that displays well on most browsers.

If a table is inserted inside another container, such as a `<div>` tag or a table with a fixed width, it doesn't change size based on the browser window but is sized based on the container.

Note: Beginning in Dreamweaver CS4, you no longer find an H (height) field. As a best practice, most designers don't specify table height, because the table's contents may change from one visitor to another. For example, the font size of text depends on a user's system and settings.

✓ **CellPad:** Specifies the space between the contents of a cell and its border.

✓ **CellSpace:** Specifies the space between table cells.

✓ **Align:** Controls the alignment of the table on the web page. The options are Default, Left, Center, and Right. As a general rule, the Default setting aligns the table from the left side of the browser window or other container.

✓ **Border:** Controls the size of the border around the table. The larger the number, the thicker the border. If you want the border to be invisible, set it to 0.

✓ **Class:** Provides easy access to style sheet options. (See Chapters 5–7 for more on CSS.)

✓ **Clear and Convert:** The icons in the lower-left area of the Property inspector (click the expander arrow in the lower-right corner to view them) provide these formatting options:

> • **Clear Row Heights** and **Clear Column Widths** enable you to remove all height and width values at one time.
>
> • **Convert Table Widths to Pixels** and **Convert Table Widths to Percents** enable you to automatically change Width settings from percentages to pixels. Pixels specify a fixed width; a percent setting means the browser automatically adjusts the specified percentage of the browser display area.

You can also apply formatting options and change the attributes of any element — such as text, an image, or a multimedia file — within a table cell. To do so, click to select the element and then use the options in the CSS or HTML Property inspector to make your desired changes, just as you would if the element weren't in a table cell. See "Specifying cell options," later in this section, for more details.

Making tables more accessible

A few simple, behind-the-scenes elements can make your tables more accessible to people who are blind or have limited sight and view web pages with screen readers. *Screen readers* are special browsers that read the contents of a web page aloud.

Make sure the table fits the contents

Be aware that table cells automatically adjust to accommodate whatever you insert into them. For example, if you create a cell that's 100 pixels wide and then insert a 300-pixel-wide image, the table cell expands to fit the image. This behavior can cause problems if the overall size of the table isn't set wide enough to accommodate all the objects within the table cells. When you build your tables, be aware of the size of the images and multimedia files you're inserting into cells or you may end up with a mess on your hands.

For example, if you set a table to a total width of 400 pixels and then insert 600 pixels worth of images, the table is forced to adjust in a way that contradicts the settings. Some content may get cut off or expand beyond the desired width of the page layout. Worse yet, the table may not appear the same in all browsers because different browsers try to accommodate these errors in different ways, which can lead to unpredictable results.

One important element is the table header (`<th>`) tag for table headings. The `<th>` tag adds bold formatting and centering to content, and identifies the content as the header of the row or column.

For example, suppose you have a table like the one in the Dexter Tree Farm website, which includes a list of trees and the number of each kind available (refer to Figures 9-1 and 9-2). Identifying text in the top row with the table header tag tells the screen reader to repeat the heading before each tree name and number. Thus, instead of just reading a long list of names and numbers, the screen reader will identify each cell by the name of the header as it reads through the contents.

You don't have to make all your table headings bold and centered just because you use the table header tag. Like any other HTML tag, you can alter the formatting of the `<th>` tag by creating a tag style (as I explain in Chapter 5).

Dreamweaver also includes Accessibility options at the bottom of the Table dialog box when you first insert a new table (refer to Figure 9-3). Here's what those options do:

- **Caption:** If you enter a table caption, it's displayed within the table. You can specify where the caption appears with the Align Caption option.

- **Summary:** The Table Summary doesn't appear in a web browser but prompts a screen reader to describe the table for visitors who can't see the contents of the table. This gives your visitors overall context before they hear the entire table read out loud.

If you don't include these Accessibility settings as you insert your table, you can't go back to a dialog box with these options in Dreamweaver to insert them later. To add a label and summary to a table after you insert it into a page in Dreamweaver, you have to re-create the table or add the code manually in Code view.

Specifying cell options

In addition to changing overall table settings, you can specify options for individual cells within a table. When you select a cell, which you can do by clicking to place the cursor anywhere inside the cell area, the Property inspector changes to display the individual properties for that cell (see Figure 9-5), such as the formatting and alignment of the contents of a particular cell.

Beginning in Dreamweaver CS4, the Property inspector features both HTML and CSS settings. CSS settings are generally preferred and work the same for the contents of a table cell as they do for content anywhere else on a web page. (See Chapters 5–7 for more on using CSS.)

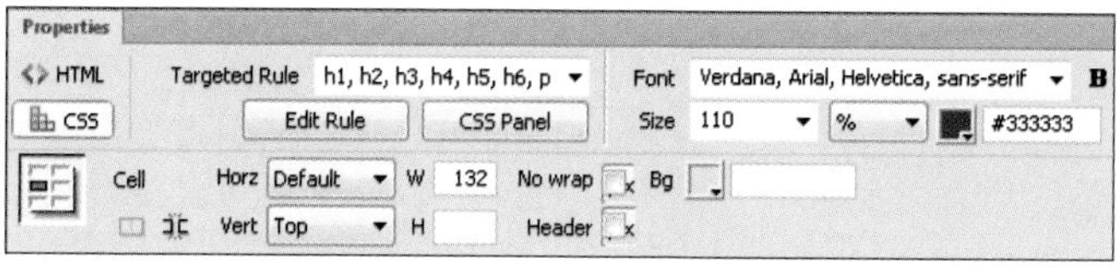

Figure 9-5: The Property inspector (in CSS mode) displays cell properties when <td> or <th> tags are selected.

You can also change multiple cells at the same time. For example, suppose that you want to format some (but not all) cells in your table with a certain background color and style of text. You can apply the same properties to multiple cells by selecting more than one cell at a time before choosing the settings in the Property inspector. Any properties you change in the Property inspector apply to all selected cells. Here are tips for selecting cells:

- **To select adjacent cells,** press the Shift key while clicking to select cells.

- **To select multiple cells that aren't adjacent,** press the Ctrl key (the ⌘ key on the Mac) and click each cell you want to select.

- **If you're having trouble selecting an individual cell because it contains an image,** click the image and then use the ← or → key on your keyboard to move the cursor and deselect the image, which activates the Property inspector and displays the options for that cell.

When one or more adjacent cells are selected, the top half of the Property inspector controls the formatting of text and URLs within the table cells. The lower half of the Property inspector provides the table cell attribute options (refer to Figure 9-5), as follows:

- **Merge Selected cells icon:** Merges two or more cells. To merge cells, you must first select two or more cells by clicking and dragging or by pressing the Shift or Ctrl key while selecting multiple cells.

- **Split Cell into Rows or Columns icon:** Splits one cell into two. When you select this option, a dialog box lets you specify whether you want to split the row (split the cell horizontally) or the column (split the cell vertically). You can then specify the number of columns or rows, which controls how many times the cell divides. Note that you can apply the Split Cell option to only one cell at a time.

  See the section, "Merging and splitting cells" later in this chapter for more details about working with these options.

- **Horz** and **Vert:** Controls the horizontal alignment or vertical alignment, respectively, of the cell contents. See "Aligning table content in columns and rows" later in this section for tips on working with the Horz and Vert alignment options.

- **W and H:** Controls the cell's width or height, respectively.

- **No Wrap:** Prevents word wrapping within the cell. The cell widens to accommodate all text while you type or paste it into a cell. (Normally, the excess text just moves down to the next line and increases the height of the cell.)

- **Header:** Formats a cell's contents by using a header tag, which displays the text in bold and centered by default in most web browsers.

- **Bg (color):** Click in the color well to select a background color from the color palette or enter a hexadecimal color code in the text field. If you use the color palette, the hexadecimal code is entered automatically in the Bg color field. Make sure you include the # sign if you add your own hexadecimal color or the color will not display properly in many browsers.

Although the alignment, color, and formatting options in the Property inspector are handy, using CSS is the preferred option. You learn more about working with CSS and creating styles to alter the appearance of HTML tags, such as the table tags, in Chapters 5–7.

Aligning table content in columns and rows

Clean alignment of elements in columns and rows makes your table neat and easy to read. Achieving that look can be tricky, however, because you don't have as much control in HTML as you have in a program such as Excel, where you can align numbers to the decimal point, for example. In an HTML table, you can align the content of columns to the left, right, or center. The following steps explain the basics of aligning rows and columns in your table (and you find tips for solving common alignment problems, too):

1. **Select the column or row for which you want to change the alignment.**

   Place the cursor in the first cell in the column or row you want to align; then, click and drag to highlight all the columns or rows that you want to change.

2. **Choose an alignment option from the Horz (horizontal) or Vert (vertical) drop-down lists in the Property inspector (refer to Figure 9-5).**

   The content of the cell adjusts to match the selected alignment option.

   Alternatively, you can access many formatting options, including alignment options, by selecting a table and then right-clicking (Windows) or Control-clicking (Mac).

If you follow the preceding steps but table contents still aren't aligning, try the following tips:

- **If you use the same number of digits after the decimal point in all your numbers, you can get them to line up in a column.** For example, if one price is $12.99 and another is $14, express the latter as $14.00; then, when you right align, the numbers line up properly. (If your columns still aren't lining up the way you want them to, consider using a monospace font, such as Courier, which lines up better.)

- **If you're having trouble aligning the contents of adjacent cells, set the vertical alignment to Top.** A common frustration when you're building tables is that you have two or more rows side by side with text in one and images in the other, and you want the top of the image and the top of the text to line up. Often they don't line up because they're different lengths, and the table is trying to adjust the contents to best use the space within their respective cells. The solution is simple: Select all the cells you want to align, and in the Property inspector, change the vertical alignment to Top. Seemingly like magic, all the content jumps to the top of the cells and lines up perfectly. This is such a common problem that I routinely set the vertical alignment of table cells to Top.

✔ **Make sure you use the same formatting, paragraph, and break tags if you want the contents of adjacent cells to line up.** Another situation in which the contents of adjacent cells don't line up properly occurs when you include paragraph tags around the text or an image in one cell but not in another. Use Split view (by clicking on the Split button at the top of the workspace) and make sure that the code in both cells matches. If you have <p> tags around the contents in one cell and not in another, make sure to include them in the second cell or remove them from the first so that both cells match.

Merging and splitting table cells

Sometimes, the easiest way to modify the number of cells in a table is to *merge* cells (combine two or more cells into one) or *split* cells (split one cell into two or more rows or columns). With this technique, you can vary the space in table sections and customize table structures. For example, you may want a long cell space across the top of your table for a banner and then multiple cells below it so that you can control the spacing between columns of text or images. The following two sets of steps show you how to merge and split cells in a table.

To merge cells in an existing table, follow these steps:

1. **Highlight two or more adjacent cells by clicking and dragging the mouse from the first cell to the last.**

   You can merge only cells that are adjacent to one another.

2. **Click the Merge Selected Cells icon, in the lower-left region of the Property inspector (and shown in this page's margin), to merge the selected cells into a single cell.**

   The cells are merged into a single cell by using the colspan or rowspan attributes. These HTML attributes make a single cell merge with adjacent cells by spanning extra rows or columns in the table.

To split a cell, create a new table or open a page with an existing table and follow these steps:

1. **Click to place the cursor inside any cell you want to split.**

2. **Click the Split Cells into Rows or Columns icon, in the lower-left region of the Property inspector (and shown in the margin).**

   The Split Cell dialog box appears.

3. **Select Rows or Columns in the dialog box, depending on how you want to divide the cell.**

   You can split a cell into any number of new rows or columns.

4. **Type the number of rows or columns you want to create.**

   The selected cell is split into the number of rows or columns you entered.

Following a workflow for creating tables

If you want to create a table from scratch, open an existing HTML page where you want to add a table or create a new, blank HTML page. Then follow these steps from the beginning:

1. **Make sure that you're in Standard mode. (Choose View⇨Table Mode⇨Standard Mode.)**

2. **Click to place the cursor where you want to create a table.**

   In both Standard and Expanded modes, tables are created automatically in the top-left area of the page, unless you insert them after other content.

3. **Click the Table icon on the Common or Layout Insert panel.**

   Alternatively, you can choose Insert⇨Table. The Insert Table dialog box appears.

4. **In the appropriate boxes, type the number of columns and rows you want to include in your table.**

   Remember, you can always add or remove cells later with the Property inspector.

5. **Specify the width, border, cell padding, and cell spacing.**

   See "Choosing your table's appearance," earlier in this chapter, for specifics about each of these options.

6. **Choose the header option that best corresponds to the layout you want for your table to create a row of header cells across the top, side, or both.**

   If you don't specify a header option, Dreamweaver will not include one.

7. **Add a caption and summary in the Accessibility section and click OK.**

   The table automatically appears on the page. If you're not familiar with the header, caption, and summary options, see "Making tables more accessible," earlier in this chapter, for details.

8. **Click to place the cursor in a cell and then type the data you want in that cell. Repeat for each cell.**

   Alternatively, you can use Edit➪Paste Special to insert columnar data from another program, such as Excel.

   If you want to import data from a table you've created in a program, such as Word or Excel, see the section "Importing Table Data from Other Programs," later in this chapter.

9. **Apply formatting options, such as bold or italic, to selected cells and their contents by choosing the option from the Property inspector.**

   The sections "Specifying cell options," "Aligning table content in columns and rows," and "Merging and splitting table cells" explain the basics of table formatting.

Sorting Table Data

When you're working with lots of columnar data, you want to be able to sort that data just as you do in a spreadsheet program, such as Excel. In Dreamweaver, you can sort data even after you format it in HTML but you don't have as many options as you do in Excel. For example, you can sort an entire table based on a specified row, but you can't sort different rows individually.

To use the Sort Table Data feature, create a new, blank HTML page, add a table with several rows and columns, and add some content. (I explain how in the preceding section.) You may also open an existing page with a table of columnar data. Then, follow these steps:

1. **Select the table you want to sort.**

   To select a table for sorting, simply place the cursor in any cell of the table you want to sort.

2. **Choose View➪Table Mode➪Standard Mode.**

3. **Choose Commands⇨ Sort Table.**

   The Sort Table dialog box appears, as shown in Figure 9-6.

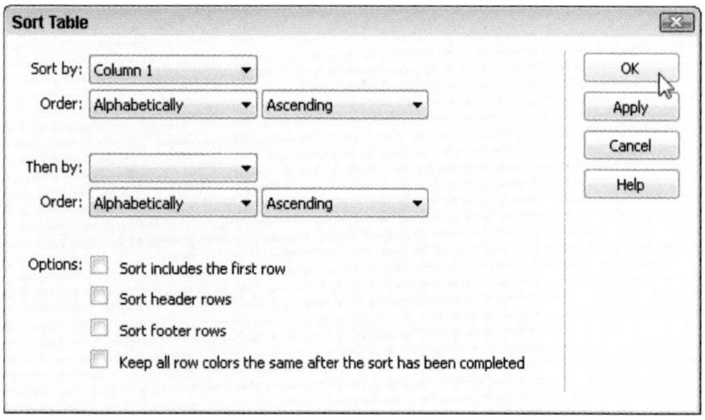

4. **Specify which column you want to sort by and then choose Alphabetically or Numerically and then Ascending or Descending.**

Figure 9-6: You can sort cell contents alphabetically or numerically, even after they're formatted in HTML.

You can set up one or two sorts to happen simultaneously and opt whether to include the first row and whether to keep the `<tr>` (table row) attributes with a sorted row by selecting Keep All Row Colors the Same.

5. **Click OK.**

   The selected cells are sorted, just as they are in a program such as Excel. (Pretty cool, huh?)

Using Tables for Spacing and Alignment

Tables have long been used on the web to create page layouts that require more than a basic alignment of elements on a page. In the early days of web design, using tables was one of the only ways you could get around many of the limitations of basic HTML and accomplish some otherwise impossible design feats, such as evenly spacing bullets, columns side-by-side on a page, and headlines or images spanned across multiple columns.

Today, CSS offers a much better option for these kinds of designs, but many people are still using tables and you may have websites that you created in this way (or you may inherit a design that uses them). If you're working on a site that's designed with tables to create a page layout for any content that isn't tabular, such as the old page from my Chocolate Game Rules website, shown in Figure 9-7, consider redesigning the page layout with `<div>` tags and CSS, which are covered in detail in Chapter 6. If you visit www. ChocolateGameRules.com, you can learn to play the chocolate game and see that I've redesigned this page with `<div>` tags.

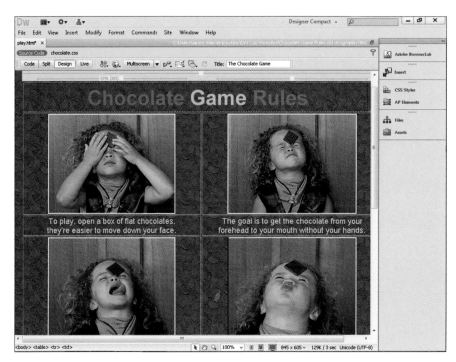

Photo by Janine Warner

Figure 9-7: Many two-column page layouts, such as the one shown here, were created with HTML tables.

Nesting Tables within Tables

Placing tables within tables, or *nested tables,* can help you create extremely complex designs. For example, with a table that contains scores of all the baseball games in a season, you could add a smaller table inside one cell to include detailed stats of an exceptional game. You create nested tables by inserting a table within a cell of another table.

The best web designs communicate the information to your audience in the most elegant and understandable way and are easy to download. To make sure that your designs don't get too messy, remember these guidelines:

✔ A table within a table within a table is nested three levels deep. Anything more than that gets hairy.

✔ Pages that use nested tables take longer to download because browsers have to interpret each table individually before rendering the page. For some designs, the slightly longer download time is worth it, but in most cases, you're better off adding or merging cells in one table, as I explain in the section "Merging and splitting table cells," earlier in this chapter. One situation that makes a nested table worth the added download time is when you want to place a table of financial or other data in the midst of a complex page design.

To place a table inside another table, follow these steps:

1. **Click to place the cursor where you want to create the first table.**

2. **Choose Insert⟳Table.**

   The Insert Table dialog box appears.

3. **Type the number of columns and rows you need for your design.**

4. **Set the Width option to whatever is appropriate for your design and then click OK.**

   The table is sized automatically to the width you set.

5. **Type the information that you want in the table cells.**

6. **Click to place the cursor in the cell in which you want to place the second table.**

7. **Repeat Steps 2–5.**

   The new table appears inside the cell of the first table.

Part III

Making Your Site Cool with Advanced Features

The 5th Wave   By Rich Tennant

WHERE'S THE DANG DOOR?!

C'mon in!

OUR AWARDS

*A*dd dynamic, interactive features to your web pages with Dreamweaver's behaviors, covered in Chapter 10, which make it easy to create rollover images, pop-up windows, and more complex image swaps with JavaScript. In Chapter 11, you discover how Dreamweaver's Spry menus help you create advanced features for your site, such as drop-down menus and collapsible panels using AJAX.

In Chapter 12, you find an introduction to multimedia on the web and instructions for adding multimedia files, such as sound, video, and Flash animations, to your web pages.

In Chapter 13, you discover that Dreamweaver has all the tools you need to create radio buttons, check boxes, and submit buttons for interactive forms for your website.

10

Adding Interactivity with Behaviors

· ·

In This Chapter

▷ Adding behaviors to your web page

▷ Creating image rollovers

▷ Using the Swap Image behavior

▷ Launching a new browser window

▷ Editing your behaviors

▷ Enhancing Dreamweaver with extensions

· ·

*W*ant to add cool effects such as rollovers and pop-up windows? Dreamweaver's behaviors make it easy to create these kinds of interactive features without having to learn the JavaScript scripting language.

Behaviors are ready-to-use scripts that you can customize to create a variety of interactive features. You can apply behaviors to almost any element on an HTML page and even to the entire page itself. For example, you can use the Swap Image behavior to create an interactive slide show within a page, or you can apply the Open Browser Window behavior to open a new browser window when you want to reveal more information or display a larger version of an image.

In this chapter, I introduce you to the Behaviors panel and show you how to use some of Dreamweaver's most popular options. Dreamweaver CS6 includes 16 options in the Behaviors panel, and you can download and install many more. For instructions on installation, see the "Installing New Extensions for Behaviors" section, at the end of this chapter.

Brushing Up on Behavior Basics

When you start working with behaviors in Dreamweaver, you can get up and running more easily if you begin with this basic introduction to how behaviors work and the terminology they use. When you set up a behavior, you can choose from a number of *triggers,* or *events,* such as OnMouseOver or OnClick (the two most popular options). Consider this slightly corny example: If you tickle someone and make the person laugh, you used an event to trigger an action. Dreamweaver would call the tickling the *event* and the laughter the *action.* The combination is a Dreamweaver *behavior.*

You may already be familiar with the *rollover* behavior, which causes one image to be replaced with another when someone rolls the cursor over an image. In a rollover, putting your mouse cursor over an image is the *event.* The *action* is the switching of the original image for the second image. In Figure 10-1, you see the effect of a rollover as the main image in the page is changed to the second image. Dreamweaver's Swap Image behavior makes it easy to create a gallery of images, like the series of galleries I created to help artist Amy Baur showcase her artwork at www.inplainsightart.com.

Rollovers are commonly used when you want to show off two or more images on a web page. You can create a simple rollover effect that uses two images, or you can create more complex designs when you use the Swap Image behavior to cause any or all the images on a page to change. As you discover in the exercises that follow, the most important factor is to make sure the images that you swap are exactly the same size.

The rollover behavior used to be a popular way to create rollover effects on links, but a better option has emerged. As you discover in Chapter 6, you can now create links with rollover effects using CSS, which is more search engine friendly, easier to update, and more accessible to people who use screen readers.

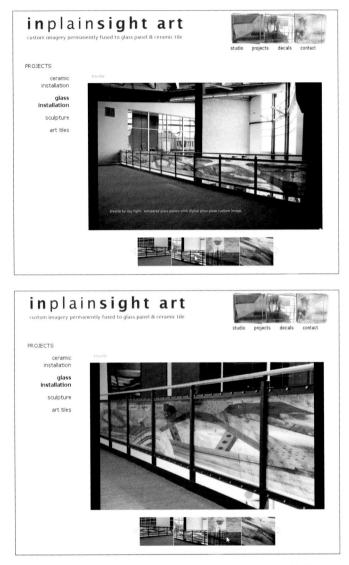

Artwork by Amy Baur, inplainsightart.com

Figure 10-1: When a cursor rolls over the images at the bottom on this page, the Swap Image behavior causes the larger images to change.

Creating a Simple Rollover Image

Rollover images, as the name implies, are designed to react when someone rolls a cursor over an image. The effect can be as dramatic as a picture of a dog being replaced by a picture of a lion, or as subtle as the color of a word changing as one image replaces another. Rollovers are such a popular feature that Dreamweaver includes a special dialog box just for rollovers: the Insert Rollover Image dialog box.

You can create more complex rollover image effects with the Swap Image option from the Behaviors panel, covered in the section that follows. The Swap Image option enables you to change multiple images at the same time.

To create a simple rollover effect with two images using Dreamweaver's Insert Image Rollover dialog box, follow these steps:

1. **Place your cursor on the page where you want the rollover to appear.**

   Rollover effects require at least two images: one for the initial state and one for the rollover state. You can use two different images or two similar ones, but both should have the same dimensions. Otherwise, you see strange scaling effects because both images must be displayed in exactly the same space on the page.

2. **Choose Insert⇔Image Objects⇔Rollover Image.**

   Alternatively, you can use the drop-down list available from the Images icon in the Insert panel and select Rollover Image.

   The Insert Rollover Image dialog box appears, as shown in Figure 10-2.

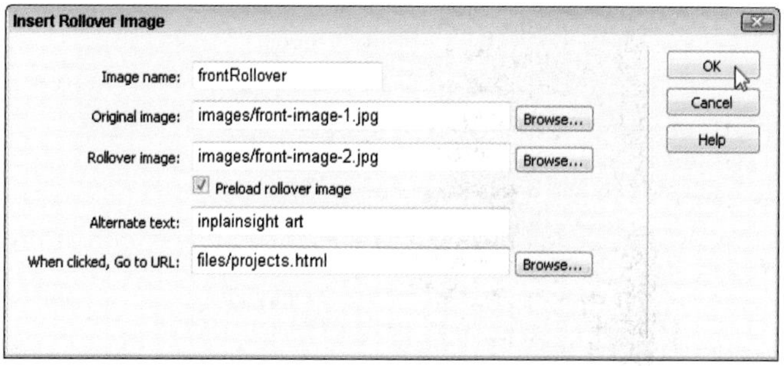

Insert Rollover Image		
Image name:	frontRollover	OK
Original image:	images/front-image-1.jpg Browse...	Cancel
Rollover image:	images/front-image-2.jpg Browse...	Help
	☑ Preload rollover image	
Alternate text:	inplainsight art	
When clicked, Go to URL:	files/projects.html Browse...	

Figure 10-2: Select the original and rollover images.

3. **In the Image Name box, name your image.**

   Before you can apply a behavior to an element, such as an image, the element must have a name so that the behavior script can reference it. You can name elements anything you like as long as you don't use spaces or special characters.

4. **In the Original Image box, specify the first image you want visible. Use the Browse button to locate and select the image.**

   If the images aren't already in your local site folder, Dreamweaver copies them into your site when you create the rollover. (If you haven't already set up your site in Dreamweaver, see Chapter 2 for more on this important preliminary step.)

5. **In the Rollover Image box, enter the image you want to become visible when visitors move their cursors over the first image.**

   Again, you can use the Browse button to locate and select the image.

6. **Select the Preload Rollover Image check box to load all rollover images into the browser's cache when the page first loads.**

   If you don't choose to do this step, your visitors may experience a delay because the second image won't be downloaded until a mouse cursor is rolled over the original image.

7. **In the When Clicked, Go to URL box, enter any web address or browse to locate another page in your site that you want to link to.**

   If you don't specify a URL, Dreamweaver automatically inserts the # sign as a placeholder in the code.

   The # sign is a common technique for creating links that don't link anywhere. Because rollover images that don't link to another page have many great uses, this technique is useful. Just remember that if you do want your rollover to link, you need to replace the # sign with a link to another page. See Chapter 2 for details about setting links.

8. **Click OK.**

   The images are set up automatically as a rollover.

9. **To see the rollover in action, click the globe icon at the top of the workspace to preview your page in a web browser.**

You can see how your rollover works in Dreamweaver's Design view or by using the Live View option. When you click the Live button at the top left of the workspace, you essentially turn Dreamweaver into a web browser that displays pages much like the Chrome browser I used for the screenshots shown in Figure 10-3.

Artwork by Amy Baur, inplainsightart.com

Figure 10-3: When you create a simple rollover, rolling your cursor over an image, such as the one shown on the top, reveals a second image, shown on the bottom.

Peeking at the JavaScript code

JavaScript is the code behind Dreamweaver behaviors. Writing JavaScript is more complex than writing HTML code, but not as difficult as writing in a programming language, such as C# or Java. (No, Java and JavaScript aren't the same.) Dreamweaver takes most of the challenge out of JavaScript by giving you a graphic interface that doesn't require you to write the complicated code yourself. When you use behaviors, Dreamweaver automatically writes the code for you behind the scenes.

To fully appreciate what Dreamweaver can do for you, you may want to switch to Code view after setting up a behavior, and then click the JavaScript file in the files list at the top of the workspace. You'll see the complex code required when you use JavaScript. If you don't like what you see, don't worry: Go back to Design view and you can continue to let Dreamweaver take care of the code for you. (I just want you to see how lucky you are that Dreamweaver includes these features.)

Adding Behaviors to a Web Page

Dreamweaver offers a number of behaviors you can choose from, including the Swap Image behavior and the Open New Browser Window behavior covered in detail in the next two sections. The process of adding other behaviors is similar to process for these two, but each behavior has its quirks. The tips and tricks you find here can help you get started with behaviors, find the location of most behavior features, and match behaviors with triggers using the Behaviors panel.

You can download many more behaviors from the Adobe Exchange website. You find instructions in the "Installing New Extensions for Behaviors" section, at the end of this chapter.

Creating swaps with multiple images

Before you start creating a more complex page design with Dreamweaver's Swap Image behavior, first look at a finished page so you can see the result before you get into the details. Note in Figure 10-4 that a collection of thumbnail images is on the bottom of the page and a larger version of one of those images is displayed in the main area of the page.

In Figure 10-5, when I roll my cursor over a different thumbnail image on the bottom, the larger image displayed above it changes to correspond to that thumbnail. With the Swap Image behavior, you can replace any or all the images on a page.

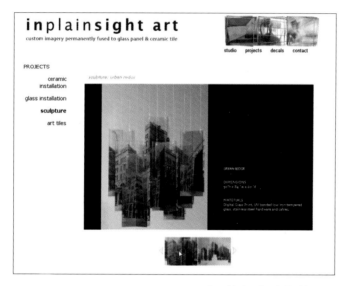

Artwork by Amy Baur, inplainsightart.com

Figure 10-4: When you use the Swap Image behavior, you can replace any or all the images on a page.

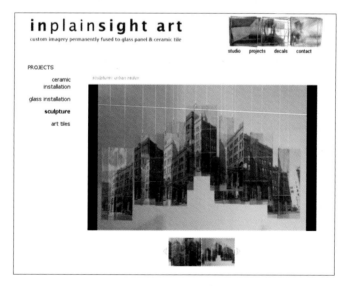

Artwork by Amy Baur, inplainsightart.com

Figure 10-5: When you preview a behavior in a browser, you can see the effect of the Swap Image behavior when the cursor is rolled over an image.

When you use the Swap Image behavior, it's important to make all of the images that you will swap the same size (height and width). If the images are not the same size, all images except the first one will be stretched or compressed to fit the space taken up by the first image inserted into the page.

If you're using the Swap Image behavior with a series of images that are not all the same height and width, you have a few of options:

- ✔ Crop the larger ones so that all images are the same size.

- ✔ Make horizontal and vertical images take up the same space in your design by combining two vertical images for every horizontal one. Simply create a file in a program such as Photoshop, insert two vertical images into the same file side by side, and then size that image so that the file is the same size as one horizontal image.

- ✔ Create one image file the size of your largest image, set the background to a neutral color, such as black or white, and then insert all other images onto the background so that you can save them all with the same file size. An example of this technique is shown in Figure 10-4, in which we inserted one vertical image into a file with a black background and then added text to the right of that image, ultimately creating a file that is same size as the image shown in Figure 10-5.

Follow these steps to use the Swap Image behavior:

1. **Create a page design with all the images you want displayed initially.**

   In the page design I created for these photos of Amy Baur's artwork, the initial page design has all thumbnail images positioned on the bottom of the page, with the first of the big images displayed in the main area just above them.

   You can use the Swap Image behavior to change images on any web page no matter how the layout is created. In the design featured in this section, I used CSS to create a layout with separate <div> tags for the row of thumbnails on the bottom and another <div> tag for the bigger image above the thumbnails. These divs are positioned with CSS. (Find instructions for creating CSS layouts in Chapter 6.)

2. **Name your images in the Property inspector, as shown in Figure 10-6.**

To target your images with JavaScript, which is how behaviors work, first give each image a unique ID. The image ID isn't the same as the image filename or the `<alt>` tag, although you can use the same or similar names. In this example, I gave each thumbnail image an ID that matched the text on the small image, to make indentifying the thumbnails easy. You can name images anything you like as long as you don't use spaces or special characters.

Although Dreamweaver automatically assigns a name to each image you insert into a web page, I find it easier to keep track when I set up the Swap Image behavior if I use names that describe the images or correspond to their order. Using the same or similar IDs for your images and the image filenames helps make it easier to match them when you create the behavior.

In contrast, I usually name the main image something simple and distinctive, such as `display_photo` or `mainImage`, as shown in Figure 10-6, to make it easier to keep track of which image I'm replacing each time.

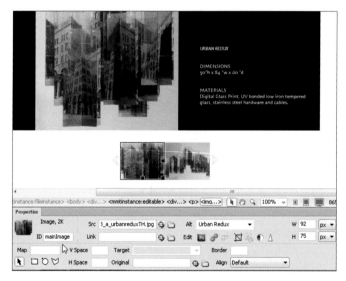

Artwork by Amy Baur, inplainsightart.com

Figure 10-6: In the top left of the Property inspector, enter an ID for each image.

3. Choose Window➪Behaviors.

The Behaviors panel opens. You can drag the Behaviors panel elsewhere on the page, and you can expand it by dragging its bottom or side. You may also want to close any other open panels to make more room by clicking the dark gray bar at the top of any panel.

4. Select an image.

First click to select the image in the page that will serve as the trigger for the action. In this example, I'm using the thumbnail images as triggers, so I select them one at a time. I started with the fashion thumbnail, but because it triggers the image that appears when the page is first displayed, I'm going to use the second one as the example here. You repeat this same process for each thumbnail. In the example shown in Figures 10-7, I've selected the second thumbnail image, with the ID urban2.

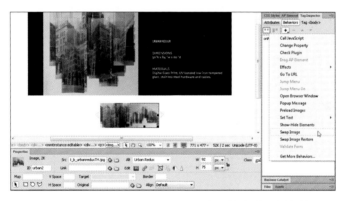

Artwork by Amy Baur, inplainsightart.com

Figure 10-7: With a thumbnail image selected, click the + to open the drop-down list in the Behaviors panel, where you can specify an action.

5. Choose the Swap Image behavior.

With the trigger image selected in the workspace, I click the Add Behavior arrow in the Behaviors panel (the small arrow under the plus sign) to open the drop-down list of actions, and choose the action I want to apply. I chose the Swap Image action, which opens the Swap Image dialog box shown.

6. Specify the images to swap.

a. In the Swap Image dialog box, select the ID for the image that will be replaced.

In Figure 10-8, I selected the image with the ID "mainImage". Note that you don't want to choose the image you selected; you want to choose the image you want to replace in the design. In this case, I'm replacing the main image in this page, which I've given the ID "mainImage". (The image is identified with an asterisk, *, because the image was inserted into the page.) In Figure 10-8, I'm replacing that first image with the second image in the sequence, using the second thumbnail as the trigger. (The process is the same when you have more than two images.)

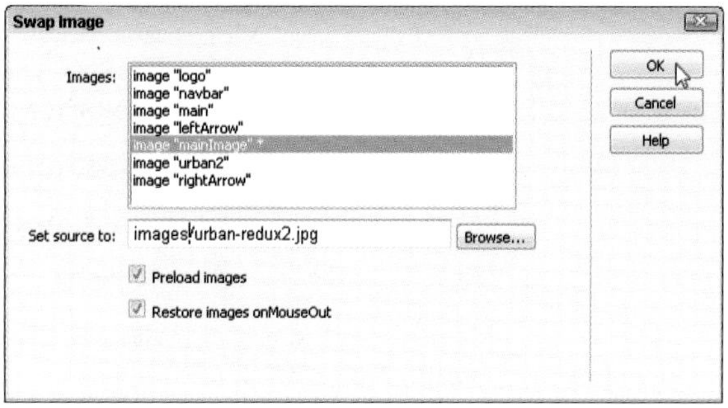

Figure 10-8: Use the Browse button to select the image you want to swap.

b. Click the Browse button to select the image that replaces the main image.

I selected the urban-redux2.jpg image, which I carefully named to correspond to the matching thumbnail, which has the urban2 ID. Now when a user rolls a cursor over the urban2 thumbnail image, the big photo of the first image will be replaced with the big photo of the second image.

Note: If the image is not already saved in the local site folder, Dreamweaver will offer to copy it there for you.

7. At the bottom of the Swap Image dialog box, select Preload Images to instruct the browser to load all the images into the cache when the page is loaded.

If you don't select this option, a delay may occur when the image swap is used.

8. **If you want, deselect the Restore Images OnMouseOut.**

The Restore Images OnMouseOut option means that when an event is completed (such as the mouse is moved off the triggering thumbnail), the original image is replaced. By default, Dreamweaver preselects this option for the Swap Image behavior, but in the example shown here, I deselected it because I found that replacing the original image each time I rolled the cursor over another thumbnail was distracting.

9. **After you specify all the settings for the behavior, click OK.**

The new behavior appears in the Behaviors panel.

10. **Specify an event for the behavior.**

After the action is applied, you can go back and specify which event will trigger the action (as shown in Figure 10-9). By default, Dreamweaver applies the OnMouseOver event when you use the Swap Image action, but you can change that event to any available one, such as OnClick, which requires that the user click the image to trigger the Swap Image action. In this example, I left the event set to OnMouseOver.

The list of behaviors and events varies depending on the element selected and the applied behavior. For more information about events and what each one accomplishes, see the "Choosing an event for a behavior" sidebar, elsewhere in this chapter.

Figure 10-9: When you set up a behavior, you can specify any available action to trigger an event.

You can display or hide events by clicking the Show All Events icon in the top left of the Behaviors panel. Note that if you're using Windows, you also see a collection of events that begin with an <a> and are for elements that are linked.

11. **Apply additional behaviors.**

To apply the Swap Image behavior to other images on a page, repeat Steps 5–10, clicking to select the image you want to serve as a trigger and then specifying the corresponding image that should be swapped. In this example, I selected each thumbnail in turn and set up a Swap Image behavior that replaced mainImage with the corresponding larger version of the photo in the thumbnail.

12. **Test your work in a browser.**

You can't see the effects of behaviors like this one until you click the Live View button at the top left of the workspace in Dreamweaver or preview your page in a web browser, such as Firefox or Internet Explorer.

Choosing an event for a behavior

Events, in interactive web-speak, are things a user does to trigger a behavior or an action in a web page. Clicking an image is an event, as is loading a page into a browser or pressing a key on the keyboard. Different browser versions support different events (the more recent the browser, the more events available). Some events are available only for certain kinds of objects or behaviors. If an event can't be used with a selected element or behavior, it appears dimmed. This list describes the most common events:

✔ onBlur: Triggered when the specified element stops being the focus of user interaction. For example, when a user clicks outside a text field after clicking in the text field, the browser generates an onBlur event for the text field. onBlur is the opposite of onFocus.

✔ onClick: Triggered when the user clicks an element, such as a link, a button, or an image.

✔ onDblClick: Triggered when the user double-clicks the specified element.

✔ onError: Triggered when a browser error occurs while a page or an image is loading. This event can be caused, for example, when an image or a URL can't be found on the server.

✔ onFocus: Triggered when the specified element becomes the focus of user interaction. For example, clicking in or tabbing to a text field of a form generates an onFocus event.

✔ onKeyDown: Triggered as soon as the user presses any key on the keyboard. (The user doesn't have to release the key for this event to be generated.)

✔ onKeyPress: Triggered when the user presses and releases any key on the keyboard. This event is like a combination of the onKeyDown and onKeyUp events.

✔ onKeyUp: Triggered when the user releases a key on the keyboard after pressing it.

✔ onLoad: Triggered when an image or the entire page finishes loading.

✔ onMouseDown: Triggered when the user presses the mouse button. (The user doesn't have to release the mouse button to generate this event.)

✔ onMouseMove: Triggered when the user moves the mouse while pointing to the specified element and the pointer doesn't move away from the element (that is, the pointer stays within its boundaries).

✔ onMouseOut: Triggered when the pointer moves off the specified element (usually a link).

✔ onMouseOver: Triggered when the mouse pointer moves over the specified element. Opposite of onMouseOut.

✔ onMouseUp: Triggered when a mouse button that's been pressed is released.

Using the Open Browser Window behavior

You can use behaviors in Dreamweaver to create many interactive features, such as opening a new browser window when someone clicks an image or a text link. As you can see in Figure 10-10, opening a new window is a great way to make supplemental information available without losing the original page a visitor was viewing. The Open Browser Window behavior enables you to specify the size of the new window and to display it over the existing window.

Artwork by Amy Baur, inplainsightart.com

Figure 10-10: Click one of the four main images on this page to open a corresponding page that provides additional information.

To add the Open Browser Window behavior to a selected image or text on a page, follow these steps:

1. **Create the page that will open in the new browser window.**

   For this art site, I created a new HTML page for each of the four sections of the Who page, and inserted the text and images that correspond to each section. The four main images in the Who page will serve as triggers. The goal is that when a user clicks the trigger image, a smaller browser window will open to reveal the content for that section.

When you name files that will be used in behaviors, such as a page that will open when the Open Browser Window behavior is used, avoid using slashes anywhere in a filename or numbers at the beginning of a filename (you can use numbers anywhere else in the name). It's also best to avoid hyphens and underscores.

2. **Select the image, text, or other element you want to serve as the trigger for the action.**

   You can select any image, text, or other element on a page and apply a behavior to it the same way.

3. **Choose Window⇨Behaviors to open the Behaviors panel.**

4. **Click the plus sign (+) and choose the behavior you want from the drop-down list.**

   In this example, I selected the Open Browser Window behavior, as shown in Figure 10-11.

If a behavior appears dimmed, it can't be associated with the selected element. For example, the Swap Image behavior can be applied only to an image, so it appears dimmed if you've selected text or another element.

Artwork by Amy Baur, inplainsightart.com

Figure 10-11: Select the image or text link to serve as the trigger, click + in the Behaviors panel, and choose the desired behavior.

5. **In the Open Browser Window dialog box, as shown in Figure 10-12, specify the settings.**

   You can set a number of options that control how the new browser window appears:

   - **Use the Browse button to the right of the URL to Display box to select the page you want to open in the new browser window.** (You can also enter a URL in this box to open a page in another website.)

   - **Set the window width and height to specify the exact pixel size of the new browser window that will open.** In this example, I set the width to the exact size of the image.

   - **Select the options Navigation Toolbar, Location Toolbar, Status Bar, Menu Bar, Scrollbars as Needed, or Resize Handles if you want the new browser window to include any of these features.** I selected Scrollbars as Needed in case my visitor's browser window is smaller than the size I specified for the photo, but I left all the others deselected because I want a clean, simple browser window without any menus or other features.

   - **Name the new window, an important step if you want to target that same window to load other pages into it.**

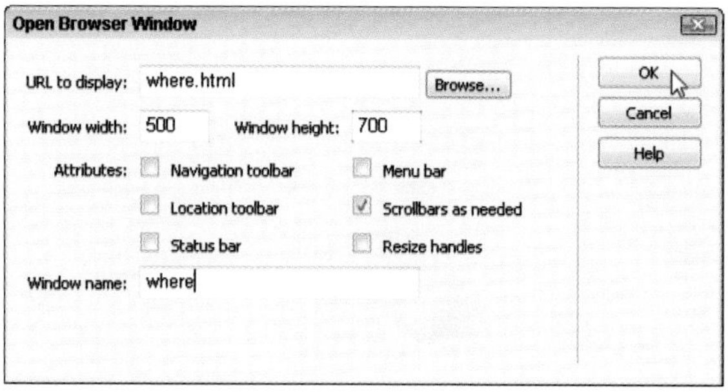

Figure 10-12: Specify settings for the display of the window.

6. **After you specify all the settings for the behavior, click OK.**

   The new behavior appears in the Behaviors panel.

7. **To change the event that triggers your behavior, select the current event from the left side of the Behaviors panel.**

   In the Events drop-down list, select any available event to serve as the trigger for the behavior. For more information about events and what each one accomplishes, see the "Choosing an event for a behavior" sidebar, elsewhere in this chapter.

8. **To test the action, choose File➪Preview in Browser.**

   Click the image to test whether a new browser window opens.

Attaching Multiple Behaviors

You can attach multiple behaviors to the same element on a page (as long as they don't conflict, of course). For example, you can attach one action that's triggered when users click an image and another when they move their cursors over the image. You can also trigger the same action by using multiple events. For example, you can open the same page in a new browser window when a user triggers any number of events.

To attach additional behaviors to an element, click the plus sign in the Behaviors panel and select another option from the pop-up list. Repeat this process as many times as you want.

Editing a Behavior

You can always go back and edit a behavior after you create it. You can choose a different event to trigger the behavior, choose a different action, or remove behaviors. You can also change behavior options after a behavior is applied.

To edit a behavior, follow these steps:

1. **Select an object with a behavior attached.**

2. **Choose Window➪Behaviors to open the Behaviors panel.**

   Here are some options you can choose in the Behaviors panel:

   • **Change a triggering event:** Choose a different event in the Events drop-down list in the Behaviors panel.

   • **Remove a behavior:** Click the action in the Behaviors panel to select it and then click the minus sign at the top of the pane. The behavior disappears.

- **Change parameters for an action:** Double-click the gear icon next to the action and change the parameters in the dialog box that opens.

- **Change the order of actions when multiple actions are set:** Select an action and then click the up arrow icon to Move Event Value Up or the down arrow icon to Move Event Value Down in the list of actions.

Installing New Extensions for Behaviors

Even with all the cool features in Dreamweaver, a day will almost certainly come when you'll want to do things that Dreamweaver can't do with the features that shipped with the program. Fortunately, the programmers who created Dreamweaver made it possible for other programmers to add features with Extension Manager. The result? You can add new functionality by adding extensions from a variety of third-party sources.

You can find extensions that do everything from adding highly customizable drop-down and fly-out menus to full-featured shopping cart systems. Keep in mind, however, that not all extensions are well supported and few come with good instructions. They're not all free, either. Some cost hundreds of dollars, but most are in the $20–$50 range. When you visit the Dreamweaver Exchange site, you'll find reviews and rankings to help you sort through the best options.

In the following steps, I explain how you find, download, and install a free Dreamweaver extension. Although how extensions work after they're installed can differ dramatically, the basic process of adding them to Dreamweaver is nearly the same.

1. **Visit the Dreamweaver Exchange site.**

   Get to the Dreamweaver Exchange site by

   - Choosing Get More Behaviors from the bottom of the Behaviors drop-down list in the Behaviors panel.

   - Visiting www.adobe.com/exchange and following the link to the Dreamweaver section.

   - Clicking the link in the bottom right of the Dreamweaver Welcome screen.

Note: If you launch Dreamweaver and find a link to download an update for Dreamweaver instead of the link to the Exchange site, by all means download and install the update first. After you're finished, the update link is replaced by the link to the Exchange site.

2. Sort through the many available extensions.

You'll find a wide range of extensions on the Dreamweaver Exchange site. You can search through extensions by category, keyword, and ranking options. Many of the extensions featured on the Exchange site include links to their creators' sites, where you'll often find even more extensions.

3. Select an extension and review its features.

When you click a link to an extension on the Exchange site, you'll find more information about the extension, including system requirements and the version of Dreamweaver for which the extension was designed. In general, you can use extensions designed for earlier versions of Dreamweaver in more recent versions. Be aware, however, that extensions designed for later versions of Dreamweaver usually won't work in earlier versions of the program.

Before you leave the extension's page, I highly recommend that you take the time to read the special instructions in the middle of the page. Some extensions include important instructions, such as where you find the new feature in the Dreamweaver interface after it's installed and warnings that some functionality of an extension will work only when previewed on a live web server (this is true for the random image extension, for example).

4. To download an extension, click the Download button (for free extensions) or the Buy button next to the extension name and save the extension to your hard drive.

5. Choose Help⇨Manage Extensions to open the installation dialog box.

Most extensions require that you close Dreamweaver before installation, and most install with the click of a button. Dreamweaver's Extension Manager launches automatically to install most extensions.

6. In the Extension Manager dialog box, choose File⇨Install Extension and then browse your drive to select the extension file you downloaded.

After the installation is complete, Dreamweaver displays instructions for using the extension. These instructions are usually the same as the ones included in the middle of the page on the Exchange site.

Pay special attention to the part of the instructions that tells you where you'll find your newly installed extensions. Extensions may be added to menus, dialog boxes, and other parts of Dreamweaver depending on their functionality and how the programmer set them up. Finding them can be hard if you don't know where to look.

7. **Launch Dreamweaver and find the new menu option, button, or other interface feature that controls your new extension.**

   In many cases, all you have to do is open an existing page or create a new page in Dreamweaver and then open the newly added dialog box or select the new option from a menu.

Adobe is constantly updating the Exchange site, which is available by clicking the Dreamweaver link at www.adobe.com/exchange. Visit it regularly to find new extensions you can download and install to enhance Dreamweaver's feature set.

11

Creating AJAX Features with Spry

Dreamweaver provides a collection of widgets known as the Spry Framework for AJAX. If you still think AJAX (Asynchronous JavaScript and XML) is just something you can use to clean the house, you're missing out on one of the greatest innovations in web design. The Spry Framework for AJAX is a JavaScript library that makes it easier to create highly interactive features, such as drop-down menus, collapsible and tabbed panels, and form validation features. In this chapter, you create menus that drop down, panels with tabs, and forms with built-in validation — even if you don't know how to write JavaScript.

Making Magic with AJAX

JavaScript has become an increasingly important part of the web, and AJAX is one of the more popular JavaScript frameworks because it enables you to create highly interactive pages that load fast. AJAX also enables designers to open and close panels and extend drop-down menus, such as the one in Figure 11-1, without reloading the page.

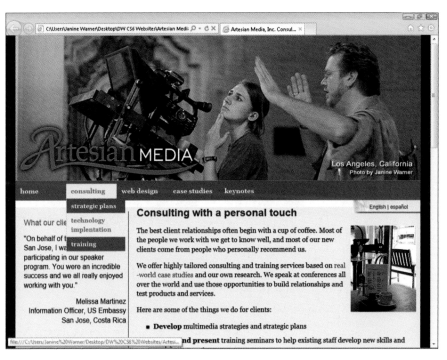

Photo by Janine Warner

Figure 11-1: You can create drop-down menus like these in Dreamweaver.

To save you from having to write the code for these kinds of features yourself, Dreamweaver includes a collection of widgets that instantly adds things such as collapsible panels and drop-down menus to your pages, and includes editing tools for customizing these features without knowing JavaScript. To view the list of AJAX widgets available in Dreamweaver, open the Spry Insert panel by choosing Spry from the Insert panel drop-down menu shown in Figure 11-2.

Figure 11-2: The Spry Insert panel provides quick access to the many Spry options.

Creating Drop-Down Menus with AJAX

An increasingly popular option for navigation bars, drop-down menus can provide a menu (or list) of links to the main sections of a website, with a secondary menu of links to the subcategories within those sections. You can even create a third layer with the Spry Menu Bar widget.

With the Dreamweaver Spry Menu Bar, you can create menus that span horizontally or vertically. As you see in the following steps, you simply choose which way you want the menu to span when you insert it from the Spry menu.

To create a drop-down menu with the Spry Menu Bar widget, follow these steps:

1. **Place your cursor on a page where you want the menu to appear.**

   If you haven't already saved your page, make sure you save it before adding Spry features, or Dreamweaver will prompt you with a warning message that you need to do so.

2. **Choose Insert⇨Spry⇨Spry Menu Bar.**

   Alternatively, you can click the Spry Menu Bar option in the Spry Insert panel, visible in Figure 11-3.

   The Spry Menu Bar dialog box appears.

3. **In the Spry Menu Bar dialog box, choose Horizontal or Vertical.**

   Horizontal creates a menu that drops down into a page; Vertical creates a menu that opens out to the right.

4. **Click OK.**

   A menu with four items and several subitems is created and inserted into the page.

5. **Enter your own text for the menu items.**

   You can edit the text for the top-level items in the main workspace by simply clicking and dragging to select the placeholder text, such as Item1, and then typing to replace it.

   In general, making changes to menu bar items in the Property inspector is best. I explain how in the remaining steps. To change formatting options, such as color, font face, and size, change the style sheet rules, described in Step 14.

6. **Click the blue Menu Bar tab on the top of the menu bar you inserted in the design area to display the settings in the Property inspector, as shown in Figure 11-3.**

   You find settings to add, remove, edit, and change the order of items and subitems in the Property inspector.

Figure 11-3: Click the blue Menu Bar tab to display the options in the Property inspector.

7. **To change the name of an item or subitem:**

   a. **Click to select the item in the Property inspector.**

   b. **Type a new name in the Text field on the far-right side of the Property inspector, as shown in Figures 11-3 and 11-4.**

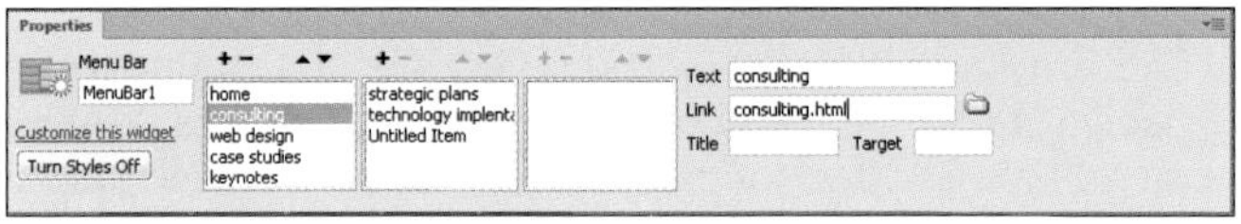

Figure 11-4: Edit any item selected in the Property inspector with the Text, Link, Title, and Target fields.

8. **To link a menu item:**

   a. **Select the item name.**

   b. **Enter a URL in the Link field or click the browse button (which looks like a file folder), and select the page you want to link to (refer to Figure 11-4).**

9. **To remove an item, select the item and then click the minus sign (–) at the top of the field in the Property inspector.**

   A deleted item is removed from the menu in the Property inspector as well as the main work area.

10. **To add an item, select the plus sign (+) at the top of the item field in the Property inspector.**

    When you add an item, it appears in the Property inspector menu as well as in the menu bar in the main work area.

11. **To add a subitem, select the item you want the subitem to appear under and then click the plus sign (+) in the item box to the right of the selected item (refer to Figure 11-3).**

12. **To change the order of items, click to select an item name and then use the arrows at the top of each item box.**

    Items move up and down the menu when you click the up or down arrows. Items appear in the web page in the order they appear in the Property inspector.

13. **Choose File⇨Save to save the page; when the Copy Dependent Files dialog box appears, click OK to automatically generate all the related files.**

    For the Spry features to work, you must upload these files to your web server when you upload the web page.

14. **To change the appearance of a drop-down menu, edit the corresponding CSS style rules.**

    CSS (Cascading Style Sheets) style rules determine the text size, font, background color, and other formatting features. When you create a menu bar, a collection of CSS styles are generated automatically and saved in an external CSS file dubbed SpryMenuBarHorizontal.CSS (for horizontal menus) or SpryMenuBarVertical.CSS (for vertical menus). You can access these styles through the CSS Styles panel, shown in Figure 11-5.

Here are a few examples of how Spry menu bar styles can be edited:

a. **To change the font size or face, double-click the style name** `ul.MenuBarHorizontal` **in the CSS Styles panel.**

This action opens the style in the CSS Rule Definition dialog box, where you can alter the corresponding Type category settings. In the example shown in Figure 11-5, I've changed the font size to 95 percent, which will make the text in the menu display at 95 percent of the size of the default text setting for the page.

b. **To remove or edit the border of a menu bar, edit the border settings in the style** `ul.MenuBarHorizontal ul`.

In the example shown here, I removed the border by simply deleting all the settings for the border.

c. **To change the text and background colors for the active links, change the colors for the rule** `ul.MenuBarHorizontal a`.

If you change the text and background colors of active links, you are effectively changing the colors of the menu bar when the page first loads.

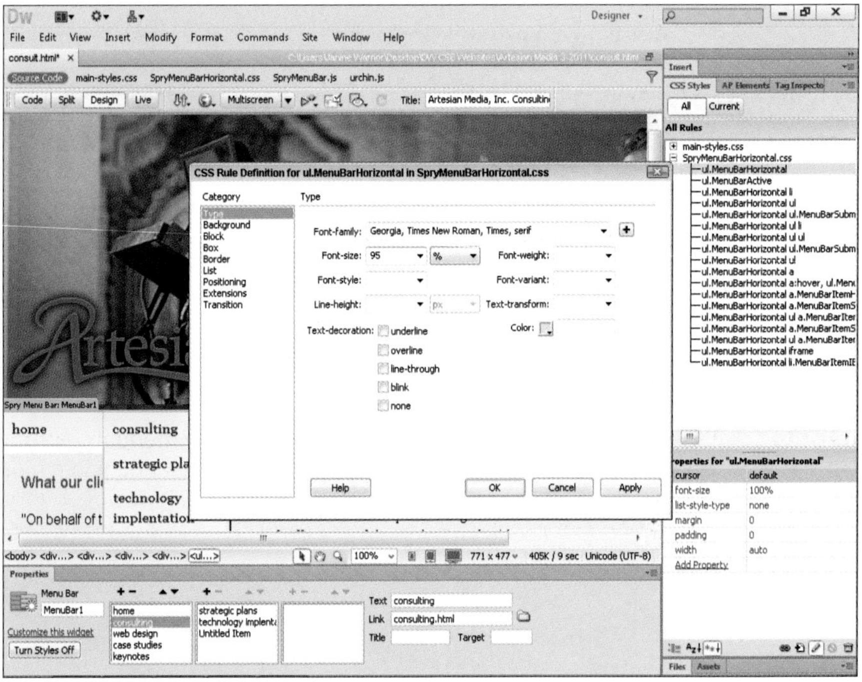

Figure 11-5: To change the appearance of a drop-down menu, edit the corresponding CSS styles.

To find other settings you may want to change, click to select each of the style names in the Spry Menu Bar style sheet and use the CSS Properties pane, in the lower half of the CSS Styles panel, to view the rules that have been defined for each style. By simply clicking through the collection of styles, you can identify each of the settings in a drop-down menu (or any other Spry feature) and determine where you'll need to edit them to change the appearance of each element. You find more detailed instructions for creating and editing style rules in Chapters 5 and 6.

15. **Click the globe icon at the top of the workspace to preview your work in a browser.**

    Here you can see how the styles appear in the menu and test the drop-down effects and links. The example in Figure 11-5 is in the Firefox browser.

Creating Collapsible Panels

The Spry Collapsible Panel option makes it easy to add panels that site visitors can open and close without refreshing the webpage. This AJAX feature enables you to make better use of the space on a page by making it easy to display more information in less space within a browser window.

In Figure 11-6, you can see how I used collapsible panels to contain the biography of each partner and consultant in a consulting firm. The result is that you can easily see the names of all the consultants on one page. To view a consultant's bio, a user need only click the tab at the top of the panel (where the consultant's name appears), and the panel opens instantly. In Figure 11-7, the bio for Designer Davi Cheng is open while the others on the page are closed. The beauty of AJAX is that the page doesn't have to be reloaded for the panels to open or close. Click once on a tab and a panel opens instantly. If a user clicks the tab again, the panel closes. Collapsible panels can be used to display text and images. You can also include multimedia files in panels, such as audio, video, and Flash files.

When you create collapsible panels with the Spry menu in Dreamweaver, you can set the panels so that they're closed or opened when a page is first loaded. Because each panel is created separately, you can create a page that displays all panels open, all panels closed, or a mix of the two options.

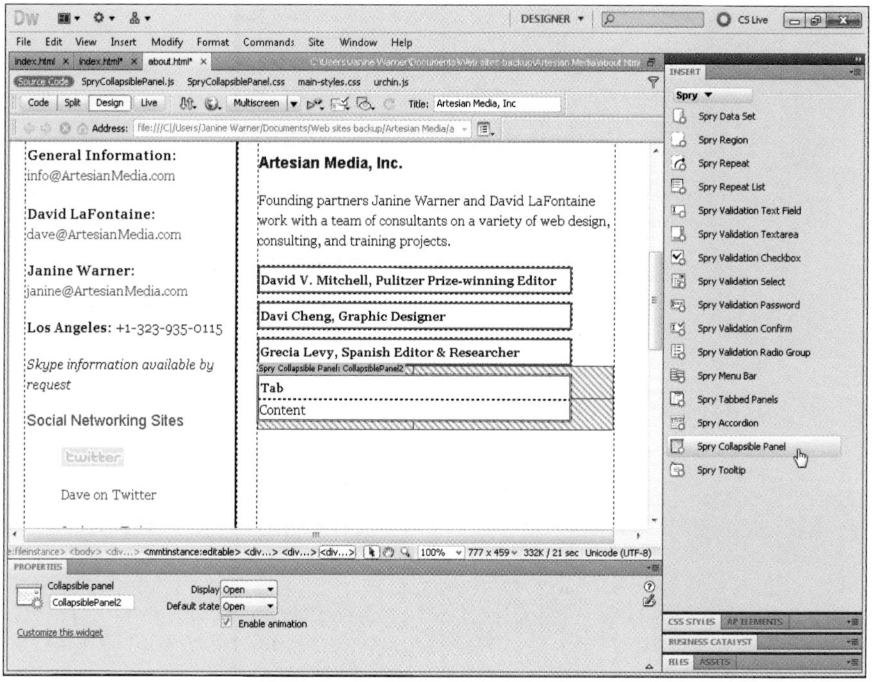

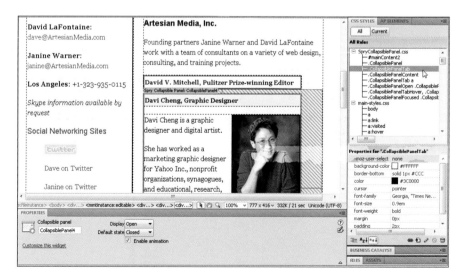

Figure 11-6: The Spry Collapsible Panel option adds one panel to a web page, but you can use it multiple times to create a series of panels.

Figure 11-7: To alter the appearance of a Spry collapsible panel tab, edit the corresponding CSS rule in the CSS Styles panel.

Follow these steps to create a collapsible panel:

1. **Place your cursor on a page where you want the collapsible panel to appear.**

2. **Choose Insert➪Spry➪Spry Collapsible Panel.**

   Alternatively, you can click the Spry Collapsible Panel item in the Spry Insert panel (refer to Figure 11-6).

   A Spry collapsible panel appears in the page, as shown in Figure 11-6.

3. **Click and drag to select the word *Tab* and replace it with the text you want to appear in the panel's Tab area.**

   By default, the text in the Tab area is bold, but you can change that by altering the corresponding CSS rule.

4. **Click to select the word *Content* in the main area of the panel and enter any text or images you want to display.**

   You can copy text into a panel by pasting it just as you'd paste text anywhere else on the page. Similarly, you insert images into panels just as you would anywhere else on a page by choosing Insert➪Image and selecting the GIF, JPEG, or PNG file you want to display. (See Chapter 3 if you need help preparing or converting images into these formats.)

   When you paste text into a panel, choose Edit➪Paste Special to choose the amount of formatting you want to preserve in the text you paste in Dreamweaver. Limiting the amount of formatting preserved can cut down on potential style conflicts.

5. **Click the blue Spry Collapsible Panel tab at the top of the panel in the design area.**

   When you click the blue tab, the panel settings immediately appear in the Property inspector (refer to Figure 11-6). (Correctly clicking the blue tab can be tricky.) Click anywhere else on the page, and the inspector returns to its default settings.

6. **From the Display drop-down menu in the Property inspector, choose Closed.**

   The Closed option immediately closes the panel in the main workspace in Dreamweaver. This setting affects the way the panel is displayed in only the Dreamweaver workspace.

7. **From the Default State drop-down menu in the Property inspector, choose Closed.**

   This setting controls how the panel displays in a web browser. Choosing Closed means the panel is closed when the page loads. If you choose Open, the panel appears open when the page is loaded.

8. **If you want the panel to open and close when a user clicks the tab, make sure the Enable Animation check box is selected.**

9. **To change the appearance of the panel, such as the font face or color, edit the corresponding CSS rule.**

   For example, to edit the background color of the tab or the font face, style, or color, select the `.CollapsiblePanelTab` style and alter the settings in the Properties panel in the lower half of the CSS Styles panel (refer to Figure 11-7). Alternatively, you can double-click any style name to launch the CSS Rule Definition dialog box to make your changes there. You find more detailed instructions for creating and editing styles in Chapters 5 and 6.

10. **Choose File⇨Save to save the page; when the Copy Dependent Files dialog box appears, click OK to automatically generate all the related files.**

    For the Spry features to work, you must upload these files to your web server when you upload the web page.

11. **Click the globe icon at the top of the workspace and select the browser you want to use to preview the page.**

Creating Tabbed Panels

The Spry Tabbed Panel option makes it easy to add a series of panels that display or hide content corresponding to a series of tabs, as shown in Figure 11-8. Similar to the collapsible panels, this AJAX feature lets you display more information in less space within a browser window.

Similar to the collapsible panels, tabbed panels can be used to display text, images, and multimedia.

When you create tabbed panels with the Spry menu in Dreamweaver, you can control the order of the tabs, effectively controlling what content appears when the page is first loaded.

Photo by David LaFontaine

Figure 11-8: Tabbed panels enable you to change the content displayed on a web page when a visitor clicks a tab.

Follow these steps to create a tabbed panel:

1. **Place your cursor on a page where you want the tabbed panel to appear.**

2. **Choose Insert⇨Spry⇨Spry Tabbed Panels.**

   Alternatively, you can click the Spry Tabbed Panels item in the Spry Insert panel.

   A Spry tabbed panel appears on the page, as shown in Figure 11-9.

3. **Click and drag to select the word *Tab* in the main workspace and replace it with the text you want to appear in the panel's Tab area.**

   You can edit the contents of the tabs only in the workspace, not in the Property inspector.

   By default, the text in the Tab area is bold and black, but you can change that by altering the corresponding CSS rule.

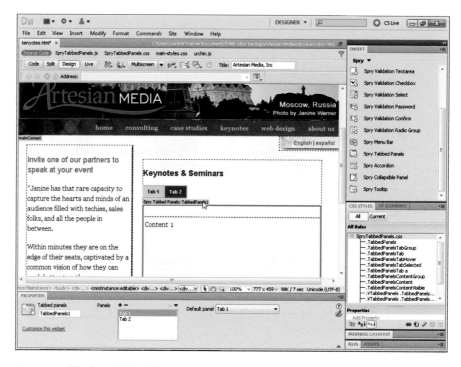

Figure 11-9: The Spry Tabbed Panels option adds a tabbed panel to a web page.

4. **Click the blue Spry Tabbed Panels tab at the top of the panel set in the design area.**

   When you click the blue tab, the settings immediately appear in the Property inspector (refer to Figure 11-9). Click outside the blue boxed area, and the Property inspector returns to its default settings.

5. **To add tabs, click the plus sign (+) icon in the Property inspector.**

   New tabs appear in the workspace.

6. **To change the order of tabs, click to select the tab name in the Property inspector and then use the arrows in the Panels field to move the panel.**

   Panel names move up and down the menu as the order is changed. Panels and their corresponding tabs appear in the web page in the order in which they appear in the Property inspector.

7. **Use the Default Panel drop-down menu to choose the tab you want to display when the page is first loaded into a web browser.**

   The drop-down menu corresponds to the names you give each tab in the workspace.

8. **To add content, select the word *Content* in the main area of any selected tab panel and enter text, images, or multimedia.**

   You can copy text into a panel by pasting it just as you'd paste text anywhere else on the page. Similarly, insert images into panels just as you would anywhere else on a page by choosing Insert➪Image and then selecting the GIF, JPEG, or PNG file you want to display. You can also add multimedia, such as Flash video files. (Find instructions for adding multimedia to web pages in Chapter 10.)

9. **To change the appearance of a tab or a panel, such as the font face or color, edit the corresponding CSS rule.**

   For example, to edit the background color of the tabs, click to select the .TabbedPanelsTab style and alter the settings in the Properties panel in the lower half of the CSS Styles panel. Alternatively, you can double-click any style name to launch the CSS Rule Definition dialog box to make your changes there. You find more detailed instructions for creating and editing styles in Chapters 5 and 6.

   In the styles for Tabbed Panels, the tab background colors are controlled by two styles — the .TabbedPanelsTab and the .TabbedPanelsTabSelected styles. As a result, you can specify a different background color and other formatting settings to distinguish the tab that's selected from the tabs that aren't selected.

10. **Choose File➪Save to save the page; when the Copy Dependent Files dialog box appears, click OK to automatically generate all the related files.**

    For the Spry features to work, you must upload these files to your web server when you upload the web page.

11. **Click the globe icon at the top of the workspace and select a browser to preview your work in a browser.**

Using Spry Validation Widgets

The Spry menu also includes a collection of validation widgets you can use to create form elements with built-in validation features. For example, you can use the Text Field Validation widget to verify whether a visitor has filled in a specified minimum number of characters — a handy way to ensure that someone has filled in all the digits in a phone number or Social Security number. You can also add hints to a text field to provide additional instructions.

Similarly, you can use the Validation Checkbox widget to verify that a check box has been selected. For example, you might use the widget when you have a legal disclaimer or contract and want to ensure that a visitor selects the Accept box before progressing into another area of your site, as shown in Figure 11-10.

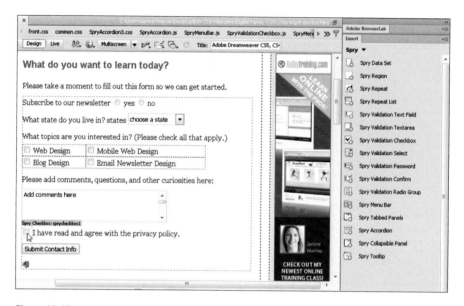

Figure 11-10: Use the Checkbox Validation widget to require that visitors select a check box before continuing to another page.

1. **Click to place your cursor in the page where you want the check box to appear.**

2. **Choose Insert⇨Spry⇨Spry Validation Checkbox.**

   Alternatively, you can click the Spry Validation Checkbox item in the Spry Insert panel.

3. **If you're not adding the check box to an area that already includes a `<form>` tag, the Add Form Tag dialog box opens. To create the `<form>` tag as you create the text box, click Yes.**

4. **Specify validation requirements in the Property inspector.**

   When you add a validation widget to a form element, such as the check box shown in this example, the Property inspector automatically displays the properties for that validation option. If those properties aren't visible, click the blue Spry tab just above the form element to display them.

5. **To require that users select a check box, choose Required from the Preview States drop-down menu in the Property inspector.**

   Dreamweaver automatically adds Please Make a Selection, just to the right of the check box in the workspace. You can edit this text by selecting it in the workspace and typing any message you want, such as, *You must accept our policy to continue.*

The validation message is displayed only if a visitor fails to select the check box before clicking the Submit button.

6. **Choose File➪Save to save the page; when the Copy Dependent Files dialog box appears, click OK to automatically generate all the related files.**

For the Spry features to work, you must upload these files to your web server when you upload the web page.

7. **Click the globe icon at the top of the workspace and select a browser to preview your work in a browser where you can test the validation features.**

Showing Off with Multimedia

*G*et your web pages singing and dancing with multimedia. Audio, video, and animation are exploding on the web and transforming static pages into rich multimedia experiences. You can use Dreamweaver to link to multimedia files, or you can insert audio, video, and other files so that they play within your pages. You can even control when and how they play for your users.

Not all websites warrant multimedia; if your goal is to provide information in the fastest way possible to the broadest audience, text is still generally the best option. If you want to provide a richer experience for your users, to *show* rather than just *tell,* or to entertain as well as inform, adding audio, video, and animation can help you share more information more vividly and even make you look more professional.

The most complicated aspect of multimedia on the web is choosing the best format for your audience, which is why you'll find a primer on audio and video formats in this chapter. You can't create or edit multimedia files in Dreamweaver. (You'll need a video-editing or audio-editing software program for that.) But after your files are ready, Dreamweaver makes adding them to your web pages relatively easy.

As you discover in this chapter, inserting video, audio, and Flash files is similar to adding image files to web pages, but with many more options, such as settings that control whether a video starts automatically or only when the user clicks the play button.

Many people surf the web in their offices, in libraries, and in other locations where unexpected sound can be jarring, disruptive, or worse. Always give people a warning before you play video or audio and always give users a way to turn audio off quickly when necessary.

In this chapter, you also find instructions for using third-party services, such as YouTube or Vimeo, to host videos. With this approach, you upload your video to YouTube, Vimeo, or another service and then use Dreamweaver to add a snippet of code into your site so that the video plays on your page (even though the video is hosted elsewhere). An advantage of this approach is that YouTube and other video sites are better at delivering video on the web than most of the commercial web servers that you're likely to use to host your site.

Understanding Multimedia Players

When you add sound, video, or any other kind of multimedia to a website, your visitors may need a special player (sometimes with an associated plug-in) to play or view your files.

Players are small programs that work alone or with a web browser to add support for functions, such as playing sound, video, and animation files. Some of the best-known multimedia players are Flash Player, Windows Media Player, and Apple QuickTime.

The challenge is that not everyone on the web uses the same player, and viewers must have the correct player to view your multimedia files. As a result, you need one or more strategies to help visitors play your multimedia easily, such as the following:

- ✔ Many web developers offer audio and video in two or three formats so users can choose the one that best fits the players they already have.

- ✔ Some developers also include the same multimedia files in different file sizes so that visitors with slower connection speeds don't have to wait as long. Optimizing multimedia for the web works much as it does with images: The smaller the file size, the lower the quality but the faster the file downloads.

✔ Many web developers also include information about how visitors can download and install the best player if they need it to view the files.

✔ Increasingly, web developers are using third-party services, such as YouTube or Vimeo to host videos and SoundCloud to host audio. You find instructions for using these services toward the end of this chapter.

You can use Dreamweaver to insert or link to any type of multimedia file, but only you can choose the format that's best for your audience. Although dozens of plug-ins are available for web pages, the most common plug-ins on the web today are Flash, Windows Media, and QuickTime.

In general, I recommend that you avoid the more obscure players unless you're offering specialized content that users have a good reason to download, such as a three-dimensional game that requires a special program to run.

Using Adobe Flash

Adobe Flash has long been a favorite among web designers, but it's losing popularity these days because Flash files don't work on Apple's popular iPhone, iPad, and iPod touch devices. That said, Flash is still well supported by desktop computers connected to the web (more than 90 percent of Internet users already have the Flash plug-in) and is still popular because you can use it to create audio files, videos, and animations, including complex games and highly interactive websites.

Because Flash is not supported by Apple's devices, more and more designers are turning to HTML5, CSS3, and JavaScript. You can find out more about using the new CSS3 features in Chapter 7. Writing JavaScript is beyond the scope of this book, but Dreamweaver's behaviors, covered in Chapter 10, provide a great alternative and make it easier to create interactive design elements, such as slide shows and drop-down menus, without using Flash.

Dreamweaver supports both of the popular Flash file types:

✔ **Flash files:** (extension `.swf`) The most versatile Flash format is the SWF file (pronounced "swiff"). Often referred to simply as a *Flash file,* this format is sometimes called a Flash movie, even when it doesn't include video. Flash files with a `.swf` extension can include illustrations, photos, animation sequences, and video. In Dreamweaver, choose Insert➪Media➪SWF for this format. You find detailed instructions for working with this type of Flash file in the following section.

✓ **Flash video:** (extension .flv) As the name implies, Flash video is a video format, although it can also be used for audio files. To convert video into the Flash video format, you need the Adobe Media Encoder. In Dreamweaver, use the Insert⇨Media⇨FLV option for this format. You find detailed instructions for working with .flv Flash files in the "Adding Flash audio and video files" section later in this chapter.

Flash files (with the .swf extension) are so flexible and so fast on the Internet in part because Flash uses *vector graphics* instead of *bitmaps.* Therefore, the graphics in Flash are based on mathematical descriptions *(vectors)* instead of dots *(bitmaps),* and those vector equations take up far less space than bitmapped images. Vector graphics can also be scaled up or down in size without affecting the image quality or the size of the downloaded file. This capability to scale makes Flash ideally suited for the many different monitor sizes that web viewers use. You can even project Flash graphics on a wall or movie screen without losing quality, although any photographs or video files integrated into a Flash file may lose quality or look distorted at higher or lower resolutions.

To create a Flash file, you need Adobe Flash or a similar program that supports the Flash format. Because Flash is an open standard, you can create Flash files with a variety of programs, including Adobe Illustrator, which has an Export to SWF option. If you want to know how to create full-featured Flash files, check out *Flash Professional CS5 and Flash Catalyst CS5 For Dummies,* by Ellen Finkelstein, Gurdy Leete, and Mary Leete.

Flash is great overall, but be aware of these important drawbacks:

✓ Flash is not supported by most mobile web browsers, including the iPhone or iPad. As a result, if you try to view a site created with Flash on a mobile device, you see only blank screen. To get around this problem, more and more web designers are creating a second version of their Flash sites designed for mobile phones and linking it to their main site. These second sites are often simplified versions of the main site, optimized with the information most likely to be useful to mobile users.

✓ If you need printouts for some reason, Flash may not print as well as you would hope.

✓ Flash may cause accessibility problems. Screen readers and other specialized viewers can't read the text in a Flash file any better than they can read text in an image file. To make Flash files more accessible, include detailed alternative text.

✓ Flash sites are generally more complicated to edit or update than sites created using HTML and CSS.

✓ Search engines may not read text in Flash files, which can hurt your page ranking in search results (although including alternative text can help with this limitation and Google is improving its capability to index Flash pages).

✓ Sites created entirely in Flash are harder to link to, especially if you want to link to a particular page within a site and not just to the front page of the site. Similarly, it's harder (or impossible) to bookmark specific pages within a site designed with Flash.

Inserting Flash SWF files

Flash files, often called Flash *movies,* use the .swf extension and can include animations, graphics, photos, and even video. Thanks to Dreamweaver, these files are relatively easy to insert into a web page. In this section, I assume you have a completed Flash file (an animation or other Flash movie), and you want to add it to your web page.

You insert a Flash file much as you insert an image file. But because a Flash file can do so much more than a still image, you have a variety of settings and options for controlling how your Flash file plays.

Before you start, make sure to save the Flash file you want to insert in the main folder for your website (that is, the local site folder you set up, as I explain in Chapter 2). I recommend creating a multimedia subfolder in your main website folder for audio and other multimedia files, just as most designers create an image folder for image files.

To add a Flash file to a website, open an existing page or create a new document and save the file. Then follow these steps:

1. **Click where you want the Flash file to appear on your web page.**

2. **If the Insert panel is not already open, choose Window⇨Insert. Then use the drop-down list to select the Common Insert panel.**

3. **From the Media drop-down list on the Common Insert panel, choose the SWF option, as shown in Figure 12-1.**

   You can also choose Insert⇨Media⇨SWF. The Select File dialog box appears.

4. **Browse to locate the Flash file that you want to insert in your page and click to select the file.**

5. **If you have accessibility options turned on, you're prompted to add alternative text to describe the Flash file. Enter a description of the file and click OK.**

   The dialog box closes, and the Flash file is inserted into your document.

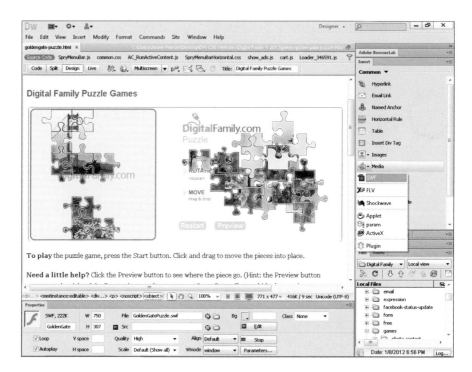

Figure 12-1: You can use Dreamweaver to insert Flash animation files, like this one, as well as Flash video files, covered later in this chapter.

TIP

When you first insert a Flash file, Dreamweaver displays it as a gray box on your web page. To display the Flash file as it will appear in a web browser when viewed with the Flash player, click anywhere in the gray box to select the Flash file and then click the green Play button on the right side of the Property inspector. (*Note:* The Play and Stop buttons are available only under Windows.) If you have the Flash player installed on your computer, the Flash file will play when you preview the page in a browser.

Setting Flash properties

Like most HTML tags, the tags that link Flash and other multimedia files to web pages have *attributes* (also called properties) that define how a file is displayed within a browser, controlling such actions as whether an animation plays automatically when a page is loaded or only when a visitor clicks a link. Dreamweaver automatically sets some of these options, such as the height and width of the Flash file, but you may want to specify others.

To display Flash attributes in the Property inspector, as shown in Figure 12-2, click to select the gray box that represents a Flash file after it's inserted into a web page.

If you don't see all the options in the Property inspector, click the expander arrow in the lower-right corner to display the more advanced options. If you still don't see all the options, you may be dealing with a .flv file, not a .swf file.

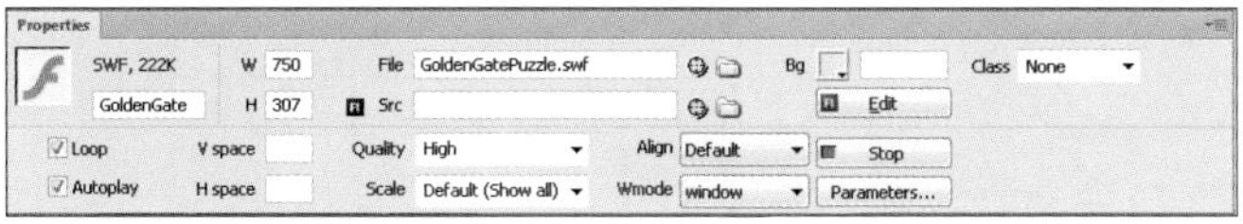

Figure 12-2: Select any Flash file to view or change its settings in the Property inspector.

The following describes the Flash options included in the Property inspector:

- ✒ **ID field:** Use the text field in the upper-left corner of the Property inspector, just to the right of the Flash icon, to assign a name to the file (in Figures 12-1 and 12-2, I've named the Flash file GoldenGate). You can enter any name; just don't use spaces or special characters other than the hyphen or underscore. The name is important if you want to refer to the file in JavaScript or other programming, but you can leave this field blank if you are not using a script with your Flash file.

- ✒ **W (width):** Use this option to specify the width of the file. The file is measured in pixels.

- ✒ **H (height):** Use this option to specify the height of the file. The file is measured in pixels.

- ✒ **Reset Size icon:** (This circular icon is visible only if you have changed the size of a Flash file.) You can change the display size of a Flash file by clicking and dragging one of its corner or by entering a number in the height or width fields. When the size of a Flash file has been altered, a small, circular icon appears just to the right of the height and width fields. Clicking this circular icon reverts the Flash file to its original size. You can resize Flash files, unlike images, video, and many other file types, without affecting image quality because they're vector-based. To keep the file proportionate, hold down the Shift key while you drag to resize the file.

✔ **File:** Dreamweaver automatically fills in this field when you insert a Flash file with the filename and path. You risk breaking the link to your Flash file if you alter this field.

✔ **Src:** Use this option to enter the name of the Flash file and the path to its location, including any folders or subdirectories.

✔ **BG:** Click the color swatch to change the background color that appears behind the Flash file, or enter a pound sign (#) followed by a hexadecimal color code.

✔ **Edit:** Click this button to open a Flash source file with the Adobe Flash program, where you can edit the file. Note that you can edit only the Flash source file. After saving the Flash file for web use with the `.swf` extension, return to the original Flash file to edit it again.

✔ **Class:** Use this drop-down list to apply any class styles defined for the document.

✔ **Loop:** Selecting this check box causes the Flash file to repeat, or *loop.* If you don't select this box, the Flash movie stops after it reaches the last frame.

✔ **Autoplay:** Selecting this check box causes the Flash movie to play as soon as it is downloaded to the viewer's computer. If you don't select this box, whatever option you've set in the Flash file itself (such as `onMouseOver` or `onMouseDown`) is required to start the movie.

✔ **V Space (vertical space):** If you want blank space above or below the file, enter the number of pixels.

✔ **H Space (horizontal space):** If you want blank space on either side of the file, enter the number of pixels.

✔ **Quality:** This option enables you to prioritize the anti-aliasing options of your images versus the speed of playback. *Anti-aliasing,* which makes your files appear smoother, can slow down the rendering of each frame because the computer must first smooth the edges. The Quality parameter enables you to regulate how much the process is slowed by letting you set priorities based on the importance of appearance versus playback speed. You can choose from these Quality options:

  • **Low:** Anti-aliasing is never used. Playback speed has priority over appearance.

  • **High:** Anti-aliasing is always used. Appearance has priority over playback speed.

  • **Auto High:** With this option, playback is set to begin with anti-aliasing turned on. However, if the frame rate supported by the user's computer drops too low, anti-aliasing automatically turns off to improve playback speed. This option emphasizes playback speed and appearance equally at first but sacrifices appearance for the sake of playback speed, if necessary.

- **Auto Low:** Playback begins with anti-aliasing turned off. If the Flash player detects that the processor can handle anti-aliasing, it is turned on. Use this option to emphasize speed at first but improve appearance whenever possible.

✔ **Scale:** Specify this option only if you change the file's original height and width settings. The Scale parameter enables you to define how the Flash movie appears within those settings. The following options in the Scale drop-down list enable you to set preferences for how a scaled Flash movie appears in the window:

- **Default (show all):** This option enables the entire movie to appear in the specified area. The width and height proportions of the original movie are maintained and no distortion occurs, but borders may appear on two sides of the movie to fill the space.

- **No Border:** This option enables you to scale a Flash movie to fill a specified area. No borders appear and the original aspect ratio is maintained, but some cropping may occur.

- **Exact Fit:** The Flash movie appears in the specified width and height. However, the original aspect ratio may not be maintained, so the movie may look squished.

✔ **Align:** This option controls the alignment of the file on the page. This setting works the same for plug-in files as for images.

✔ **Wmode:** Choose the Window option to display the Flash file in a rectangular window on a web page. Choose Opaque to hide everything behind a Flash file when you move or resize it using JavaScript. Choose Transparent to show the background of the HTML page through any transparent portions of the Flash file.

✔ **Play button:** Click the green Play button to play a Flash file in Dreamweaver. Note that when the Play button is activated, the button changes to Stop (refer to Figure 12-2). *Note:* The Play button is available only under Windows.)

✔ **Parameters:** This button provides access to a dialog box where you can enter parameters specific to your Flash files.

Finding Flash resources online

One of the best places to read more about creating Flash files is on the Internet, where a wide range of websites offers everything from predesigned Flash files you can easily customize to great ideas for getting the most from this award-winning technology. You may find these websites useful if you want to find out more about Flash:

✔ www.adobe.com: At the Adobe site, you'll find loads of tips and tricks for creating and using Flash files (as well as many inspiring examples of Flash in action).

✔ www.swishzone.com: If you're looking for an alternative to Adobe Flash, Swish from Swishzone.com is a great little program that's more reasonably priced.

✔ www.flashkit.com: You'll find a wide range of resources for Flash developers at the Flash Kit site.

✔ www.gotoandlearn.com: Go to gotoAndLearn when you want free Flash tutorials as well as videos about developing Flash animations and working with ActionScript, the programming language used in Flash.

✔ www.coldhardflash.com: The Cold Hard Flash site is both a gallery of short Flash animations and a resource center, with tutorials and links to other sites.

Using scripts to make Flash function better

When you insert Flash or other multimedia files with Dreamweaver, the program creates a collection of JavaScript files that help the Flash file play properly.

The files are named according to the format swfobject_modified.js and are stored in a Scripts folder, which Dreamweaver automatically creates in your local site folder. The first time Dreamweaver creates this file, a dialog box alerts you that you need to upload the script for your multimedia file to work properly. Make sure you include this script when you publish your site on your web server.

If you don't include the script, your multimedia file may not play properly, or your visitors may be required to click the green Play button twice before the file begins to play. (Remember, the Play and Stop buttons are available only under Windows.)

With each new version of Dreamweaver, Adobe has changed the scripts included with Flash and other multimedia files. If you're editing a site that was created with an earlier version of Dreamweaver, update these scripts by deleting and then reinserting the multimedia file to generate new scripts. Then, make sure you upload the page with the Flash or other multimedia file, as well as the Scripts folder.

Working with Video and Audio on the Web

As bandwidth has grown on the web, the use of video files has grown more dramatically than almost any other multimedia file type. From YouTube to small personal websites, millions of video files are added to the web every day. Adding a video file to a web page with Dreamweaver is relatively easy, especially if you use the Flash video format described in the "Adding Flash audio and video files" section later in this chapter.

If you use another video format, such as Windows Media Video or QuickTime, you find instructions for adding files in those formats in the section, "Inserting audio and video files," also later in this chapter. You can specify video and audio settings, such as Autoplay, by changing setting parameters, an option that is a little more complicated if you use any format other than Flash video. You find instructions for managing these settings in Dreamweaver in the "Setting options for audio and video files," later in this chapter.

You don't have to host your video and audio files on your own web server. You can upload video files to YouTube, Vimeo, or another video site and then include special code from that site in the HTML code of your web pages so that the video plays within your pages, even though it's hosted on YouTube. For audio files, I recommend SoundCloud. You find instructions for using these kinds of services in the sections "Using YouTube, Vimeo, and Other Online Services," and "Using SoundCloud to Host Audio Files," later in this chapter.

The first challenge to working with multimedia is choosing the right format and optimizing your video so it downloads quickly and still looks good. Unfortunately, no single video format works perfectly for everyone on the web, but most new computers come with preinstalled video and audio players that play the most common file formats. If you use a Windows computer, you probably have Windows Media Player. If you use a Mac, you have QuickTime. Both video players can handle multiple video formats, so anyone with a relatively new computer can likely view video in common formats.

Streaming media plays faster

To *stream* multimedia means to play a file while it's downloading from the server. This trick is valuable on the web because video and audio files can take a long time to download. Here's how streaming works. When you click a link to a video file, your computer begins to download it from the server. If the video is hosted on a web server that supports streaming, the video or audio file begins to play as soon as enough of the file downloads successfully to ensure an uninterrupted experience.

If you don't use streaming, the entire file may have to download before the media can play. Although the download time for streaming or nonstreaming files may be the same, streaming can greatly reduce the time your visitors wait before they can start viewing a video online. Because web servers that stream video are very expensive (part of why more and more people are hosting their videos on sites such as YouTube or Vimeo, covered later in this chapter), Flash offers an option called *Progressive Download*. This option offers many of the same advantages of streaming because a video embedded with the Progressive setting will start playing before the entire file is downloaded. However, the option has some limitations. For example, you can't fast forward or back up as well with a video that is downloading using Progressive settings as you can with a video hosted on a web server that supports streaming.

Comparing popular video formats

You can convert video from one file format to another relatively easily with most video-editing programs. You can open a video in AVI (Audio Video Interleave) format in a program, such as Adobe Premier Elements (a good video editor for beginners), and then choose File⊅Export to convert it to any of a dozen formatting and compression options. For example, you could convert an AVI file to the Windows Media format with the compression setting for a 56K modem or into the QuickTime format with the compression setting for a cable modem.

Editing video can get complicated, and optimizing video for the best quality with the fastest download time is both an art and a science, but the most basic process of converting a video file isn't difficult after you understand the conversion options.

Table 12-1 provides a brief description of the most common digital video formats, their file extensions, and a web address where you can find out more about each option.

Table 12-1		Common Digital Video Formats	
Format	*File Extension*	*Website*	*Description*
Flash video	`.flv`	`www.adobe.com`	You can create Flash videos with Adobe Flash. Because the Flash player is almost ubiquitous on the web, many developers still consider Flash a viable option.
WebM	`.webm`	`www.webmproject.org`	WebM is an open source video format championed by Google. Although WebM is still somewhat rare, many designers are starting to take it seriously due to the increasing popularity of Android mobile devices.
MP4	`.mp4`	No official site for this technology	Part of MPEG-4, the MP4 format can be used for audio or video. This format is becoming increasingly popular, partly because most mobile phones, including the iPhone, support it, making it a good alternative to `.flv`.
Windows Media Video	`.wmv`	`www.microsoft.com/windows/windowsmedia`	Defined by Microsoft and popular on the PC, the Windows Media Video format supports streaming and plays with Windows Media Player as well as many other popular players.
Quick-Time	`.qt`, `.mov`	`www.quicktime.com`	The QuickTime player is built into the Macintosh operating system and is used by most Mac programs that include video or animation.
AVI	`.avi`	No one site about AVI exists, but you can find information if you search for *AVI* at `www.microsoft.com`.	Created by Microsoft, AVI (Audio Video Interleave) is an uncompressed video format that is fine if you're viewing video on a CD or on your hard drive, where the file doesn't have to download, but tends to result in file sizes that are unwieldy for Internet use. If your files are in AVI, convert them to one of the other formats before adding them to your website. Otherwise, you force your visitors to download unnecessarily large video files.

Comparing popular audio formats

Audio works much like video on the web. You can link to a sound file or embed the file into your page; either way, your visitors need to have the right player to listen to the file. You find instructions for adding both audio and video files to your pages in the following section, "Adding Audio and Video Files to Web Pages."

Table 12-2 provides a brief description of the most common digital audio formats, their file extensions, and a web address where you can find out more about each option.

Table 12-2		Common Digital Audio Formats	
Format	*File Extension*	*Website*	*Description*
MP3	`.mp3`	No official site for this technology	One of the most successful audio compression formats, MP3 supports streaming audio. Most music you can download from the Internet is in MP3 format, and it's clearly the first choice of many web developers. Most popular multimedia players on the web can play MP3 files.
Windows Audio	`.wma`	`www.micro soft.com/ windows/ windows media`	Microsoft's Windows Audio format supports streaming and can be played with Windows Media Player as well as many other popular players. It also offers digital rights management functionality.
WAV	`.wav`	No official website exists for WAV files, but you can find some documentation at `www.micro soft.com` if you search for *WAV.*	The WAV file format is popular in digital media because it offers the highest sound quality possible. Audio files in this format are often too big for use on the web, averaging 12MB for a minute of audio. (In comparison, an MP3 file that is five times longer can be less than one-third the size.) Although WAV files are commonly used on the Internet because of their nearly universal compatibility, I recommend that you convert WAV files (especially for long audio clips) to one of the other audio formats.

Adding Audio and Video Files to Web Pages

Like other multimedia files, you can link to an audio or a video file or you can insert multimedia files into a page. Linking to a multimedia file is as easy as linking to any other file, as you see in the instructions that follow. Inserting an audio or a video file is a little more complicated, but it lets a visitor play the file without leaving the web page. Inserting audio and video files is covered in this section. If you're using Flash video or audio, see the "Adding Flash audio and video files" section, later in this chapter.

Linking to audio and video files

To use Dreamweaver to link to a video or an audio file, follow these steps:

1. **Click to select the text, image, or other element you want to use to create a link.**

   If you're linking to a video file, a good trick is to take a single still image from the video and insert that into your web page. Then create a link from that image to the video file.

2. **Choose Insert⇨Hyperlink or click the Hyperlink icon in the Common Insert panel.**

   The Hyperlink dialog box opens, as shown in Figure 12-3.

   Alternatively, you can click the Browse icon just to the right of the Link field in the Property inspector. (The Browse icon looks like a small file folder.)

3. **In the Text field, enter the text you want to serve as a link.**

   If you selected a section of text on the page before opening the Hyperlink dialog box, that text automatically appears in the Text field.

4. **In the Link field, enter the URL where the audio or video file is located.**

   Alternatively, click the Browse icon (the small file folder icon) to the right of the Link field and browse your hard drive to find the video or audio file you want to link to.

   As with any other file you link to, make sure you've saved your audio or video files into your local site folder (which I explain how to set up in Chapter 2).

   Note that you can link to an audio or a video file on another website, as I did in the example shown in Figure 12-3, but you need to have the exact URL of the file's location.

   To specify Accessibility settings, enter a title, an access key, and a tab index.

5. **When you have finished specifying settings, click OK.**

The dialog box closes, and the link is created automatically.

6. **Click the Preview button (at the top of the work area) to open the page in a browser, where you can test the link to your multimedia file.**

Dreamweaver launches your specified web browser and displays the page. If you have the necessary player, the file downloads, your player launches, and your file automatically plays.

Many people like to have multimedia files, such as video, pop up in a new browser window. To do this, create an HTML file and embed your multimedia file in it. Then use the Open Browser Window behavior in Dreamweaver to create a pop-up window that displays your multimedia page. For more on how to work with Dreamweaver behaviors, see Chapter 10.

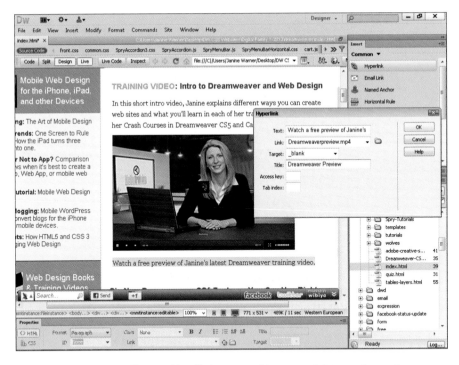

Figure 12-3: Link to an audio or a video file just as you'd create a link to another web page.

Inserting audio and video files

When you insert an audio or a video file into a web page, you can set the file to play automatically when the page loads (as long as your visitor has the necessary player), or you can require that your visitors click the play button in the video or audio player first. I recommend the second option. I like to give users control over when and how a video plays because I never want to get anyone in trouble if they're surfing the web in an office or library where unexpected audio can be distracting, embarrassing, or worse.

Whether or not you set the file to play automatically, the advantage of embedding it into the page is that file will play within your web page instead of opening in a separate window or player.

To use Dreamweaver to embed an audio or a video file (in any format other than Flash) into a web page, follow these steps:

1. **Click where you want the file to appear on your web page.**

2. **Select Common from the Insert panel, and in the Media drop-down list, choose Plugin (see Figure 12-4).**

   You can also choose Insert⇨Media⇨Plugin. The Select File dialog box appears.

   Use the Plugin option for all audio and video file types — except Flash video (`.flv`) files, covered in the next section.

3. **Browse your hard drive to locate the sound or video file you want inserted in your page and then click to select it.**

4. **Click OK.**

   The dialog box closes, and the file is inserted automatically into the page. A small plug-in icon (resembling a puzzle piece) represents the file.

5. **Click the plug-in icon that represents the file in the web page to display the file options in the Property inspector and specify your desired settings.**

Figure 12-4: Use Plugin to insert an audio or a video file.

When you add audio or video, Dreamweaver doesn't automatically determine the height and width of the file, so you need to add the dimensions in the Property inspector after you insert the file. You find a description of these and other options in the next sections, "Setting options for audio and video files."

6. **Click the Preview button (at the top of the work area) to open the page in a browser.**

   If you have the necessary player on your computer and set the file to Autoplay (the default setting), your file plays automatically when the page loads into the browser. To change video and audio settings that aren't included in the Property inspector, such as Autoplay, see the "Setting multimedia parameters" section later in this chapter.

Setting options for audio and video files

When you select an inserted multimedia file, such as a sound or a video file, the Property inspector displays the options for the file, as shown in Figure 12-5. Among these settings, the height and width are the most important. Unlike image files or Flash files, Dreamweaver can't automatically detect the height and width of other audio or video formats, so it's important to set these options in the Property inspector. To determine the height and width of a video file, you may need to open the file in a video-editing program. For audio files, set the height and width based on the size required for the player you're using. You can find the dimensions of a video file by opening it in a video-editing program and looking for the height and width.

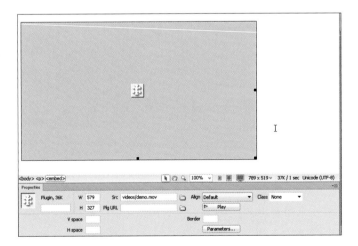

Figure 12-5: Select an audio or a video file in Dreamweaver to display the properties for the file in the Property inspector.

The following describes the multimedia options available from the Property inspector:

- ✔ **ID field:** Use the text field in the upper-left corner of the Property inspector, just to the right of the plug-in icon, if you want to assign a name to the file. If you leave this field blank, Dreamweaver doesn't enter a name automatically unless you are using a file in a Flash format. The name is important only if you want to refer to the file in JavaScript.

- ✔ **W (width) and H (height):** Specify the measurement of the file in pixels. If you make the video much bigger than its actual size or fail to maintain its proportions, the video may be distorted or lack quality.

- ✔ **Src (source):** This option specifies the name and path to the file. You can type a filename or click the Browse icon (which looks like a small folder) to browse for the file. This field is filled in automatically when you embed the file.

- ✔ **Plg URL:** This option enables you to provide a URL where viewers can download the plug-in if they don't already have it.

- ✔ **Align:** This option enables you to specify how the element aligns on the page. Alignment works just as it does for images.

- ✔ **Play button:** (Available only under Windows.) Click the green Play button to preview the media file. The media plug-in must be installed in Dreamweaver (in the Configuration/Plugins folder) for it to be previewed in Dreamweaver.

- ✔ **Class:** Use this drop-down list to apply any style sheets defined for the document.

- ✔ **V Space (vertical space):** If you want blank space above and below the plug-in, enter the number of pixels here.

- ✔ **H Space (horizontal space):** If you want blank space on either side of the plug-in, enter the number of pixels or use a percentage to specify a portion of the browser window's width.

- ✔ **Border:** This option specifies the width of the border around the file when it's displayed.

- ✔ **Parameters:** Click this button to access a dialog box where you can enter additional parameters specific to the type of multimedia file you inserted. For more information, see the following section.

Setting multimedia parameters

You can use parameters to control a wide range of multimedia options, such as whether a video file or an audio file starts playing as soon as a page is loaded. Setting parameters isn't intuitive, and Dreamweaver doesn't do the best job of helping with these settings. However, by researching the options for the file type you're using and being careful when using the Parameters dialog box in Dreamweaver, you can have a lot more control over your multimedia files.

In fairness to the programmers who created Dreamweaver, including all the parameters for all the possible multimedia file types in use on the web today would be difficult. However, they could have included the common file types. Because they don't, I offer you this brief primer on using the Parameters setting and a few typical options for a few common file types. You also find web addresses where you can find more complete lists of parameters for a few of the most popular audio and video formats.

In Figure 12-6, you see the Parameters dialog box with settings for a Windows Media Video file. The following steps outline how the process works:

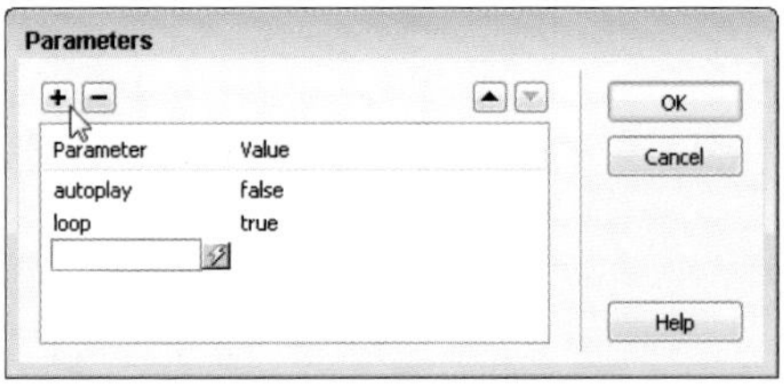

Figure 12-6: Add parameters for additional audio and video settings.

1. **To access the Parameters dialog box, click to select the multimedia file in the web page and then click the Parameters button in the Property inspector.**

   The Parameters dialog box opens. The dialog box is blank unless you have already entered parameters for the selected file.

2. **Click the plus sign (+) at the top of the dialog box to add a parameter.**

   If you wanted to delete a selected parameter, you'd click the minus sign (–).

3. **On the left side of the dialog box, enter the name of the parameter; on the right side, enter the value you want.**

   I entered *autoplay* as the parameter and *false* as the value, to prevent the Windows Media Video file from playing automatically.

You can move from the name side of the Parameters dialog box to the value side by pressing the Tab key or by clicking to insert your cursor.

To help you get started with parameters, here are some of the most common and valuable parameters:

✔ **autoplay (or autostart, depending on the file type):** By default, when you add video or audio to an HTML file, most browsers play the file as soon as the page loads. If you want to prevent your multimedia files from playing automatically, set the autoplay or autostart parameter to false. Think of true and false as on and off when it comes to parameters.

✔ **loop:** This parameter enables you to control whether a video file or an audio file loops or continues to play over and over.

✔ **showControls:** This option makes it possible to hide the video or audio controls for a file.

Be careful about combining options like these. For example, if you set autoplay to false and showControls to false, your visitor can never play your file. By default, the controls for most multimedia files are visible unless you set the showControls parameter to false.

Find more attributes for the Windows Media format at `www.microsoft.com` when you search for *Windows Media Player properties*, or go directly to `http://msdn.microsoft.com/en-us/library/ms930698.aspx`. For QuickTime attributes, visit `www.apple.com` and search for *QuickTime Embed tag attributes* or go directly to `http://support.apple.com/kb/TA26486`.

Adding Flash audio and video files

Flash video has long been the video format of choice because so many people have the Flash Player and the player is such a small and easy download for those who don't have it. Adobe owns both Flash and Dreamweaver, so you find much better support for Flash files in Dreamweaver.

The Insert FLV dialog box makes it easy to set parameters for Flash. Dreamweaver can even automatically detect the size of Flash video files. You can also use Flash to create and insert audio files, displaying only the player (called a *skin* in Flash).

Follow these steps to insert a Flash video file into a web page:

1. **Click where you want the file to appear on your web page.**

2. **Choose Insert⊏⟩Media⊏⟩FLV.**

   Alternatively, you can choose FLV from the Media drop-down list in the Common Insert panel select (refer to Figure 12-1).

   The Insert FLV dialog box appears, as shown in Figure 12-7.

them to a *script* (essentially a short program that executes a limited set of commands). Most forms are processed by Common Gateway Interface (CGI) scripts or some other program. These scripts can be written in different programming languages, including PHP, ASP.NET, C, C#, Java, Ruby on Rails, and Perl. CGI scripts are far more complex than simple HTML files. Even experienced web designers often purchase scripts created by a third party or hire experienced programmers to develop CGI scripts for them — especially for complex features, such as discussion boards or shopping carts.

Fortunately for those who don't have a computer science degree or a huge budget for programmers, many free and low-priced scripts are available on the web. Search the Internet for *CGI scripts* and you'll find an impressive collection of ready-to-use programs, many of them free. Be aware, however, that when you download a program, you could be creating a security risk for your server, so look for trustworthy scripts with good reviews and support.

You also have to know how to configure and install any script you download on your web server, which may require special access. How you install a script on your server depends on how your server is set up. Unfortunately, this book can't show you everything there is to know about working with all the different kinds of scripts available on the web on all the different kinds of servers. (That task would require a shelf full of books.) But I do try to give you an idea of what's involved in working with CGI scripts — and what to do in Dreamweaver to make sure your HTML form will work with a script.

The first part of this chapter includes instructions for creating the common elements in an HTML form, from radio buttons to text boxes. In the last part of the chapter, I include instructions for configuring a form to work with a common CGI script that you can use to send the contents of a form to any specified e-mail address. The steps and features covered in the final exercise also help you with other kinds of CGI scripts, but you should note that how you work with forms will depend on your web-hosting service and the specific configuration and requirements of your server.

 You also need to create forms when you build dynamic websites using Dreamweaver's ColdFusion, ASP.NET, or PHP features. If you're creating a dynamic or database-driven site, use the features specific to those technologies and the site you are working on.

Creating HTML Forms

No matter what kinds of fields you put in your form — radio buttons, check boxes, and text areas, for example — you start by inserting the `<form>` tag itself. Think of a `<form>` tag as the container for all other elements — the buttons, boxes, and so on that you place in your form.

You must have a `<form>` tag around any form field, even if you're including only a simple text box or radio button. If you don't insert a form field before you add a form element, Dreamweaver will add one for you, but it's good practice to set up the form field yourself. Start by creating an HTML form before you move on to other exercises in this chapter.

The following exercise walks you through creating an HTML form. Start with an open page — either a new page or an existing page to which you want to add a form:

1. **Choose Insert⇨Form⇨Form or click the Form icon on the Forms Insert bar.**

   An empty `<form>` tag is inserted in your document and displayed as a rectangle outlined by a red dotted line, like the one shown in the Document area in Figure 13-1. This dotted line defines the boundaries of a form in the HTML code.

   You can control the display of invisible elements, such as `<form>` tags. Choose Edit⇨Preferences (Windows) or Dreamweaver⇨Preferences (Mac). Then, in the Invisible Elements category, select or deselect the Form Delimiter box. When the box is selected, the form outline is visible in the Dreamweaver workspace, as you see in Figure 13-1.

2. **Click the red outline to select the `<form>` tag and display the `<form>` tag options in the Property inspector (as shown at the bottom of Figure 13-1).**

3. **In the ID text box, type a name.**

   You can choose any name for this field as long as you don't use spaces, special characters, or punctuation. With your basic HTML form set up, you're ready to add elements to it, as explained in the following sections.

Before you begin filling your form with options, keep the following tips in mind:

 ✔ **The best way to align your form fields is to use CSS.** By creating styles that control the spacing and padding of form elements, you can make all your fields, buttons, and other elements line up neatly. (Chapters 5–7 cover CSS.)

 ✔ **After you design your form, your work isn't quite done; your form won't do anything unless you configure it to work with a script.**

Although Dreamweaver doesn't provide any scripts, it does make linking your HTML forms to a script — or to a database — relatively easy. The section "Understanding How CGI Scripts Work" (later in this chapter) offers more details on making your form work with a script.

✔ **Match the script.** Most fields displayed in the Property inspector when the `<form>` tag options are on-screen should be set to match those in the CGI script or other program used to collect and process the data from the form. You find instructions for filling in these fields in the "Configuring your form to work with a script" section, at the end of this chapter.

✔ **Use accessibility settings.** The accompanying sidebar, "Making forms accessible," offers some practical examples of how the accessibility settings in Dreamweaver can help you tweak your forms' characteristics to make them easier to use for all of the visitors to your site.

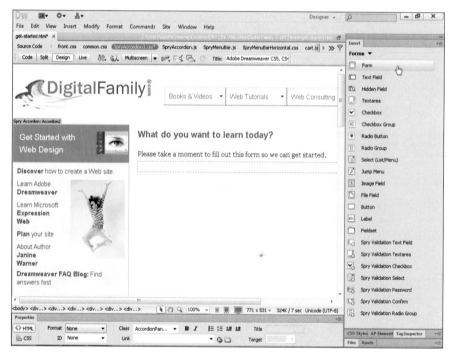

Photo by Jasper Jahol

Figure 13-1: The Forms Insert bar provides easy access to all common form elements.

Making forms accessible

You can make your forms much easier to use and more accessible to all your visitors by using the <label> tag and other accessibility attributes with form items. Dreamweaver makes adding these tags easy by including an Input Tag Accessibility Attributes dialog box, as shown in the figure. For this dialog box to appear when you insert a form item such as a radio button or a check box, you must have accessibility features turned on in Dreamweaver's Preference settings. To turn on these features, choose Edit⇨Preferences (Dreamweaver⇨Preferences on a Mac); in the Preferences dialog box, click the Accessibility category, and select the Form Objects option.

With the accessibility options turned on, the Input Tag Accessibility Attributes dialog box opens automatically when you insert a form item (such as a radio button or a text box). Use this dialog box to specify the following options:

✔ **ID:** Use the ID field to assign a name to a form element. The name is important because it can be used to refer to the field in a script. The ID is used also if you choose the Attach Label Tag Using 'For' Attribute option under the Style options. If you're not using the form with a script or a label, you can leave this field blank, and Dreamweaver won't enter a name automatically.

✔ **Label:** Enter a name that describes the form element (radio button, check box, text field, whatever). For example, you might enter *E-mail Address* for a text field where you want users to enter their e-mail address. The text you enter in the Label field will appear next to a form field in the web page and will have special meaning to a *screen reader.* (The screen reader program provides audible descriptions of screen elements to visually impaired users and relies on the added instructions provided by labels to help identify the type of text.)

✔ **Style:** Select one of these three options to specify how the label should be included with the form field in the HTML code. The option Attach Label Tag Using 'For' Attribute is recommended as the best option for accessibility because it wraps the label tag around the entire form field, ensuring that the label and the form field will always be associated with each other. This option makes it easier for users to select a form field, such as a check box or radio button, because they can select the field by clicking anywhere in the text associated with it, instead of having to click precisely inside the check box or radio button.

✔ **Position:** Select the corresponding box to specify whether the label text should appear before or after each form item.

✔ **Access Key:** This attribute enables you to create a keyboard shortcut for each of your form items. You can enter any letter in this field, and your users can select the form item by holding down the Alt key (Windows) or the Control key (Macintosh) and typing the letter you specify. For example, if you enter *Q* as the access key, a visitor to your site who uses a Windows computer could press Alt+Q to select the form item.

✔ **Tab Index:** By default, a visitor to your site can use the Tab key to move from one form field to another in the order in which the form items appear on the page. With the Tab Index, you can specify the order

(continued)

in which the Tab key progresses from one form item to another. This is especially helpful if you have links and other form items on a page, and you want the user to be able to tab through them in a specific order. To control the order, assign a number to each form. Be sure to number your form items in ascending numerical order (as with 1, 2, 3); don't skip any numbers or the tab order will revert to the visual layout order.

Input Tag Accessibility Attributes

ID:	textfield
Label:	Name
Style:	○ Attach label tag using 'for' attribute
	○ Wrap with label tag
	○ No label tag
Position:	○ Before form item
	○ After form item
Access key:	n Tab Index: 1

OK
Cancel
Help

If you don't want to enter this information when inserting objects, change the Accessibility preferences.

Creating radio buttons and check boxes

Radio buttons and check boxes make filling in a form easy for viewers of your site. Instead of making users type a word (such as *yes* or *no*), you can provide radio buttons and check boxes so users can simply click boxes or buttons to make a specific and consistent choice. Using buttons, check boxes, and multiple-choice lists, covered later in this chapter, can also help ensure that the data collected in a form is consistent.

What's the difference between radio buttons and check boxes? *Radio buttons* (like the pushbuttons on old car radios) enable users to select only one option from a group. Thus, radio buttons are good for either-or options — or in situations where you want users to make only one selection. *Check boxes,* on the other hand, enable users to make multiple choices, so they're good for choose-all-that-apply situations or for situations that require approval, such as *Check this box if. . . .*

Creating radio buttons

To create radio buttons on a form, follow these steps:

1. **Click to place your cursor inside the boundary of the** `<form>` **tag where you want to add a radio button.**

   If you haven't yet inserted the `<form>` tag, follow the steps in the section "Creating HTML Forms," earlier in this chapter.

2. **Click the Radio Button icon on the Forms Insert bar.**

   You can also choose Insert⟳Form⟳Radio Button. Either way, a radio button appears inside the form's red boundary line.

If you have accessibility options turned on in Preferences, the Input Tag Accessibility Attributes dialog box opens. (See the sidebar "Making forms accessible" to find out more about these options.)

3. **Repeat Step 2 until you have the number of radio buttons you want.**

4. **Select one of the radio buttons on the form to reveal the radio button's properties in the Property inspector, as shown in Figure 13-2.**

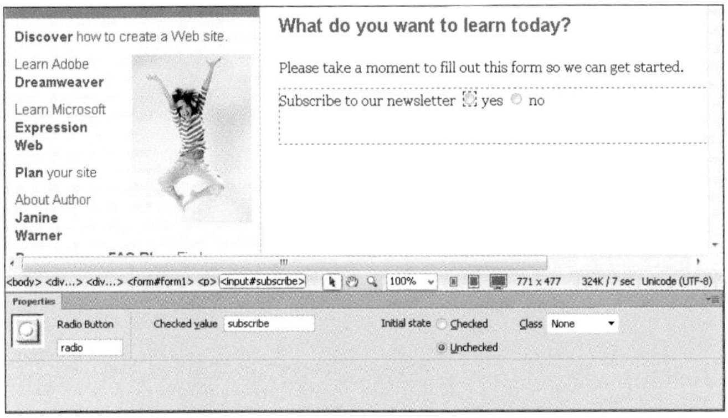

Photo by Jasper Jahol

Figure 13-2: Properties of radio buttons.

5. **In the Radio Button text box on the far left of the Property inspector, type a name.**

All radio buttons in a group should have the same name so that the browser associates them with one another and prevents users from selecting more than one. If you want users to be able to choose more than one item from a list, use check boxes instead, as described in the following section.

6. **In the Checked Value text box, type a name.**

Each radio button in a group should have a different Checked Value name so it can be distinguished from the others. Naming radio buttons for the thing they represent is often a good practice; for example, *yes* when the choice is yes and *no* when it's no. If you're asking users about their favorite ice cream flavors, you might use as values the flavor each button represents.

The Checked Value name is usually included in the data you get back when the form is processed and returned to you (the data collected by a form can be returned in an e-mail message or sent directly to a database or other data-storage option). How the data is returned depends on the CGI script or other programming used to process the form. If you're looking at the data later, interpreting it is easier if the name is something that makes sense to you.

7. **For the Initial State option, select Checked or Unchecked.**

These two options determine whether the radio button on your form appears already selected when the web page loads. Select Checked if you want to preselect a choice. You should set only one radio button option to be preselected; remember that the user can always override this setting by selecting another radio button.

8. **Select the other radio buttons one by one in the main design area and repeat Steps 5–7 to specify the properties in the Property inspector for each one.**

If you want to create a series of radio buttons, you'll find some advantages to using the Radio Group button in the Insert Form panel. Dreamweaver creates IDs for each radio button automatically. If you want to change these IDs, you may find it easier to change them in Code view. You can split the screen between Code and Design views by clicking the Split View icon at the top of the workspace.

If you want to format your form with CSS styles, you can create tag styles for the form, radio button, and other tags, or you can create class styles and apply them to any or all of your tags using the Class drop-down list in the Property inspector. (You find more information about creating and applying styles in Chapters 5 and 6.)

If your form is complete, jump ahead to the "Finishing your form with Submit and Reset buttons" section, later in this chapter.

Creating check boxes

To create check boxes, follow these steps:

1. **Click to place your cursor inside the boundary of the** `<form>` **tag where you want to add a check box.**

If you haven't yet inserted a `<form>` tag, follow the steps in the "Creating HTML Forms" section, earlier in this chapter.

2. **Click the Check Box icon on the Forms Insert bar.**

You can also choose Insert⊏>Form⊏>Check Box.

If you have accessibility options turned on in Preferences, the Input Tag Accessibility Attributes dialog box opens. (See the sidebar "Making forms accessible," to find out more about these options.)

3. **Repeat Step 2 to place as many check boxes as you want.**

4. **Select one of the check boxes on your form to reveal the check box properties in the Property inspector, as shown in Figure 13-3.**

Figure 13-3: Properties of check boxes.

5. **In the Checkbox Name text box, type a name.**

   Use a distinct name for each check box. Users can select more than one check box, and you want to ensure that the information submitted is properly associated with each individual check box.

6. **In the Checked Value text box, type a name.**

   Every check box in a group should have a different Checked Value name so the CGI script can tell the boxes apart. Naming them for the things they represent is a good practice. As with radio buttons, the checked value is usually included in the data you get back when the form is processed and returned to you.

   If you're looking at the data later — say, reading an e-mail message that lists the text in the Checked Value text box and whatever the user entered into the field — the data is easier to understand if the name is something that makes sense to you. For example, entering the word *Chocolate* instead of *Option2* will result in data that looks like this: *Chocolate=yes* instead of *Option2=yes.*

7. **For the Initial State option, select Checked or Unchecked.**

   This option determines whether the check box appears already selected when the web page loads. Select Checked if you want to preselect a choice. A user can always override this preselection by clicking the text box again to deselect it.

8. **Select the other check boxes one by one and repeat Steps 5–7 to set the properties in the Property inspector for each one.**

If you want to create a series of check boxes, you'll find some advantages to using the Checkbox Group button in the Insert Form panel.

If your form is complete, jump ahead to the "Finishing your form with Submit and Reset buttons" section, later in this chapter.

Adding text fields and text areas

When you want users to enter text, such as a name, an e-mail address, or a comment, use a text field. To insert text fields, follow these steps:

1. **Click to place your cursor inside the `<form>` tag where you want to add a text field.**

   If you haven't yet inserted a `<form>` tag, follow the steps in the "Creating HTML Forms" section, earlier in this chapter.

2. **Click the Text Field icon on the Forms Insert bar.**

   You can also choose Insert⇨Form⇨Text Field. A text field box appears.

   If you have accessibility options turned on in Preferences, the Input Tag Accessibility Attributes dialog box opens. (Refer to the "Making forms accessible" sidebar to find out more about these options.)

3. **On the form, click to place your cursor next to the first text field and type a question or other text prompt.**

   For example, you may want to type *E-mail Address:* next to a text box where you want a user to enter an e-mail address.

4. **Select the text field on your form to reveal the Text Field properties in the Property inspector, as shown in Figure 13-4.**

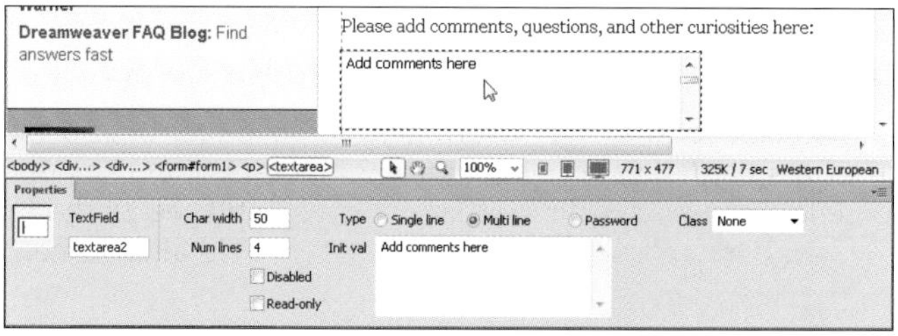

Dreamweaver FAQ Blog: Find answers fast

Please add comments, questions, and other curiosities here:

Add comments here

`<body> <div...> <div...> <form#form1> <p> <textarea>`   100%   771 x 477   325K / 7 sec   Western European

Properties

TextField   Char width 50   Type ○ Single line ⦿ Multi line ○ Password   Class None

textarea2   Num lines 4   Init val Add comments here

☐ Disabled

☐ Read-only

Figure 13-4: Use the Text Field options to enable users to enter text.

5. In the TextField text box, type a name.

Each text area on a form should have a different text field name so the CGI script can distinguish it from the others. Naming text areas for the things they represent is usually best, but don't use any spaces or special characters (other than the hyphen or underscore). In Figure 13-4, you can see that Dreamweaver automatically includes the name `textarea`, `textarea2`, and so on. You can replace that name with your own text as long as you don't use spaces or special characters. Many scripts return this name next to the contents of the text field a visitor enters at your website. If you're looking at the data later, you can interpret it more easily if the name corresponds to the choice.

6. In the Char Width box, type the number of characters you want visible in the field.

This setting determines the width of the text field that appears on the page. In the example shown here, I've set the character width to 50 to create a text box that's more than wide enough for most e-mail addresses. How wide you make your text boxes depends on the amount of information you expect users to enter — and on the constraints of your design.

7. In the Max Chars box, type the maximum number of characters you want to allow.

Note: The Max Chars field is visible only if you choose the Single Line radio button. If you leave the Mac Chars field blank, users can type as many characters as they choose, even if their entries exceed the physical length of the text box specified in the Char Width field.

I usually limit the number of characters only if I want to maintain consistency in the data (for example, I like to limit a State field to a two-character abbreviation). Creating drop-down lists, which require users to make a selection rather than risking that they might make a typo, is an even better way to ensure consistent data. You find instructions for creating drop-downs in the exercise that follows.

You can set the Char Width field to be longer or shorter than the Max Chars field. If users type more characters than can appear in the text field, the text scrolls so that users can still see all the text they enter, even if it can't be displayed in the text field all at once.

8. Next to Type, select one of the following options:

    • **Single Line** creates a one-line text box.

- **Multi Line** gives users space to enter text. (Note that if you select Multi Line, the Num Lines field appears, where you specify the number of lines you want the text area to cover.)

- **Password** is used if you're asking users to enter data that they might not want to display on-screen. This type of field causes entered data to appear as asterisks — and disables copying from the field (essential if you're going to keep the password secure).

9. **Use the Class drop-down list to apply any class CSS styles that may be defined in the site.**

    You can create class styles for many purposes, including formatting form elements. (For more about creating and applying class styles, see Chapters 5 and 6.)

10. **In the Init Val text box, type any text you want displayed when the form loads.**

    For example, you can include *Add e-mail address here* on the form in the text field. Users can delete the Init Val text or leave it and add more text in the same text field.

11. **Select the other text areas one by one and repeat Steps 5–10 to set the properties in the Property inspector for each one.**

If your form is complete, jump ahead to the "Finishing your form with Submit and Reset buttons" section, later in this chapter.

Creating drop-down lists

When you want to give users a multiple-choice option but don't want to take up lots of space on the page, a drop-down list, such as the one shown in Figure 13-5, is an ideal solution. Drop-down lists are a good option also if you want to make sure that data collected in the form is consistent. For example, if you give users a list of state names instead of a text field, you don't have to worry about the fact that some people may enter the full state name, others may enter two letters, and still others may misspell the name. If the data collected in your form is simply e-mailed to you, consistency may be no big deal. But if the data goes into a database where it needs to match other related data, misspellings and other variations can cause big problems.

Photo by Jasper Jahol

Figure 13-5: The List/Menu option enables you to create a drop-down list.

To create a drop-down list with Dreamweaver, follow these steps:

1. **Click to place your cursor inside the** `<form>` **tag where you want to add a drop-down list.**

   If you haven't yet created a `<form>` tag, follow the steps in the "Creating HTML Forms" section, earlier in this chapter.

2. **Click the Select (List/Menu) icon on the Forms Insert bar.**

   You can also choose Insert⇨Form⇨Select (List/Menu). A drop-down list appears.

   If you have accessibility options turned on in Preferences, the Input Tag Accessibility Attributes dialog box opens. (Refer to the "Making forms accessible" sidebar, earlier in the chapter, for more about these options.)

3. **Click to place your cursor next to the List field and enter a question or other text prompt.**

   I typed *What state do you live in?*

4. **Select the field that represents the list on your page to reveal the List/Menu properties in the Property inspector.**

5. **In the List/Menu text box, type a name.**

   Each list or menu on a form should have a different name so you can differentiate the lists when the form data is returned.

6. **Next to Type, select the Menu or List option.**

   This step determines whether the form element is a drop-down list or a scrollable list. If you select List, you can specify the height and control how many items are shown at a time. You can also specify whether a user can select more than one item. If you select Menu, these options aren't available.

7. **Click the List Values button, at the upper-right of the Property inspector.**

   The List Values dialog box appears, as shown in Figure 13-6.

List Values		
+ −		OK
Item Label	Value	Cancel
choose a state		
Alabama	AL	
Alaska	AK	
Arizona	AZ	
Arkansas	AR	Help

   Figure 13-6: Create the options in the List form field.

8. **Enter the choices you want to make available.**

   Click the plus sign (+) to add an item label and then type the label text you want in the text box that appears in the dialog box. Item labels appear on the menu or are listed on the web page in the order in which you enter them. Use the minus sign (–) to delete a selected option.

   Press the Tab key to move the cursor to the Value side of the dialog box, where you can enter a value. Values are optional, but if they're present, they're sent to the server instead of the label text. This feature provides a way of including information that you don't want to display directly on the drop-down list. For example, if you enter *Alabama* as a label on the left, you can enter the abbreviation *AL* as a value on the right. If you enter *Alaska* as a label, you can enter *AK* as a value, and so on. That way, you visitors can select from a list that displays the full name of each state, but your script can collect only the two-letter abbreviations. If you don't enter a value, the label is used as the submitted data when the form is processed.

   The first label entered in the List Values dialog box is the only one that's displayed on the page until a user clicks the drop-down arrow. Thus, it's good practice to include an instruction in this space, such as *Choose a State,* as shown in the examples in Figures 13-5 and 13-6.

9. **Click OK to close the dialog box.**

Using jump menus

Many designers use *jump menus* (which take the user immediately to a different online location) as navigational elements because they can provide a list of links in a drop-down list without taking up lots of room on a web page. You can also use a jump menu to launch an application or start an animation sequence. Jump menus are generally used as standalone features on a web page, but they can be integrated into a form with other form items.

To create a jump menu, follow these steps:

1. **Click to place your cursor inside the** `<form>` **tag where you want to add a jump menu.**

   Alternatively, you can create a jump menu anywhere on a page. If no `<form>` tag is in place, Dreamweaver adds one automatically around the jump menu's tag.

2. **Click the Jump Menu icon on the Forms Insert bar.**

   You can also choose Insert➪Form➪Jump Menu. The Insert Jump Menu dialog box opens.

3. **In the Text field, under Menu Items, type the name you want to display in the drop-down list.**

   Click the plus sign (+) to add more items. As you type items in the Text field, they appear in the Menu Items list, as shown in Figure 13-7.

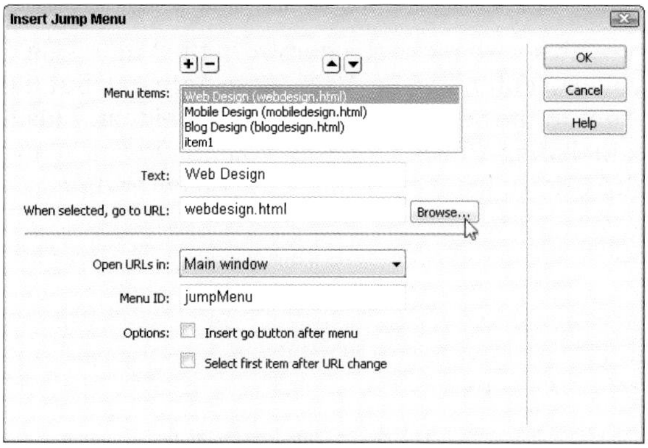

Figure 13-7: Items added in the Text field appear in the Menu Items list.

4. **Click the Browse button to locate the page you want to link to or type the URL for the page in the When Selected, Go to URL field.**

   You can link to a local file or enter any URL to link to a page on another website, and you can use the Browse button to specify the URL you want to link to.

5. **If you're using frames, use the Open URLs In field to specify a target.**

   If you're not using frames, the default is Main Window. When the user selects an option, the new page replaces the page he or she is viewing. (I explain how to target links in frames in Chapter 8.)

6. **If you want to enter a unique identifier for this menu, use the Menu ID field.**

   This option can be useful if you have multiple jump menus on a page. You can use any name you want, but you can't use spaces, special characters, or punctuation.

7. **If you want to force users to click a button to activate the selection, select the Insert Go Button after Menu option.**

   If you don't add a Go button, the linked page loads as soon as the user makes a selection. The Go button works like a Submit button for the jump menu options.

Finishing your form with Submit and Reset buttons

For your users to be able to send their completed forms to you, create a Submit button that, when clicked, tells the user's browser to send the form to the CGI script or other program that processes the form. You may also want to add a Reset button, which enables users to erase any information they've entered if they want to start over.

Many developers don't use the Reset button because they find it can be confusing to visitors (and annoying if it means they accidentally erase all the information they just entered). Because visitors can always leave a page before clicking the Submit button if they choose not to complete a form, the simplest way to avoid this problem is to avoid using a Reset button.

To create a Submit, Reset, or other button in Dreamweaver, follow these steps:

1. **Click to place your cursor inside the** `<form>` **tag where you want to add a button.**

   If you haven't yet inserted the `<form>` tag (which appears as a red outline around your form), follow the steps in the earlier section "Creating

HTML Forms" before continuing with these steps. You might also want to enter at least one text field or other field option. There's not much point in having a Submit button if you don't provide any fields where a user can enter data to be submitted.

2. **Click the Button icon on the Forms Insert bar.**

   You can also choose Insert⇨Form⇨Button.

   If you have accessibility options turned on in Preferences, the Button Accessibility Attributes dialog box opens. (The "Making forms accessible" sidebar, earlier in the chapter, details these options.)

   A Submit button appears.

3. **Click to select the button.**

   The Property inspector changes to reveal the form button properties, as shown in Figure 13-8. You can change the button to a Reset button or other kind of button by altering the attributes in the Property inspector, as shown in the remaining steps.

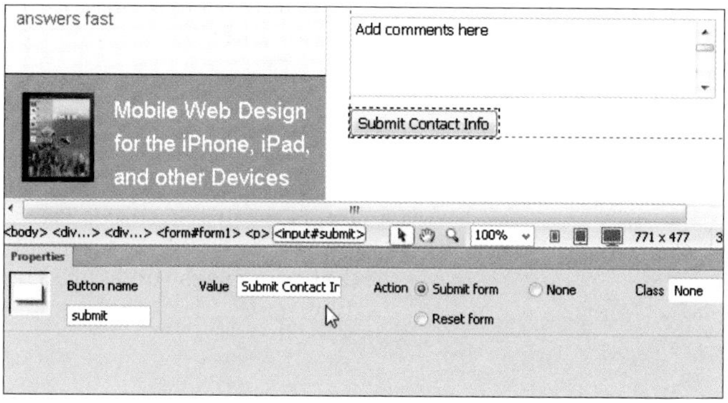

Figure 13-8: The form button properties.

4. **Next to Action, click the Submit Form or Reset Form option.**

   The Submit Form option invokes an action, such as sending user information to an e-mail address. The Reset Form option returns the page to the way it was when the page loaded. You can also select the None option, which creates a button that can be used for many purposes by combining it with a script.

5. **In the Value text box, type the text you want to display on the button.**

   You can type any text you want for the label, such as Search, Go, Clear, or Delete.

Having the user click a Submit button in a form doesn't do much unless you've configured the form to work with a CGI script or other program that collects or processes user-entered data.

Understanding How CGI Scripts Work

As mentioned, *Common Gateway Interface (CGI) scripts* are programs written in a programming language (such as Perl, Java, C++, ASP, or PHP) that work with your web server to process data submitted by a user. Think of CGI scripts as the engine behind an HTML form and many other automated features on a website. These scripts are much more complex to create than HTML pages — and these languages take much longer to figure out than HTML. CGI scripts reside and run on the server and are usually triggered by an action a user takes, such as clicking the Submit button on an HTML form.

A common scenario with a script may go like this:

1. A user loads a page (such as an order page), fills out the HTML form, and clicks the Submit button.

2. The browser gathers all the data from the form and sends it to the web server in a standard format.

3. The web server takes the incoming data and hands it off to the CGI script, which unpacks the data and does something with it — such as placing it in an e-mail message and sending the message to a specified e-mail address, or processing the credit card to complete the order.

4. The CGI script then sends instructions or a block of HTML back to the browser through the web server to report on the outcome of the script and to complete any final actions, such as displaying a Thank You page.

Configuring your form to work with a script

After you create a form using the features covered in the previous sections of this chapter, configure the form to work with a CGI script or a program. To help you understand how this process works, I use the common `formmail.pl` script in the following exercise. This clever little script is designed to collect data entered into an HTML form and send it to a specified e-mail address. You can find out more about `formmail.pl` at `www.scriptarchive.com` (a great place to find lots of free CGI scripts).

Every script is different. The details of how you install and configure a script depend on the individual program — and on how your server is set up.

If your service provider doesn't offer a mail script to use in your form, you can download and configure the script if you have the right access on your server (*and* knowledge of how your server is configured). Ask your service provider for more information. If your service provider doesn't provide the interactive scripts you want, you may want to consider moving your site to a hosting service that does provide CGI scripts you can use.

The following exercise shows you how to use Dreamweaver with the `formmail.pl` script. This gives you a good introduction to how you'd set up any form to work with any script — but be aware that you may have to alter some of the steps to work with the program you're using:

1. **Select the** `<form>` **tag that surrounds your form by clicking anywhere on the red outline that represents the boundary of the** `<form>` **tag (or by clicking the** `<form>` **tag in the tag selector at the bottom of the work area), as shown in Figure 13-9.**

   With the `<form>` tag selected, the Property inspector changes to feature the `<form>` tag options. ***Note:*** All HTML forms must be enclosed by the `<form>` tag. If your script doesn't have a `<form>` tag, add one around the entire contents of your form by following the steps in the "Creating HTML Forms" section found earlier in this chapter.

   To select the `<form>` tag in Dreamweaver, place your cursor anywhere in the body of your form and then use the tag selector at the bottom of the work area to select the `<form>` tag. Make sure you've selected the `<form>` tag and not just one of the form elements, such as the text box I created in this form for comments.

2. **In the Property inspector, give your form a name.**

   Dreamweaver automatically gives each form you create a distinct name (form1, form2, and so on) — but I prefer to change the name to something that has more meaning, such as *contact* for this contact form. You can name your form whatever you like; just don't use spaces or special characters.

3. **Specify the action for the form.**

   For the `formmail.pl` script used in this example (as well as many other scripts you might use), the action is simply the path to the script's location on your server. In Figures 13-9, you can see that I've entered the address `/cgi-bin/formmail.pl`. The address you enter depends on your service provider; a common convention is to call the folder where CGI scripts are stored `cgi-bin`. The last part of the address (`formmail.pl`) is the name of the script. (In this case, it's a Perl script, indicated by the `.pl` extension.)

   You can use the Browse icon (the folder icon in the Property inspector) to enter an address automatically in the Action field only if you're working on a live server — and Dreamweaver has identified the location of your script — or if you have the script on your local system in the same directory structure that exists on your server. In most cases, it's simplest just to ask your service provider or programmer for the address and type it in the Action field.

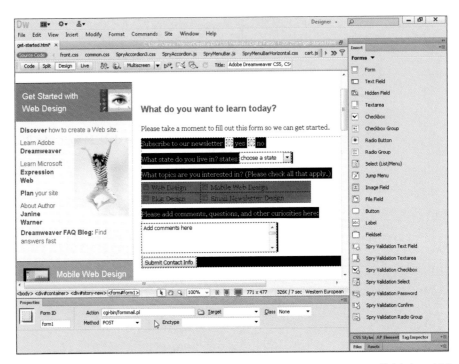

Figure 13-9: Use the tag selector to select the <form> tag and display form properties in the Property inspector.

4. In the Method field, use the drop-down arrow to choose Get, Post, or Default.

Again, what you choose depends on your script, but Dreamweaver's default is Post. If you're using a script, such as `formmail`, which is featured in the final sections of this chapter, the best option is Post.

The Get option is generally used for nondestructive, safe form transactions that may be repeated, such as those done with a search engine. Transactions with the Get option are generally stored in the log files on a server and in a browser's history files, so this option isn't recommended for sensitive data, such as financial information. The Post option is generally used for transactions that occur only once — such as sending an e-mail with the data from a form, registering for a service, or unsubscribing to a newsletter. The Post option can also handle larger chunks of data than Get.

5. **Click the Target option and specify what the browser does when the submit action is completed.**

   If you choose _blank, the results page opens in a new browser window. If you leave this field blank, the browser window is simply replaced with the results page. A results page is usually a simple HTML page with a message (such as *Thanks for playing*) delivered when the Submit button is clicked.

6. **Use the Enctype field to specify how the data is formatted when it's returned (see Figure 13-10).**

   For example, if you're using a form mail script, the Enctype field determines how the text appears in your e-mail when the contents of the form are sent to you. By default, this field is blank.

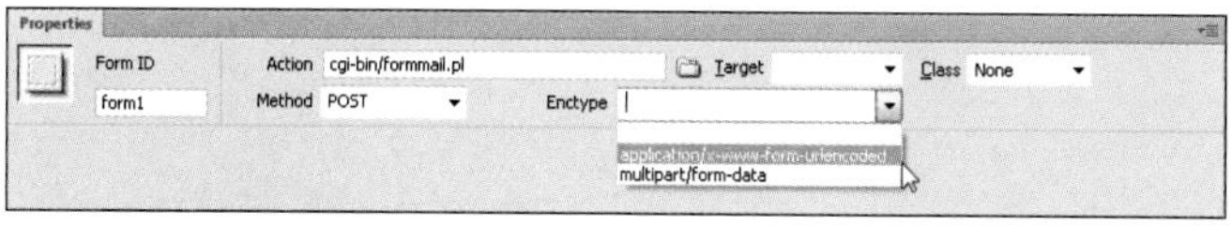

Figure 13-10: Enter a type in the Enctype field.

7. **Use the Class field at the far right of the Property inspector to apply a CSS style to the form.**

   In this example, I applied CSS to some elements in the form, such as the text, but not to the entire form.

Completing this set of steps takes care of all the options in the Property inspector. You still have one more task, however: inserting a hidden form field into this form to make it work with the `formmail.pl` script, as shown in the next exercise.

Using form validation to check data

When you create a form, including features that validate the form as a user submits it is a good practice. For example, you can use form validation to ensure that a user has entered an e-mail address in a text field. If they have not, you can return the form with a message stating that the e-mail address field is required. You can set up validation for forms in many ways, but the simplest method in Dreamweaver is to use the Spry form fields, which are covered in Chapter 11.

Using hidden fields

Many scripts, including the `formmail.pl` script, require the use of *hidden fields* — fields that hold data you want associated with a form but not shown to visitors to a site (such as the e-mail address to which a form is sent when a visitor clicks the Submit button). To insert and use a hidden field, follow these steps:

1. **Click to place your cursor inside the** `<form>` **tag.**

   If you haven't yet inserted the `<form>` tag (which appears as a red outline around your form), follow the steps in the first exercise in the "Creating HTML Forms" section before continuing with this exercise.

2. **Choose Insert⇨Form⇨Hidden Field or click to select the Hidden Field icon from the Insert panel.**

   Even though the hidden field doesn't appear in the form area, make sure that it's inside the `<form>` tag before you add a hidden field. Placing your cursor at the top or bottom of the form area before inserting a hidden field is a good option because it makes the hidden field easier to find in the HTML code.

   After the hidden field is inserted into the `<form>` tag, the Property inspector changes to feature the Hidden Field options (shown in Figure 13-11).

Properties		
HiddenField		
recipient	Value	janine@digitalfamily.com

Figure 13-11: The Hidden Field properties.

3. **In the Property inspector, enter a name.**

   If you're using `formmail.pl`, you'd enter **recipient** as the name and the e-mail address where you want the form data sent as the value. You can even enter more than one e-mail address, separated by commas. So, for example, I could enter *janine@jcwarner.com, janine@digitalfamily.com* in the Value field, and the data from the form would be e-mailed to both these e-mail addresses when a user clicks the Submit button.

4. **Click to place your cursor inside the** `<form>` **tag and then click the Hidden Field icon in the Forms Insert Bar to add another hidden field.**

5. **Create a subject line.**

6. **In the Property inspector, enter the name *subject*.** In the Value field, include a subject line you want inserted into the e-mail message automatically when a user submits the form.

   In this example, I entered *Contact Information from DigitalFamily.com* as the value.

   You can add many other hidden fields to a form, depending on the script you're using and on how much you want to customize the results.

That's it. Assuming all fields are filled in correctly and `formmail.pl` (or a similar script) is properly installed and configured on your server, you should receive via e-mail any data a user enters into your form and submits.

People have many reasons for creating forms on the web, but e-mailing the contents of a contact form is one of the most common. I hope this little exercise has helped give you an idea of what to do to make your HTML forms interact with a CGI script on your server.

Most service providers offer a collection of scripts you can use to create forms for common features of websites, such as order forms and contact forms. All you have to do is create the HTML part of the form and then specify the form fields to interact with the script on your server. Check the website of your web-hosting service for instructions specific to the scripts available on your server.

Part IV
The Part of Tens

The 5th Wave   By Rich Tennant

"Evidently he died of natural causes following a marathon session animating everything on his personal website. And no, Morganstern — the irony isn't lost on me."

*T*he Part of Tens features a collection of time-saving tips and great online resources. In Chapter 14 you find a collection of websites that can help you with some of the things you won't find in Dreamweaver, such as domain registration. You also discover how to add detailed traffic tracking and e-commerce features and how to design and manage e-mail newsletters and other bulk e-mail messages.

In Chapter 15, you find ten ways to promote your website. From social media sites to search engine optimization (SEO), the tips in this chapter will help you attract the audience that your site deserves.

Ten Resources You May Need

*A*lthough Dreamweaver is a wonderful tool for creating websites, it can't do everything you need to put a site online. For example, you can't register a domain name using Dreamweaver and you can't create a favicon, a special kind of image that appears in the top of a web browser.

I added this chapter to offer you a handy list of online resources that can help you finish your site when you need to go beyond the features in Dreamweaver.

Registering a Domain Name

The address for your website is its *domain name*. The domain name is what visitors need to know to find your website. For example, you can visit my Digital Family website at www.DigitalFamily.com.

Even before you start building your website, I recommend that you register your own domain name. The process is simple, painless, and costs less than $10 per year, but it can take from a few hours to a few days for the domain registration process to be completed.

You can register any domain name that hasn't already been taken by someone else. Just visit any domain registrar, such as www.godaddy.com or www.1and1.com, and enter the domain name you want into the search field on the main page of the registrar's site. If the name you want is no longer available, most registration services will give you a list of recommended alternatives.

Most domain registration services also provide web-hosting services, but you don't have to host your site at the same place where you register the name. You can set up a web server anywhere you want and then use the domain management settings at your domain registration service to point your name to the server where your website is hosted.

After you buy that killer new URL that will undoubtedly lead to a life of fame and fortune and a ten-figure exit strategy, you'll probably be bombarded with offers to buy all the variants of your website's name. Before you go splurging on the .tv, .org, .net, and .biz versions of your site, you should know that most people still default to the good old .com when looking for a site with a catchy name.

When you enter a domain name into a web browser, everything before the extension (the .com, .net, or .org part) can be written in uppercase or lowercase, and it will work just fine. However, if you want to go to a specific page within a website, such as www.DigitalFamily.com/videos, the text that comes after the extension is often case sensitive. Because the part before the .com doesn't matter, I find it easier to recognize domain names when they're written with capital letters. So, for example, I use *www.DigitalFamily.com* on my business cards instead of *www.digitalfamily.com*.

Dressing Up the Address Bar with a Favicon

Have you ever wondered how to add a *favicon* — a custom graphic that appears in the address bar at the top of browsers such as Internet Explorer or Firefox — to your site? Google adds a capital G, Adobe adds its logo (shown in Figure 14-1), and you can add an image, too. But first you have to get the image in the right format.

Figure 14-1: Distinguish your site by adding a favicon.

To convert an image into a favicon, visit www.Favicon.com, where you can upload a graphic and have it converted for free. Then just add that image to the root level of your main site folder (that is, your local site folder). The next time you preview your page in a browser, the image appears automatically in the address bar.

Highlighting Links with Pop-Ups

An innovative online service creates a small pop-up preview of any page you link to on your site. You simply sign up (for free) at www.snap.com and use its online tool to generate special code that you then copy and paste into the code in your web pages.

With Snap.com's unique pop-ups, your visitors see a preview of the page or site that you've linked when they roll their cursors over a link. Adding this feature is a great way to give visitors a little more information as they peruse your pages and to highlight the links on your site.

Selling Stuff on the Web

You can sell things online in many ways. As a general rule, I recommend that you start simple and add more complex and expensive options after you know that you'll make money with your site.

At the simple end of the spectrum, you can add a purchase button or a simple e-commerce shopping cart with the services offered at www.PayPal.com and checkout.google.com. These services require no upfront costs, and they are as easy as copying and pasting to use, but they are suited only for relatively small shopping carts. For a slightly more advanced, Dreamweaver-compatible solution, consider www.cartweaver.com.

If you're selling hundreds of products, you'll want to move up the scale in complexity and price and choose a service such as www.bigcommerce.com or www.shopify.com. At the high end of the shopping service, you could create a site as complex as Amazon.com with the tools offered at www.Magento.com.

Sharing Your Computer Screen Remotely

Often when you're designing a website, you will want to show your site to someone (a client, a friend) before you publish it on the public web. That's where remote screen sharing can really come in handy.

You can show what you're doing on your computer to anyone who has access to the Internet with a growing list of online collaboration tools. At the high-end of the spectrum, Adobe Connect, at www.adobe.com/adobeconnect, provides a collaborative sharing environment with chat features and the ability to moderate questions, making it ideal for large presentations and online classes and webinars.

If you just want to share your screen with one other person, my new favorite tool is Skype. I've long loved Skype for its capability to make phone calls over the Internet for little or no cost, but the latest version includes a Share My Screen option that is free and super easy to use. Both computers must have the Skype software and accounts on Skype (download the program and set up your account for free at www.skype.com). After you've logged in and initiated a call between your two computers, click the Sharing icon (just to the right of the Video icon) and choose Share My Screen from the pop-up window.

Another useful sharing service can be found at https://join.me, a quick and easy-to-use service that works on Mac and Windows computers, as well as many mobile devices.

Keeping Track of Traffic

Most web-hosting services provide basic log reports and traffic information, but if you want to know for sure how people are finding your website and what they're doing after they arrive, consider using a service such as Google Analytics (www.google.com/analytics), StatCounter.com (www.statcounter.com), or WebSTAT.com (www.webstat.com).

To use any of these services, set up an account and copy a bit of code from the site into your web pages. (The procedure is a simple copy and paste that you can do in Code view in Dreamweaver.) Google Analytics, StatCounter, and other services then use that bit of code to track your traffic.

Visit any of the services, such as Google Analytics (the most popular of these tools), for a demo and a sample report that illustrates the kind of information you can collect, including what search terms someone used to find your site through a search engine. Studying how people use your website is one of the best ways to determine how to improve your site's content and design.

For instructions on how to copy and paste code from a site such as Google Analytics into the pages of your site in Dreamweaver, read the tutorial on the similar service, Google AdSense, on my website at `www.DigitalFamily.com/dreamweaver`.

Taking Your Site's Temperature with a Heat Map

Adding a heat map to your website is a great way to discover what people find most interesting on each page of your site. Analytics, covered in the preceding section, measure overall traffic patterns on the different pages of your site; heat shows you the popularity of the different elements on each page of your website.

When you add a heat map to your site, you get a visual snapshot showing "hot areas" — the links, text, images, and other elements on a page that attract the most attention from your visitors. To learn more about how heat maps work, visit `www.clickdensity.com` or `www.crazyegg.com`, shown in Figure 14-2.

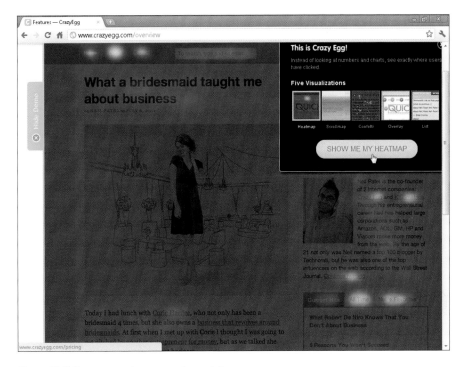

Figure 14-2: Heat maps show you where visitors go on your pages.

Surveying Your Visitors

Want to know what your visitors really think? Ask them. You can create a free online survey at www.SurveyMonkey.com and link to it from your website. With SurveyMonkey, you create the survey using a web browser. The site then automatically tallies the results and presents them in a series of reports and pie charts. The survey results are a great way to impress your board of directors at the next annual meeting.

Prefer to create an interactive quiz you can embed directly into the pages of your site? Visit www.quizrevolution.com, where you can design quizzes with a service that automatically scores each quiz taker and includes the option to add bonus instructions or tips.

Keeping Up with Web Standards at W3.org

If you want to keep up with the latest developments in web design and make sure you're following standards, you'll find no better place than www. W3.org, the official website of the organization that sets web standards. This nonprofit site provides loads of information, including the full specification for HTML, CSS, and much more.

In Chapter 4, you find instructions for testing your web pages with Dreamweaver's validation tools. For more advanced testing, or for testing sites you've already published to the web, the W3C offers online testing tools. You can use these sites to test your web pages for compliance with W3C standards by entering a page's URL into the CSS validator at http://jigsaw.w3.org/css-validator/ or the MarkUp validator at http://validator.w3.org/.

Extending Dreamweaver at Adobe.com

Visit the Dreamweaver Exchange Site at www.adobe.com/cfusion/exchange/ to find a vast collection of extensions you can use to add behaviors and other features to Dreamweaver. To install them, use Extension Manager, which I cover in Chapter 10.

While you're at the site, check out the growing collection of Adobe tutorials, updates, and resources at www.adobe.com/devnet/dreamweaver. Among the resources, check out the new CSS section, where you'll find the latest in CSS tips, tricks, and workarounds.

Ten Ways to Promote Your Site

*W*hat if you build a website and nobody comes? Unfortunately, that problem is all too common, which is why I've chosen to end this book by pointing you to a few places where you can promote your website. Driving large amounts of traffic to the pages of a site often requires an investment of time, a compelling product or message, money, or dumb luck. Improve your odds and save your budget with this chapter's tips, which are designed to help you attract the best people to your website.

Scoring High in Search Engines

Search engine optimization, or *SEO,* has evolved from an esoteric dark art to the hottest buzzword on the web. Basically, SEO is a process designed to help you attract more attention from search engines such as Google, Bing, and Yahoo! The goal is to get your site higher on the search results page than your competitors.

Why all this search engine secrecy?

Because much money can be made at the top of search results lists, web marketers spend countless hours testing how search engines work to come up with their best guesses about the criteria that search engines are using and how best to move their sites up the list. The people who run sites such as Google and Bing, however, want to deliver the best results when someone conducts a search — not just a list of the sites that reflect the ability of smart web marketers to figure out how to trick their way into top position. The result is sort of a cat-and-mouse game, with search engines changing the rules to thwart the most calculated efforts of specialists in SEO, and people who specialize in SEO charging big bucks to figure out the secret formula that can put you on top.

Scoring high in web searches is complicated because millions of sites vie for the top spots and search engines use complex formulas to determine which website should match any given keyword search. Search engines also guard their formulas for prioritizing website more carefully than Coca-Cola guards its recipe. And if all that secrecy doesn't make search engine optimization complicated enough, most search engines change their formulas regularly. (*How* regularly is also secret.)

Building a website today without considering SEO is like opening a store in a dark alley with no advertising. Letting people know that your site exists is vital. A detailed explanation of SEO and how best to optimize your pages is beyond the scope of this book, but I've added a section on my website with a collection of the most important tips and instructions for making make sure your website is optimized for search engines. Visit www.digitalfamily.com/seo.

Buying Traffic (Yes, You Really Can!)

In addition to the natural results that search engines deliver when someone does a keyword search, buying keywords on search engines helps to ensure that your site is listed when someone searches for words that are relevant to your site, although the process is far more complex than most people realize. Search engine ads generally appear at the top and right side of most search result pages.

Not all keywords sell for the same price. Using a complex bidding process, most search engines charge significantly more for the most popular keywords. Adding to the complexity, the results of those keywords for your site can vary dramatically based on a dizzying array of factors. For example, the expensive keyword *Hawaii* may bring the most amount of traffic to your site, but the lower-priced keyword *luau* may result in more reservations to your hotel. Because it's possible to measure not only the traffic from a keyword search but also the actions of the person who clicks that keyword, you can calculate and compare the effectiveness of nearly every aspect of search engine advertising.

Again, this process can be highly complex. Just consider the following:

- ✓ **The real art of developing a list of keywords for search engine advertising requires more than just brainstorming a few words related to your business.** The best SEO companies come up with hundreds or thousands of keywords and phrases and then track the results to find the best return on each dollar spent for the keywords (for example, how many paying customers arrive via each keyword or phrase and how much they buy). Thus, running a campaign with 10,000 words might not cost much more than running a campaign with 100 words and might prove much more effective over time.

- ✓ **The most sophisticated ad campaigns involve creating special web pages to go with each keyword ad.** For example, you can create a special page (often called a *landing page*) on your Hawaiian hotel site for people who click the search term *scuba diving* that is different from the page for those who click the search term *health spa.*

You can learn more about how to make the most of your keyword ads by carefully reading the instructions and tips on any site where you plan to advertise.

Google AdSense offers the largest online advertising program for keywords. Just visit www.google.com/adsense to find detailed instructions and a number of tips and tools to help you develop the best campaign and measure the results.

In addition to buying ads on Google, you can include Google Ads on your own website to earn advertising income. This program is called Google AdWords, and you can learn more about it at adwords.google.com. Google often gives away $100 coupons in AdWords to web developers who use their Webmaster Tools (including Google Analytics). Signing up for a Google Webmaster tools account at www.google.com/webmasters/ is also a valuable way to build traffic to your website.

Using Social Networking Sites for Promotion

Social networking, the art of meeting and building contacts on the web, has become the most popular activity on the Internet. As we live more of our lives online, connecting through social networks is becoming a powerful way to build your network, attract new clients, find discounts, or get a new job. On top social media sites, you can create personal profiles as well as professional pages, which are an increasingly important way to drive traffic to your website and promote your business, brand, or organization.

Here's what you can expect to find among the most popular social networking sites:

- **Facebook** (www.facebook.com): Facebook wins top place as the fastest growing social networking site on the web, and its broad appeal makes it an excellent place to promote your website. Facebook was originally considered a vanity site and a place for college students, but its professional power is growing with its ever-expanding audience. With more than 800 million members, Facebook is by far the most important, and most active, of the social media sites to date.

- **LinkedIn** (www.linkedin.com): LinkedIn is *the* site for professional connections and online business networking. If you're online to develop business contacts with other professionals, especially if you're job hunting or trying to attract new business clients, LinkedIn is a powerful place to promote yourself and your website. Unlike Facebook and myspace, LinkedIn is all business.

- **myspace** (www.myspace.com): Once the most popular social networking site, myspace now exists mostly to help musicians promote new songs and for movie studios to release movie trailers. The best evidence of myspace's fall from popularity as Facebook has grown is the fact that they now encourage you to log on to their site using your Facebook ID.

- **Ecademy** (www.ecademy.com): Similar to LinkedIn, Ecademy is a site where professionals network, seek new clients, hunt for jobs, and recruit employees. What makes Ecademy different is that it's more international, with an especially strong audience in Europe and Asia.

- **Twitter** (www.twitter.com): Once derided as an insipid waste of time, where people fired off short messages about trivial details of life, Twitter has evolved into an international force to be reckoned with. Best described as microblogging, Twitter makes it easy to connect with people online and share brief bursts of information, called *tweets*. Twitter limits you to no more than 140 characters per post, but that brevity seems to be the secret to Twitter's success. Athletes, celebrities, politicians, and all types of so-called experts use Twitter to connect directly with their audiences, one brief message at a time. It takes a while to get the hang of the terse, abbreviation-heavy tweetspeak language, which includes the use of special characters, such as the hash tag (#) to indicate a topic (such as *#Dreamweaver* in posts about the software) or the at sign (@) in posts about a person.

Because you can post to Twitter from a computer, a cell phone, or any other Internet-enabled device, and because the posts are so brief, people tend to update Twitter more frequently than other services, making it a great place to follow trends, news events, and other information in real time. Like all social networks, Twitter is constantly evolving, so it's a good idea to read other people's posts for a while to get the hand of it before you start to participate. Follow a few friends or experts to see how they use the service. You can follow me @janinewarner.

✔ **Google+** (www.plus.google.com): The newest entry in the social media scene is Google's competitor to Facebook, known as Google+. Launched in the summer of 2011, Google+ quickly turned into a must-have for every self-respecting web geek because membership was initially limited to only people who managed to wangle an invitation. The principal difference between Google+ and other social networking sites (such as Facebook) is that Google+ starts out by encouraging you to put your friends into circles, as shown in Figure 15-1. Google circles provide a way to organize the people you know into categories, allowing you to choose what information and updates you share with each group.

Figure 15-1: Google+ makes it easy to categorize friends and other contacts into circles.

One of the more controversial features of Google+ is the +1 button, which Google encourages website owners to put on their pages. You can get the code for these buttons at `www.google.com/webmasters/+1/button/`. Ostensibly, these buttons are added to your website to allow users to publicly approve your content and post it to their Google+ wall. However, Google has publicly announced that the buttons are being used also to determine page ranking in their search engine results. Many website owners have complained that Google using its own social media site as a factor in search ranking constitutes a form of blackmail — that is, if you don't accede to Google's demands to install this code on your site, Google may penalize you by lowering your page ranking.

Increasing Your Ranking on Social Bookmarking Sites

Social bookmarking sites rank the popularity of web pages by the number of votes they get. As a result, these sites are excellent resources for people who want to keep up with what's popular online. Most enable anyone to vote on a site.

Getting your site listed on social bookmarking sites is a highly effective way to increase traffic. Dozens of these sites and services exist (with more sure to come), and they feature catchy and unusual names, such as Delicious (`delicious.com`), StumbleUpon (`www.stumbleupon.com`), and reddit (`www.reddit.com`).

Although you can submit your own pages on any of these sites, that practice is generally frowned upon and you can be banned if you do it too frequently. Besides, your one little vote won't make much difference anyway. A better method is to add a button to your site from each of these services so that visitors can easily vote for you. If you're a blogger, you can add a button each time you post. You can get the buttons (called *chiclets*) for free and add them to your pages by simply inserting a little code you generate on the social networking site.

Spreading the Love with Social Media Share Buttons

Want to know about one of the best ways to attract new visitors to your website? Make sure that current visitors can easily tell a friend about your site by enabling them to share your site's content on Facebook, Twitter, and other social media sites. Simply add social media share buttons to your pages. You'll find many services designed to help facilitate the connection between your site and social media sites, but `www.addthis.com` (see Figure 15-2) and `share.lockerz.com` are among my favorites. Simply sign up for a free account and then copy and paste a little code into your web page. Your visitors can then click an icon on your page to add a post about your site to their pages on social media sites.

Figure 15-2: Include social media share buttons so your site visitors can tell their friends about you.

Enticing Visitors to Return for Updates

One of the best ways to improve traffic to your site is through repeat visitors, and regular updates to your site can make all the difference. If you want your visitors to know when to look for updates, consider making regular changes to your website. Add a post to your blog every Thursday morning, for example, or post your newest photos to the site on Saturday mornings. Regular updates help get people in the habit of visiting your site.

Marketing a Website to the Media

Attracting traditional media attention to your website is like attracting it to any other business. The trick is to tell a good story and get the attention of someone who can write about it in a publication that your target audience reads. If you're looking for press coverage, make sure to include a Press section on your website with contact information, story ideas, and any other press coverage you've received.

Don't wait for journalists to come to you! You should never pester a reporter with a barrage of e-mails, press releases, or phone calls, but a well-timed or well-pitched message can get the attention of a reporter *and* the desired result — your web address in the press. One good way to find journalists who might be interested in your site is to visit related sites and study their Press sections to find out who has been writing about the site. Note not only the publication but also the writer. Then send a note directly to that person with a message that starts like this:

> Dear *fabulous journalist* <insert *that person's name,* of course>:
>
> I enjoyed reading the article you wrote on the XYZ company and thought that you might be interested in what we're doing.

Keep your message brief, and try to include a news hook and story idea that go beyond just promoting your business. For example, rather than tell a reporter that you have the best B&B site in northern California, pitch a story about the best hikes in the area. With any luck, the article on great hikes will include a quote from you and a mention of your B&B's website (especially if the reporter can send readers to your online list of hiking tips).

Unleashing the Power of Viral Marketing

Viral marketing is another marketing industry buzzword for the digital age. The idea is that a message (a video, an article, or a photo, for example) is so exciting, fun, and compelling that people share it by passing it on to their friends, who then pass it on to their friends, until the message spreads like a virus. Such messages are often sent by e-mail, blogs, or chat, which can make the ever-expanding impact happen at an almost instantaneous pace.

Tap in to the power of viral marketing, and you can become an overnight sensation. Humor seems to be the most effective strategy. Among the mainstays of the viral phenomena are those silly photos of cats with clever sayings. Known as the LOL cats, these photos have spawned several websites, such as www.icanhascheezburger.com. Funny video clips — the kind you would expect to see featured on a show such as *America's Funniest Home Videos* — are also highly viral because they're shared around the web.

To use viral marketing to attract traffic to your website, include a section with funny photos, industry jokes, or a top-ten list, and you might just get visitors to tell their friends about your site.

Blogging, Blogging, Blogging

Blogs are designed for frequent updates, so creating a blog for your website makes it easy to add fresh content. If you become a blogger, you'll also join the ranks of a prolific group of writers who regularly refer their readers to each other's website.

Don't launch a blog without considering the commitment it requires. For your blog to attract traffic and serve as an effective marketing tool, you must

✔ Feature interesting, relevant information for your audience.

✔ Update the blog regularly.

✔ Take the time to participate in other blogs. Adding relevant tips and thoughtful comments to other people's blogs is an excellent way to get their visitors to come to your website.

Check out *Blogging For Dummies,* 4th Edition, by Susannah Gardner and Shane Birley, if you're interested in exploring blogging.

Gathering Ideas from Other Websites

One of the best ways to create good habits in web design is to visit the websites of others and study what works and what doesn't on their pages. In particular:

✔ Pay special attention to the title of the page, descriptive text, and keywords used throughout the site.

✔ Ask yourself what you like about the site and why you like it.

✔ Determine whether you can easily find the information you're most interested in and how easily you can navigate around the site.

Sometimes the best way to discover the problems in your own website is to look for problems on someone else's site and then return to yours with a fresh perspective. The Internet changes every day. Keeping an eye on what other sites are doing is a great way to stay informed about new technologies, new social media sites, and other ways of promoting your site.

Index

Apple & Mac

iPad 2 For Dummies,
3rd Edition
978-1-118-17679-5

iPhone 4S For Dummies,
5th Edition
978-1-118-03671-6

iPod touch For Dummies,
3rd Edition
978-1-118-12960-9

Mac OS X Lion
For Dummies
978-1-118-02205-4

Blogging & Social Media

CityVille For Dummies
978-1-118-08337-6

Facebook For Dummies,
4th Edition
978-1-118-09562-1

Mom Blogging
For Dummies
978-1-118-03843-7

Twitter For Dummies,
2nd Edition
978-0-470-76879-2

WordPress For Dummies,
4th Edition
978-1-118-07342-1

Business

Cash Flow For Dummies
978-1-118-01850-7

Investing For Dummies,
6th Edition
978-0-470-90545-6

Job Searching with Social
Media For Dummies
978-0-470-93072-4

QuickBooks 2012
For Dummies
978-1-118-09120-3

Resumes For Dummies,
6th Edition
978-0-470-87361-8

Starting an Etsy Business
For Dummies
978-0-470-93067-0

Cooking & Entertaining

Cooking Basics
For Dummies, 4th Edition
978-0-470-91388-8

Wine For Dummies,
4th Edition
978-0-470-04579-4

Diet & Nutrition

Kettlebells For Dummies
978-0-470-59929-7

Nutrition For Dummies,
5th Edition
978-0-470-93231-5

Restaurant Calorie Counter
For Dummies,
2nd Edition
978-0-470-64405-8

Digital Photography

Digital SLR Cameras &
Photography For Dummies,
4th Edition
978-1-118-14489-3

Digital SLR Settings
& Shortcuts
For Dummies
978-0-470-91763-3

Photoshop Elements 10
For Dummies
978-1-118-10742-3

Gardening

Gardening Basics
For Dummies
978-0-470-03749-2

Vegetable Gardening
For Dummies,
2nd Edition
978-0-470-49870-5

Green/Sustainable

Raising Chickens
For Dummies
978-0-470-46544-8

Green Cleaning
For Dummies
978-0-470-39106-8

Health

Diabetes For Dummies,
3rd Edition
978-0-470-27086-8

Food Allergies
For Dummies
978-0-470-09584-3

Living Gluten-Free
For Dummies,
2nd Edition
978-0-470-58589-4

Hobbies

Beekeeping
For Dummies,
2nd Edition
978-0-470-43065-1

Chess For Dummies,
3rd Edition
978-1-118-01695-4

Drawing For Dummies,
2nd Edition
978-0-470-61842-4

eBay For Dummies,
7th Edition
978-1-118-09806-6

Knitting For Dummies,
2nd Edition
978-0-470-28747-7

Language &
Foreign Language

English Grammar
For Dummies,
2nd Edition
978-0-470-54664-2

French For Dummies,
2nd Edition
978-1-118-00464-7

German For Dummies,
2nd Edition
978-0-470-90101-4

Spanish Essentials
For Dummies
978-0-470-63751-7

Spanish For Dummies,
2nd Edition
978-0-470-87855-2

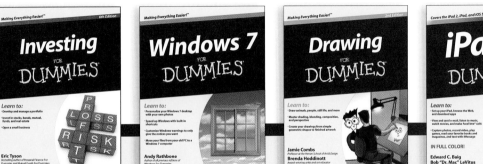

Math & Science

Algebra I For Dummies,
2nd Edition
978-0-470-55964-2

Biology For Dummies,
2nd Edition
978-0-470-59875-7

Chemistry For Dummies,
2nd Edition
978-1-1180-0730-3

Geometry For Dummies,
2nd Edition
978-0-470-08946-0

Pre-Algebra Essentials
For Dummies
978-0-470-61838-7

Microsoft Office

Excel 2010 For Dummies
978-0-470-48953-6

Office 2010 All-in-One
For Dummies
978-0-470-49748-7

Office 2011 for Mac
For Dummies
978-0-470-87869-9

Word 2010
For Dummies
978-0-470-48772-3

Music

Guitar For Dummies,
2nd Edition
978-0-7645-9904-0

Clarinet For Dummies
978-0-470-58477-4

iPod & iTunes
For Dummies,
9th Edition
978-1-118-13060-5

Pets

Cats For Dummies,
2nd Edition
978-0-7645-5275-5

Dogs All-in One
For Dummies
978-0470-52978-2

Saltwater Aquariums
For Dummies
978-0-470-06805-2

Religion & Inspiration

The Bible For Dummies
978-0-7645-5296-0

Catholicism For Dummies,
2nd Edition
978-1-118-07778-8

Spirituality For Dummies,
2nd Edition
978-0-470-19142-2

Self-Help & Relationships

Happiness For Dummies
978-0-470-28171-0

Overcoming Anxiety
For Dummies,
2nd Edition
978-0-470-57441-6

Seniors

Crosswords For Seniors
For Dummies
978-0-470-49157-7

iPad 2 For Seniors
For Dummies, 3rd Edition
978-1-118-17678-8

Laptops & Tablets
For Seniors For Dummies,
2nd Edition
978-1-118-09596-6

Smartphones & Tablets

BlackBerry For Dummies,
5th Edition
978-1-118-10035-6

Droid X2 For Dummies
978-1-118-14864-8

HTC ThunderBolt
For Dummies
978-1-118-07601-9

MOTOROLA XOOM
For Dummies
978-1-118-08835-7

Sports

Basketball For Dummies,
3rd Edition
978-1-118-07374-2

Football For Dummies,
2nd Edition
978-1-118-01261-1

Golf For Dummies,
4th Edition
978-0-470-88279-5

Test Prep

ACT For Dummies,
5th Edition
978-1-118-01259-8

ASVAB For Dummies,
3rd Edition
978-0-470-63760-9

The GRE Test For
Dummies, 7th Edition
978-0-470-00919-2

Police Officer Exam
For Dummies
978-0-470-88724-0

Series 7 Exam
For Dummies
978-0-470-09932-2

Web Development

HTML, CSS, & XHTML
For Dummies, 7th Edition
978-0-470-91659-9

Drupal For Dummies,
2nd Edition
978-1-118-08348-2

Windows 7

Windows 7
For Dummies
978-0-470-49743-2

Windows 7
For Dummies,
Book + DVD Bundle
978-0-470-52398-8

Windows 7 All-in-One
For Dummies
978-0-470-48763-1

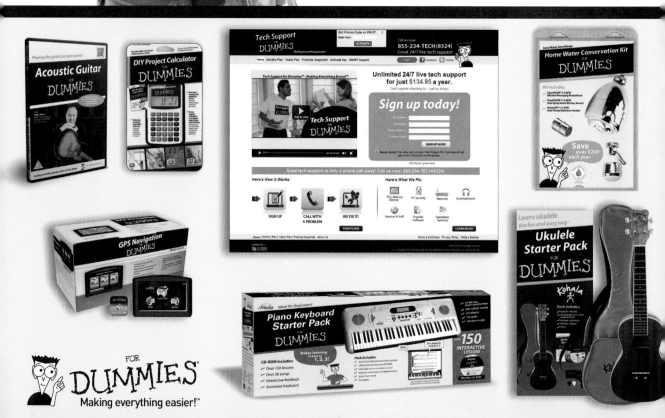